Porsche 928, 924, 944 and 968

Porsche 928, 924, 944 and 968

The Front-Engined Sports Cars

MARC CRANSWICK

McFarland & Company, Inc., Publishers
Jefferson, North Carolina, and London

Library of Congress Cataloguing-in-Publication Data

Cranswick, Marc.
Porsche 928, 924, 944 and 968 : the front-engined sports cars /
Marc Cranswick.
p. cm.
Includes bibliographical references and index.

ISBN 978-0-7864-3040-6
softcover : 50# and 70# alkaline papers ∞

1. Porsche automobiles — History. I. Title.
TL215.P75C72 2008 629.222'2 — dc22 2007050978

British Library cataloguing data are available

On the cover: (top) The Porsche 944 in a wind tunnel; (bottom) front view of a Porsche 968 (Photographs courtesy Dr. Ing. h.c. F. Porsche AG)

Manufactured in the United States of America

McFarland & Company, Inc., Publishers
Box 611, Jefferson, North Carolina 28640
www.mcfarlandpub.com

TABLE OF CONTENTS

PREFACE

Why turn attention to the front-engined, water-cooled Porsche sports cars in the 21st century? The answer is that they are important cars, and particularly important to Porsche. Draw a line in the lifetime of the company at the point when the final 968s and 928s were produced, and the water pumpers represent half the German manufacturer's history. The lesser known half, the overshadowed half, but half nonetheless. In terms of resources put forward to develop the model range, marketing attention given to incorporating the new cars into the Porsche plan, numbers produced and public profile, these transaxle cars were highly significant for Zuffenhausen.

The 924 to 928 family is also key to the German auto industry, and to understanding the interrelations between various manufacturers. The 924 would use parts in common with the Volkswagen Beetle, so closely linked with the dawn of the Autobahn. The extent of the relationship between Porsche and VW is exaggerated in the minds of many, but their paths did cross several times in the story of the cars at hand. More indirectly, a prototype 924 chassis would be seen clothed in the bodywork of a BMW, or testing the Weissach Axle principle on an Opel. The historical convergences with other companies are such that to learn about these Porsche models is to learn about the German car industry as a whole.

The Wirtschaftswunder, or postwar German economic miracle, is well known, but what happened after that? The front-engined cars take up the experience of Porsche and how German manufactured goods were viewed after 1970, once their value in the world had become established. This is indeed part two of the industrial revival. So what exactly will be observed in this account? The best way to truly understand a company, arguably, is to consider the products it made during any given period. To this end all 924, 944, 968 and 928 variants produced and sold at various points between 1975 and 1995 will be described.

The engineering background, specifications and intrinsic qualities of these four and eight cylinder coupes and convertibles in relation to their rivals will be examined. Forays into racing are also recounted, even if these are limited in extent compared to the exploits of the 356 and 911 series. However, this was an era when showroom success was much more important to car makers than racetrack prowess. Buyers were more concerned with smooth style, reliability and badge cachet in the period under consideration. To sell in the great numbers that the water pumpers achieved, Porsche would be catering to many that didn't follow motorsport as closely as the typical diehard of the fifties and sixties had done.

In researching this book, I found firsthand experience to be a valuable asset. Over the past five years I have had the pleasure and privilege to sample a number of the privately owned collector cars presented here. I offer my thanks once again to those individuals for helping to refresh the memory concerning the driving experience afforded by the front-engined Porsche range. It also proved convenient to draw upon the resources of a manufacturer to confirm or deny points of interest and dispute. In that respect I owe special thanks to Jens Torner of Porsche AG and Marita Niemann of Strosek Design KG, for helping to determine innumerable details.

The contribution of car clubs and organizations must also be noted. They are a guard against information being lost, and sometimes even aid the manufacturer where the record is unclear. There is also a time to stop playing with cars and get down to some serious research, using internationally recognized motoring and business journals and other helpful materials referenced herein. The University of Western Australia proved to be a nice place to escape the European winter. There is also the convenient truth that there can be few places quieter than the Reid Library during a mid-semester study break. So here it is, the distillation of experience, fact and thought on a Porsche family that has just received much greater attention!

Introduction

In 1985 Porsche president Peter Schutz was asked why Americans perceived German cars as possessing the highest quality. The normally talkative Schutz gave a brief reply: "There are three reasons for that, Mercedes. BMW. Porsche."* From the mid–1970s to the mid–1990s a large number of car fans all over the world received their heavenly slice of Porsche pie courtesy of the new front-engined, water-cooled models.

Porsche AG, the small, headstrong German automaker long associated with rear-engined, air-cooled matters, adopted a changed game plan for an important new era in the company's history. That era would be shaped by looming national laws concerning safety, air pollution, and noise pollution, as well as altered buyer needs and desires. The promise of financial security from expanded production and a larger customer base also couldn't be ignored. So it was that the new Porsche 924 arrived in late 1975, ushering in a new kind of Porsche.

The wheels were set in motion. Porsche may be small, but it's also smart. Plans were in place for a cohesive range of models, serving a wide spectrum of buyers with two things in common: a love for driving and a hunger for quality. Voices of dissent never swayed Porsche's plan; the 924 made a 1980 Le Mans debut and snatched 6th, 12th and 13th overall during Group 4 travails. Porsche's new kid on the block had made its mark.

Ever since Ferry Porsche and Karl Rabe got that first 356 going in 1948, people have expected speed and entertainment from Porsche. During the 1980s Porsche honed earlier 924 work to create the 944. The 944 range, in normally aspirated and turbocharged forms, has given the world some of the most enjoyable and respected sporty cars of the modern era. There is little doubt that the four-banger, front-engined family possesses the true Porsche essence.

In an auto world often challenged by compromise, the 968 could only have come from a company like Porsche AG. This final development in Porsche's front-engined, four-pot dynasty confirmed the company's single-minded devotion to the driving experience. Single-minded, but certainly not narrow-minded. The auto connoisseur with a penchant for luxury discovered the 1977 Porsche 928. Everything one could ask for in a Porsche — but just a tad larger.

The 928 fulfilled dreams of flying along continental autoroutes during business trips and vacations. In truth there wasn't a continent the 928 didn't take to; it became a default standard for GT comparison. Not only did it boast a full complement of luxury toys, the 928 remained faithful to Porsche's fast ways, albeit with greater handling decorum. From Salzburg to Seattle the 928 gave auto enthusiasts another ultimate Porsche to desire. The 1978 Euro-

***Popular Science*, Vol. 227, no. 2, August 1985, p. 11.

pean Car of the Year progressed through increasingly powerful iterations, culminating in the 350 bhp 928 GTS.

The front-engined, water-cooled Porsche family notched up over 350,000 sales, got the critics talking non-stop for two decades, and made a bunch of new Porsche friends.

Chapter 1

Creating a Porsche—The How-to Manual for 1970

914—Little Car Out of Control!

The Porsche 914 left one *Consumer Reports* road tester startled. He was pushing the Fourteener though a high-speed turn when the little Porsche suddenly spun out. The tester said the car felt really good, and then at a certain point didn't feel so good anymore. The problem turned out to be underinflated tires, but that bad experience back in 1970 seemed to sum up the life of the poor little 914: A good start, but then something went wrong.* In contrast, that other 1970 newcomer, the Datsun 240Z, was the standout car of the sports car test and went on to unbridled sales success. But what of the 914? What was this littlest Porsche, what was its plan, and what exactly did it achieve? Answers to these weighty questions may help us better understand the Porsche 924 because one can't have 924, without first having 914!

A Gentleman's Agreement

The Porsche 914 arose out of the mutual need of Volkswagen and Porsche for an affordable, volume-selling sports car. Volkswagen had relied on the stylish Karmann Ghia. These coupes and convertibles were Type 1 VW Beetle-based, had looks courtesy of the Italian house of Ghia's Luigi Segre, and were constructed by coachbuilder Karmann in Osnabruck. Accompanying this model was the Karmann Ghia version of the Beetle-evolved Type 3, but unlike the Type 1–based Karmann Ghia, this car wasn't available in convertible form. The 1962 Type 3 coupe was styled by Sergio Sartorelli. The Type 1–based Karmann Ghia lasted from October 1955 to June 1974; the Type 3 Karmann Ghia ran from 1962 to 1969. Add the production totals of these sporting VWs and one gets 487,798.

Over in the Porsche camp the new upmarket six-cylinder 911's arrival had left a gap in the Porsche model range. To fill the gap resulting from the move upscale with a larger, more powerful model, a junior Porsche variant was called for. This position was nicely catered for by the final Porsche 356C cars of 1964/65. The ultimate refinement in the 356 series sold alongside the early 911-series cars. By the end the 95-bhp, four-cylinder, 1.6-liter 356C 1600SC coupe retailed at $4,577, while the more modern six-cylinder, 2-liter 911 cost $6,490. With yet more overlap with the 356C, Porsche introduced the somewhat tamer 912 in May 1965.

**Consumer Reports*, Vol. 35, no. 9, September 1970, p. 554.

The enduring Type 1 Karmann Ghia, the sporty upscale Beetle derivative. A 1971 convertible is featured (courtesy Patrick Baptist).

The Porsche 912 was basically a 356-powered 911. Brought to the U.S. with a price tag of $4,690, the 912 utilized a further refined version of the proven Super 90 flat-four motor. The 912 came with a four-on-the-floor as standard equipment, and just three rather than the 911's normal quota of five dash dials. The 911's wooden dash trim was also absent in a bid to keep the 912's base sticker down.

By 1968 Porsche seemed to have a well-spaced model hierarchy. The 356 was gone, and the 911/912 family went from the 90-bhp 912 to the budget 110-bhp 911T, through the plush 130-horse 911L, followed by a larger horsepower leap to the 160-pony 911S. If you liked the 356, you were going to love the 912. It had much the same turn of speed as the final 356C 1600SC, and if a bit extra was paid your 912 could have a 5-speed stick.

The 912 was a well-balanced machine, the favored choice of a select band of experts because of the noises it made and the reduced weight bias of having a flat four rather than a flat six hanging over the rear axle. However, Porsche couldn't maintain the price disparity between the 912 and 911. Many folks either opted for the cheapest 911 they could get their hands on, or selected from one of the new breed of cheaper yet equally quick sports cars. The 912 was in the middle of nowhere, and although Porsche kept it up to date with the 911 A and B series upgrades, 1969 would be its last model year — for the time being.

Styled by Sergio Sartorelli, the Type 3 based Karmann Ghia was relatively short lived and available only as a coupe (courtesy Chris Wright and www.kgoc-gb.org).

So VW needed a front line sportster to replace the aging Karmann Ghia, and Porsche were searching for a replacement for the 912 that was cheaper to produce. It's at times like these when you need your friends. Fortunately such a friendship did exist between the two companies with so much shared history. The cordial relationship was that between Ferry Porsche and VW's boss, Professor Heinz Nordhoff. They agreed that Porsche should design and develop the new fun car, Karmann would make the bodies, and Porsche would get a supply of Fourteener bodies at a super low price.

A competitive price on 914 bodies was assured because the car was going to come in two versions. There would be a VW-badged 914 with VW flat-four power, and a Porsche-badged edition with Porsche 911 flat-six punch. Porsche would be getting the bodies on the cheap, because VW would be ordering so many. After all, the production total for Type 1 and Type 3 Karmann Ghias came to almost half a million, so sales volume was potentially large if the Fourteener took off.

For a first draft Porsche looked towards the work of a German company called Gugelot. This industrial design firm had cooked up a sports car proposal, and submitted it to various German companies in 1966. Porsche liked what they saw, bought the rights to the Gugelot design in the fall of 1966 and promptly converted the sportster from front-engine to the Fourteener's mid-engine configuration. The mid-engine layout was certainly in vogue at the time

75·96·GD

AE·88·55
75·96·GD

Ferry's first car, the immortal 356! Time and distance haven't wearied the appeal of the 356 (courtesy Eric Stice).

as a recipe for victory in sports car racing, in which Porsche were high profile exponents with the 904, 908 and 917 racers. Racing improves the breed: win on Sunday and sell in the showrooms on Monday. The Fourteener would give Porsche the opportunity to put such old adages into effect, especially since Porsche's road and race models had diverged since the golden 356 era. Image aside, the mid-engined benefits of even weight distribution and an ability to change direction quickly were inescapable. In addition, the mid-engined style was receptive to various types of powerplant, and as mentioned it was in the cards for the Fourteener to feature both a VW flat four and a Porsche flat six.

The Fourteener story was moving along quite speedily, with Volkswagen giving its production blessing in 1967. On March 1, 1968, the first four-cylinder 914 prototype was moving around under its own steam when disaster struck! Professor Heinz Nordhoff, major architect in guiding VW to being Europe's biggest car maker, and major Porsche amigo, passed away on April 12, 1968. A minute's silence was held on VW's assembly lines for the man who

Opposite, top: **For many years the Karmann Ghia was the stepping stone between VW's cars and the cheapest Porsche 356s. Over time some have had their original motors replaced by high performance 356/911 flat fours and sixes (courtesy Patrick Baptist).** ***Opposite, bottom:*** **Combined production of Type 1 and Type 3 based Karmann Ghia models was almost 500,000 units by June 1974. VW needed a modern replacement, and Porsche could help (courtesy Patrick Baptist).**

Accompanying the new 911 was the cheaper 356-engined 912 (courtesy Barwaut Verhoeven www.912.nl).

had been in charge of VW since the late 1940s and had seen VW rise to become the third largest automaker in the world. The question now was, where did Nordhoff's passing leave the little Fourteener? "None too safe" was the answer.

Professor Nordhoff had been scheduled to retire in 1970 anyway, and Dr. Kurt Lotz had been brought in as his deputy in June 1967 with an eye towards learning the ropes and taking over the top spot in 1970. Nordhoff's death put Dr. Lotz into the driving seat ahead of schedule, and he had two concerns with Type 914. Lotz wasn't happy about the arrangement concerning the Fourteener being an informal gentleman's agreement and wasn't aware of the specifics of the deal struck between Ferry Porsche and Professor Nordhoff. He was also not pleased about this super-low price Porsche was going to pay for 914 bodies.

Even though 1965–71 contained the million-selling-Beetle years, VW needed the cash. The competition from Opel, Ford Europe and Japanese car makers was heating up, and a satisfactory Beetle successor had yet to be found. Kurt Lotz wasn't going to let Porsche have what could have been a fast-selling 356 replacement below economic cost. Lotz felt VW had sole

Opposite, top: **The 912 combined the 911 body with the 356's 1600 flat four during 1965–69, offering better balance than the 911 (courtesy Barwaut Verhoeven, www.912.nl).** ***Opposite, bottom:*** **The 912's flat four, an expensive powerplant for a relatively expensive car. Porsche needed a more competitively priced entry model (courtesy Barwaut Verhoeven www.912.nl).**

rights to the Fourteener, and that if Porsche wanted the car they would have to pay a price that would realistically contribute to offsetting VW's tooling costs.

The friendship between VW and Porsche may have seen better times, but the two entities reached a compromise in January 1969, and formalized the Fourteener joint venture with the creation of a special company. In April 1969 VW-Porsche VG GmbH was commenced with an initial 5 million deutschmarks on hand. VW and Porsche had equal stakes in the new Stuttgart company, which largely formalized a setup that already existed between the two companies. Historically Porsche automobiles had been sold through VW dealers in many countries. However, just for the record, VW-Porsche VG GmbH would formally market and distribute the Fourteener and 911 series in most world markets.

Greater distribution changes were afoot for the U.S. market in 1970. Up to that time VW-Porsche dealerships conveniently offered a historically intertwined, but diverse, line of cars under the same roof. However, with a perceived need to distance economy-oriented VW from sports-luxury Porsche, Porsche+Audi was established on October 1, 1969. So VW-Porsche dealerships in the U.S. had to decide whether to remain VW only, or become a Porsche+Audi dealer. The latter path was a bit onerous, because to go with that upmarket side a dealership owner would have to find a quarter of a million dollars for a dedicated Porsche+Audi showroom.

VW had purchased the sole surviving post–World War II member of Auto-Union, DKW, in 1965. VW had revived Audi, one of the dormant members of the once-great Auto-Union quartet, as an upmarket brand in the VW empire. Thus, it was in keeping with the new U.S. arrangements that the reactivated Audi marque should be paired off with Porsche to create the new Porsche+Audi franchise.

Naturally the Fourteener would be sold in Porsche+Audi showrooms, alongside the Audi 100, also new for 1970, as well as the already famous 911. Note that the four-cylinder car tested by *Consumer Reports* in 1970 was referred to as a Porsche 914. All 914/4 variants were sold as Porsches in the U.S., and as VW-Porsches in other markets, as part of the plan

A 1972 Porsche 914. The Fourteener had its origins in a sports car design proposed by the German firm Gugelot (courtesy Victor Manzano).

for marketing and distribution. Two names for the Fourteener, but also two versions, one exclusively denoted with a Porsche tag for all countries.

914—Meet the Twins

The four-pot 914 was completely finished at Karmann's Osnabruck facility. This 914/4 model utilized a very interesting variation of the familiar VW air-cooled flat four. It was the motor from the Type 4, the 411E to be precise. The Type 4 was yet another larger and more refined attempt by VW to move on from the Beetle. The engine had bore and stroke dimensions of 90 × 66 mm, displacing 1,679 cc. It also featured the world's first computer controlled, multipoint, electronic fuel injection. The "E" in 411E stood for Einspritz, German for injection, and came courtesy of Bosch D-Jetronic fuel injection. This 1968 electronic system metered exactly the correct amount of fuel/air mixture based on intake manifold pressure.

As one of the most advanced family-car motors produced in West Germany at the time, the 914/4's version of the overhead-valve 411E's 1.7-liter produced 80 horsepower, just 10 horses shy of the final 1.6-liter Porsche Super 90's 90 horses, the overhead-valve flat four fitted

The 914 had a mid-engine configuration, two seats and two trunks! Powerplants were either a VW flat four or a 911T-sourced 2 liter flat six for the 914/6 (courtesy Rev. C. Emerson Strain).

to the Porsche 356C 1600SC and the 912. For Europe the 914/4's arrival was timely, given the Type 3 Karmann Ghia's 1969 demise. In the U.S.A. the Fourteener's high-tech 1.7 would usefully combat American emissions regulations. This enlarged "E" version of the fabled 948 cc "E-Motor," designed to power the Beetle on early 1930s Autobahnen, would be pushing the Fourteener along U.S. freeways and turnpikes in the 1970s.

There was good news for fresh air lovers too. The 912 had featured a Targa top from 1966, and so did the new Fourteener. The removeable top was stored in the 914's rear trunk. The 914/4 arrived with an East Coast price of just $3,595; for a lot less money than the previous 356C 1600SC and 912 you got a car that was just as quick. It was good enough to secure the Fourteener the title of *Motor Trend*'s "Import Car of the Year" for 1970. Its modernity was beyond question.

For even greater performance, enthusiasts could chose a Porsche-powered version of the Fourteener, known as 914/6. This six-cylinder model was completed by Porsche in Zuffenhausen on the same assembly line as the 911, using 914 bodies supplied by Karmann. At the heart of the 914/6 was the 110-bhp Porsche overhead-cam flat six straight from the junior 911, the 911T. The 911T was the lowest priced 911 variant, and its 2-liter flat 6 featured cast-iron pistons. In another move to distance the Fourteener from the 911, the 1969-specification 911T motor was chosen. The 911 C series cars for 1970 were using a new 2.2-liter engine, but the 914/6 utilized the outgoing 2-liter powerplant.

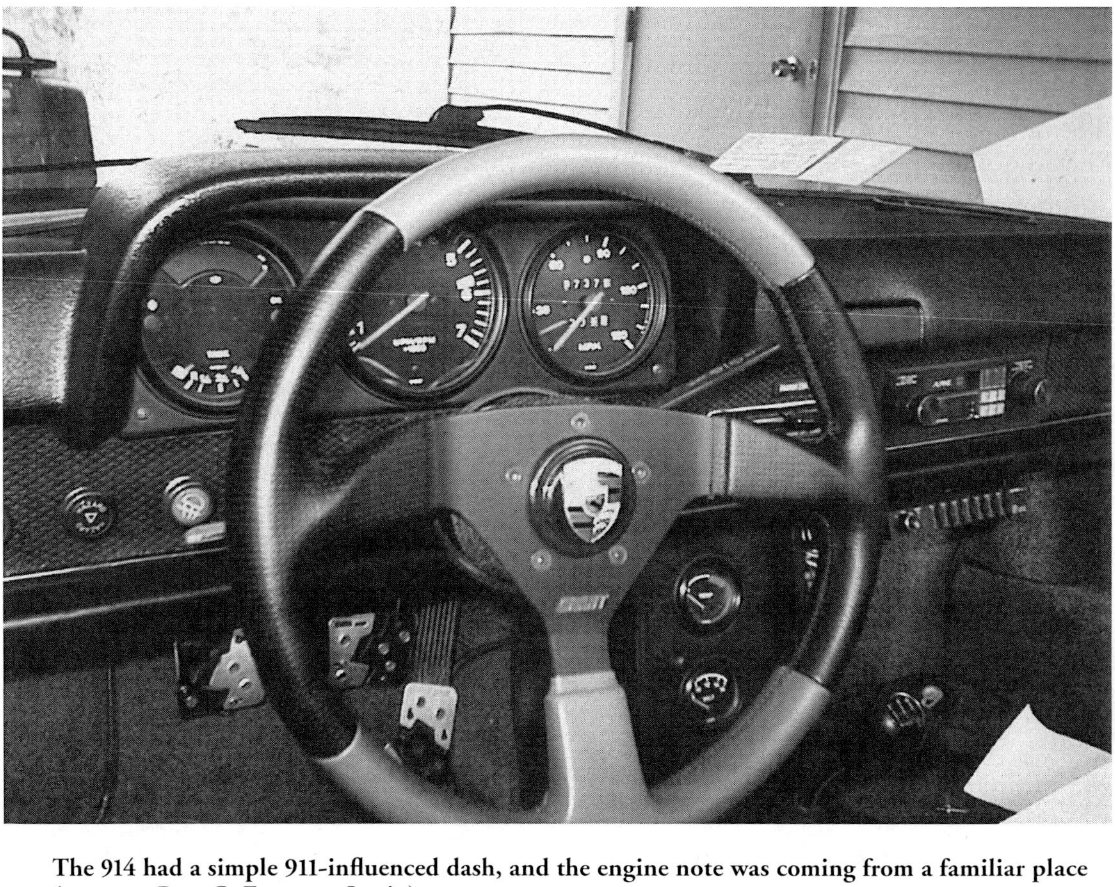

The 914 had a simple 911-influenced dash, and the engine note was coming from a familiar place (courtesy Rev. C. Emerson Strain).

With a zero to sixty time of 8.8 seconds and a top end of 120 mph, the 914/6 was scarcely any slower than the early 130-horse 911. Less palatable was the 914/6's West Coast $6,099 price tag, compared to $7,205 for the 2.2-liter 911T Targa. It was appreciably higher than the 914/4, but once you overcame the sticker shock, you realized the 914/6 enjoyed advantages beyond just its extra 30 horses.

Designed by Porsche, assembled by Porsche, the 914/6 used Porsche hubs, wheels and brakes all around. Indeed, the 914/6 could be visually distinguished from the 914/4 by its use of a 5-stud wheel pattern, rather than the VW-powered edition's four-stud wheel pattern. As a little side note, Vee Dubs up to 1965 used a five-stud pattern, but that was before the Fourteener's day of course! More obviously, the 914/6 was badged and sold as a Porsche for all world markets, not just America. However, in other respects the two versions were similar; both featured 4-wheel disk brakes, Porsche 5-speed manual gearbox, and the option of Porsche's excellent "U-shift" semi-automatic Sportomatic.

The underlying truth was that the 914/4 could lay an even greater claim than the 914/6 to having Porsche DNA. The first prototype 356 completed featured a backwards-facing, souped-up VW flat four which limited the car to a 2-seater due to space constraints, and exactly the same could be said of the 914/4. Carrying on the Porsche family connection, this time in keeping with the 911, the car featured rack and pinion steering, MacPherson strut independent front suspension with longitudinal torsion bars, and independent semi-trailing-

Also known as the "Square Porsche," the 914 brought the promise of neutral handling to the Porsche marque (courtesy Rev. C. Emerson Strain).

arm rear suspension. The only deviation from 911 practice was the use of rear coil springs rather than torsion bars; this was to make room for the space-hungry, back-to-front-facing 1.7-liter flat four.

Business at the Track

As Porsche was the reigning sports car racing king, by virtue of clinching the World Manufacturer's Championship in 1969, it seemed fitting that the Fourteener should take to the track to uphold Porsche family honor, and to boost its public profile among fans of speed. Once the first 500 stock 914/6 road cars were built, the 914/6 GT could be homologated for the FIA's Group 4 category. So Porsche's Competition Department in Zuffenhausen constructed twelve 914/6 GT racers. The first big outing for the Fourteener was at the 1970 Nürburgring 1000 km event. The four 914/6 GTs secured second, third, fourth and fifth in the 2-liter GT class.

Nineteen seventy also saw the 914/6 GT win the Grand Touring class and finish sixth overall at Le Mans, driven by the driver pairing of Guy Chasseuil and Claude Ballot-Léna. In contrast, the two 914/6 GTs entered for Le Mans 1971 expired prior to the race's completion. Nineteen seventy-one would mark the 914's final outing to the famous 24-hour endurance race. However, there were other competition highlights for the 914.

After the success of the Fourteener at the Nürburgring 1000 km event in May 1970, the six-pot mid-engined Porsche was back at the old "Ring" in August for the Marathon de la Route. At this 84-hour stamina test, three factory 914/6 GTs were piloted by lead drivers Gerard Larrousse, Claude Ballot-Léna and Bjorn Waldegaard. The orange-and-red-painted diminutive dynamos came in first, second and third overall! Add in a first and second in class at the Österreichring in October 1970, and the 914/6 GT was on its way to grabbing the 1970 International GT Trophy title.

Emulating the 356's and 911's earlier forays into rallying, the Fourteener tested the waters by entering the 1970 RAC Rally, in preparation for the Monte Carlo Rally the following year. Porsche had won the Monte Carlo Rally in 1970, and for 1971 entered three 914/6 GT works racers driven by the same crew that had brought them success in 1970. The drivers were Björn Waldegaard, Gerard Larrousse and Ake Andersson. Although Bjorn Waldegaard came third equal overall, and first in class, Porsche were hoping for even more, and the 1971 Monte Carlo Rally would prove to be the last time a factory-backed Fourteener was entered in a rally.

Greater success for the 914/6 GT came in the very early days of IMSA racing (International Motor Sports Association Championship). Backed by North America's Porsche+Audi, the 914/6 GT driven by Peter Gregg won three races and achieved three additional class victories. It allowed the 914/6 GT to win the 1971 IMSA GTU Championship for under–2.5-liter machinery. The 914 also enjoyed good times on the Targa Florio. The Fourteener came in 13th overall and second in class in 1971, following this up with a class victory which equated to 9th overall in 1972, piloted by Schmid and Floridia.

Factor in the Fourteener's appearances in smaller scale events and SCCA races, and the competition tally starts to add up. And of course at Le Mans and other places the 914 was the only thing from the Porsche stable that looked remotely like a normal road car. The 914/6 was pictured alongside a 917K on the racetrack, and in May 1971 the public was invited to own a 914/6 GT clone! Porsche offered the M471 appearance and rim pack on the 914/6 production car exclusively.

The M471 package consisted of steel wheel-arch extenders enveloping 15 × 6-inch forged Fuchs aluminum rims, front airdam, and fiberglass side skirts to incorporate with the car's flared arches. More extravagant still was a bona fide eight-cylinder Fourteener. To bring the 914 into the racing fold and underline its racing links, Zuffenhausen built two 8-pot Fourteeners. These 914/8s utilized the air-cooled flat eight from the 908 race car, and were officially referred to as 914Ss.

VW & Porsche — Forever Friends

It was all about image, and Porsche had more image than most. Consider the cachet in Europe of the VW's circular logo next to the traditional style Porsche script on the tail of non–U.S.-spec 914/4s. It's good for a mainstream auto giant to get some halo glow from the glamorous world of motor sport, and Volkswagen wasn't alone. Think about what the Corvette has done for all things Chevy. Closer to home, Renault would subsequently take over competition car maker Alpine of Dieppe, proudly placing Le Regie's diamond logo on the nose of the new Alpine A310 sports car. Even closer to the relationship between VW and Porsche was that which existed between Fiat and Ferrari involving the various "Dino" cars.

By the time production ceased in 1976, nearly 120,000 914s had been assembled. The 914 was very popular in America where it was exclusively sold as a Porsche (courtesy Rev. C. Emerson Strain and www.914fan.net).

The 1966 Fiat Dino helped Ferrari homologate a V6 motor for Formula 2, and it helped Fiat gain some prestige. The Dino-marketed 206/246 mid-engined cars also helped to bridge the image chasm between Fiat and Ferrari, especially since the former had bought out the latter by the close of the 1960s. Naturally VW didn't buy out Porsche, and Porsche continues as an independent car maker to this day. But in other respects the Fiat Dino/Dino 206/246 Ferrari analogy holds. Fiat built the Dino V6 engine in Turin, just as VW constructed the 914/4's injected Type 4 motor.

VW were creating avenues away from their economy-car-only status. The activation of the Audi marque was a convenient instant entry point to compete with the upper Ford, Opel and lower BMW sports/luxury sedans. And with the Fourteener there was the seamless progression from Karmann Ghia and its successor, to the VW-Porsche 914/4 through the Porsche 914/6, and finally culminating in the 911 zenith: a clear path of progression from Wolfsburg to Zuffenhausen. Collectively the VW and Porsche entities could supply just about any passenger or light commercial vehicle the European buyer desired — even a cross-country buggy in the form of the Type 181 "Thing"!

This close association between VW and Porsche has led people to believe that the two companies are indeed one. This sentiment was especially heightened when VW-Porsche VG

VW enlisted the help of Porsche to come up with a successor to the long lived Beetle. Unfortunately Zuffenhausen's EA-266 proposal was considered too pricey by Wolfsburg (author's collection).

GmbH was formed, and Porsche had to issue a clear statement that VW and Porsche were not merging. The VG was simply a means to handle a joint-venture sportster and formally tie up some distribution arrangements, no more than that. Indeed, fast-forwarding to the present, it is the little guy that is helping the big guy out.

As of September 26, 2005, Porsche announced plans to increase its stake in Volkswagen from under 5 percent to 20 percent. The German state of Lower Saxony has around 18 percent. Put together the holdings of Porsche, Lower Saxony and Volkswagen, and one has a 51.2 percent stake in total shares. Porsche increased its holding to stave off any hostile takeover of VW that might place in jeopardy their longstanding relationship as development partners.

What does that relationship embody in the 21st century? For a start, the high-profile Porsche Cayenne SUV based on the VW Touareg. This big butch Porsche accounts for the lion's share of the 30 percent content VW supplies to Porsche to create motor vehicles wearing the Zuffenhausen shield. Behind the scenes, VW and Porsche are working on a gas-saving hybrid system to help deal with the greater strain placed on finite fossil fuel reserves and higher gasoline prices, caused by the rising demand from emerging economies, oil supply problems and other factors.

VW greeted Porsche's increased shareholder commitment with a sigh of relief, but then again the two parties have always needed each other. Dr. Ferdinand Porsche was the father of the Love Bug, and with project EA-266 Dr. Kurt Lotz asked Porsche to come up with a successor to Beetle Type 1. Project EA-266 was a mid-engined, water-cooled sedan. Ferry Porsche's nephew Ferdinand Piech headed the project for this model family, which had its four-cylinder engine transversely mounted beneath the rear seat. Work on the car cost 250 million deutschmarks, and EA-266 was seen in Lapland flanked by a few of the then-new VW Super Beetles as escorts. However, in October 1971 Dr. Lotz was replaced as VW supremo by Rudolph Leiding from VW Brazil. Leiding dropped EA-266 on the grounds that it would be too pricey to produce.

914 — When Things Go Wrong

Shared history with Beetle I and II, and a rosy 20th-century relationship, were of little help to the Fourteener. After appearing at the 1969 Frankfurt Show, the 914/4 was going to enter production in October 1969, with projected annual output of 30,000 cars. The 914/6 would come into production slightly later. An initial hitch was the absence of right-hand-drive models for markets like the U.K., Japan and Australia, due to VW's penny-pinching desire to recover the money expended on tooling costs as quickly as possible.

As things transpired, a factory designed right-hand-drive car never became a reality, so those wanting right hand drive had to have a special conversion done, once the car landed in the importing country. This was an expensive procedure, and in the U.K., where one has the choice of driving a left-hand-drive car, most buyers didn't bother. In Australia, where conversion for new cars is compulsory, consumers had to swallow the inflated price. Regardless of market, the Fourteener bore a hefty price tag. Economic analysis will explain why, and the reasons were beyond Porsche's control.

The absence of a factory right-hand-drive model was a relatively minor deterrent in the grander scheme. A principal problem for Porsche was the supply of bodies from Karmann. As already mentioned, the "Nordhoff" discount was off the table. This condition was exac-

The VW Old Beetle conquered all world markets. This example is pictured in front of the Dubai InterContinental hotel/apartment complex in the early 1980s (author's collection).

erbated when the 914/6 came into being. It was originally agreed that Porsche would receive the bodies from Osnabruck in bare-bones form. However, under the formalized VG agreement, Porsche received fully painted and trimmed Fourteener bodies, which would then be completed into full blown 914/6s at Zuffenhausen.

Economics 101—How to Buy Your Porsche

Under Dr. Lotz's pricing formula, a 914 body cost more than a 911 body, and the whole point of getting out of the 912 was to move towards a less costly design. So once the 911T motor was fitted and the 914/6 completed by Porsche, the cost advantage compared to a normal 911 was lost, and the rear-engined car was more powerful even in "T" specification. Making matters worse for Zuffenhausen, and for other German manufacturers, was the rising value of the deutschmark. Slowly but surely the U.S. dollar or U.K. pound sterling possessed by buyers in export markets was purchasing fewer West German deutschmarks. It was bad for the overseas buyers because it cost them more to buy an imported Fourteener, and it was also bad news for Porsche. As the deutschmark was revalued against a weaker dollar, the dollars paid for each U.S.–export car were worth less and less to Porsche when converted back to deutschmarks.

The situation from the consumer's perspective was described by the U.K. journal *Motoring Which?* in 1974, comparing the price of an imported 1968 BMW 1600-2 to a 1974 BMW 2002. The 1974 version cost more than double what the 1600-2 was priced at in 1968. In contrast, equivalent U.K.-produced sports sedan prices had risen by less than half.* This relative rise was largely attributable to the strength of the deutschmark, because U.S. and U.K. manufactured goods were affected by the same 1970s economic factors, such as the stagflation intensified by the first fuel crisis.

By the time of the example of the 1974 imported BMW, the exchange rate phenomenon was even worse for Porsche because of the breakdown of the Bretton Woods agreement, the post–World War II exchange rate system of fixing the value of a currency in relation to the U.S. dollar.† As with the earlier breakdown of holding the value of the pound sterling under the gold standard, the exchange rate regime wasn't reflecting underlying economic conditions, specifically the speedy rise of the West German economy in the postwar years known as the "Wirtschaftswunder" or economic miracle.‡

The U.S. was importing relatively more from Western Europe, and Japan than it was exporting. In the face of a worsening balance of payments, the U.S. dollar was overvalued. This precipitated the move to floating exchange rates in March 1973. The value of a nation's currency was now determined by demand and supply on the foreign exchange market. This implied a faster-rising deutschmark to reflect Germany's strong economic position and the sizable demand for its goods and services. With floating rates, the rise is known as an appreciation.

Still, economic reality proved to be little comfort for Porsche+Audi. In the face of a rising deutschmark and falling dollar, the only way to maintain profit for management back at Zuffenhausen was to raise the U.S. price of a 914. This was another part of the shocking price for the U.K.-imported 1974 BMW mentioned previously. Importing concessionaires were lifting prices there just to maintain profit margins. Another item to factor into the price of German goods would be labor costs.

Although known for low strike rates and wage restraint, the union movement too requested and received the gains of the West German economic miracle. The exchange rate and labor cost pressures brought to the foreground the idea of a U.S. factory for VW. All those hundreds of thousands of Beetles sold in 1960s America were imported.** If VW's U.S. Westmoreland factory had come along earlier it could have insulated VW from the economic crunches of the seventies. And if that factory could have assembled the Fourteener, the 914 might have mimicked the U.S. Spartanburg-built BMW Z3 two-seater a quarter of a century early!

Sadly this was not to be; Westmoreland was a friend of the Rabbit rather than the Beetle or Fourteener. A pity, given the large percentage of Porsches sold in the U.S. Yes, high pricing didn't get the 914 off to a robust start. In fact, by the close of the Fourteener's first model year, VW-Porsche VG GmbH had registered a loss of 200 million deutschmarks. There were noises made about shelving the entire joint venture! However, that didn't mean the VG was giving up on the 914, but things got close for a while. Fortunately VW-Porsche persevered, but the 914/6 was skating on thin ice.

**Motoring Which?*, January 1974, p. 23.

†Edward M. Bernstein, "The Making and Remaking of the Bretton Woods Institutions," in *The Bretton Woods-GATT System, Retrospect and Prospect After Fifty Years*, ed. Orin Kirshner (M.E. Sharpe, 1996), pp. 93–94.

‡Raymond, Vernon, "The U.S. Government at Bretton Woods and After," in *The Bretton Woods-GATT System, Retrospect and Prospect After Fifty Years*, ed. Orin Kirshner (M.E. Sharpe, 1996), p. 65.

***National Geographic*, Vol. 152, no. 2, August 1977, pp. 161-162.

Just to show how scary the price of the six-pot Fourteener was, as of November 1970 the 914/4 started from DM 11,955 and the 914/6 was yours from DM 19,980! The six-cylinder was quick, but couldn't make a strong argument against the purchase of a 911. Even the mid-engined layout established little discernible advantage over the 911 family; the Fourteener also was susceptible to sudden rear-end breakaway when pushed. At least Porsche didn't fettle the 914 for safety with handling-numbing predominant understeer, as had happened with the mid-engined Pantera. The Fourteener had the steering reflexes to catch out well-heeled American buyers new to Porsche world, but the abrupt oversteer was disappointing.

It had been hoped that placing the flat six amidships would bring improved control, but Porsche's continual development of the 911 into the long-wheelbase B series of 1969 had somewhat leapfrogged the Fourteener. Next to the pre–1969 911s, the 914's improved handling of on-the-limit oversteer would have been clear; against the new 911 the gain was smaller. A small gain in handling, but at what cost? The 914 had only 2 seats compared to the 2+2 911. The 914/6's first year production total was 2,657, as opposed to the 6,000 sales volume hoped for. It was a sad response to the only roadgoing series production Porsche outside the 911 to contain the classic air-cooled flat six.

Porsche didn't give up on the 914/6, even after its glacially slow start. They had plans to develop the initial 914/6, and place it on par with the 911 family by adding the 2.4-liter flat six. The 911 had gone to 2.2 liters upon the Fourteener's debut, and for 1972 jumped to 2.4 liters. It was this long-stroke flat six that Porsche inserted into the 916. The 916 was a special Fourteener Porsche built to investigate the prospects of a larger-engined 914/6. This hot Fourteener had the wide-arched appearance of the 914/6 GT racer, and an 80-bhp shot in the arm compared to the normal 914/6 2-liter.

916—Fourteener of Dreams

Porsche bypassed "T" specs. and went all the way to the 911S's 190-horse, 2.4-liter flat six, making the 916 a genuine 145-mph road rocket. Bigger rims, fatter tires, a no-compromise suspension and the hefty power increase necessitated structural rigidity, so the 916 had a fixed roof rather than a Targa top. Out of the eleven 916 prototypes, a number had front-mounted oil coolers, with the 915 gearbox modified to suit this application. The constructed cars had very posh interiors. As studies of what an ultimate Fourteener might resemble, the prototypes were loaded with all the goodies, and one car was even air conditioned.

Unfortunately the 916 project was axed, deemed too expensive to produce by the bean counters. After all, Porsche was having a tough time selling the regular 914/6. Porsche had cleared matters so that the 2.4-liter motor could be used by the Fourteener in America, but plans for a 914/6 2.4 seemed to have reached the end of the road. The 1971 M471 GT "racer clone" pack had failed to spark life into the flat-six Fourteener. Rather than 1972 model year being the time for the 914/6 2.4's debut, it represented the virtual demise of the 914/6. The six-pot Fourteener was only available in the U.S. to special order.

1973—Year of the 914

As the final curtain was lowered on the 914/6, just 229 1972 examples were made, with a total of a mere 3,318 created during its short life. It was bye-bye to the 914/6, but better things lay in store for the Fourteener. Nineteen seventy-three turned out to be the 914's best year ever. There was a new 2-liter powerplant for the top 914 which was of VW origins. The VW flat four displaced 1,971 cc, producing exactly 100 horses (DIN net rating) and 115 lbs./ft. torque.

Inserted into the Fourteener, this 2-liter version of VW's ubiquitous air-cooled, overhead-valve flat four was unique to the 914, and predated the use of a 2-liter in the Type 2 Transporter by 3 years. In 914/4 application it was just 10 horses shy of the expensive Porsche overhead-cam, 2-liter flat six used in the outgoing 914/6. Its performance figures were practically identical with the Porsche-powered variant, with zero to sixty and top-speed figures of 9.1 seconds and 116 mph, virtually equal to the 914/6's 8.8 seconds and 120 mph.

It had 2 liters, and performance similar to the 914/6, but the new 2-liter Fourteener was much better value than the Zuffenhausen-completed 914. Previously the 914/6 wasn't much less than the 911T, but just look at the 914 prices for 1973. The regular 914 1.7-liter was listed at $4,499, with the 911T Targa costing a pricey $8,760. However, the new high-performance 914 with 2-liter flat four was only a tad higher than the 914 1.7, a veritable steal at $5,049. It was a marketing coup reminiscent of the time BMW axed the slow-selling 2500/2800 and replaced it with the sharply priced and hot-selling 1971 Bavaria sedan.

The public shouted a collective "yippee!" If history offers anything, it is the lesson that people know and like a bargain when they see it. There were other improvements for 1973, such as softer ride comfort, and better sound/heat insulation. Luxury and sports accoutrements

The new 2 liter VW-powered 914 2.0 invigorated the 914 range and helped make the 1973 model year the Fourteener's best sales effort (courtesy Rev. C. Emerson Strain).

were conveniently grouped into an appearance package. This pack was extremely extensive on the 1973 914 2.0, including desirable items like Fuchs aluminum rims, center console with auxiliary instruments, quartz driving lights, front and rear sway bars, plus an armrest!

A key change for the new model year was the 914's gearbox shift linkage change from tail-shifter to side-shifter. Pre-1973 Fourteeners had their shift forks on the end of the transmission case. For 1973 the forks were repositioned to the side of the transmission casing. This modification simplified the shift linkage and improved shift quality. However, since all 914s have a rather convoluted shift linkage, shift quality was still somewhat vague — another issue to be addressed on its successor, the Porsche 924.

The upgrades, plus the hot new 914 2.0, helped the Fourteener to a career-best sales figure, only 10 percent below the originally envisaged 30,000 sales per year. However, it wasn't all glad tidings for '73. Californian 914 1.7s lost 8 horses, with compression falling from 8.2 to just 7.3 to one, partly due to tight emissions regulations, and partly due to the absence of high-test gas in California. That said, both 1.7 and 2.0 flat fours continued with Bosch D-jet injection. One thing that didn't continue was the use of the "S" nomenclature for the new 2-liter 914.

The VW-powered 2-liter 914 was originally launched in Europe as the 914S, and it even carried this nameplate in some early U.S. advertising. However, the 914S description was soon changed to 914 2.0, and the new variant was sold under this designation in North America. That said, the model continued to be called 914SC in the U.K. and Australia, the SC tag evoking a glamorous 911 connection. Another anomaly was the earlier existence of the popular "S" pack on the 914/4 in Europe.

Porsche weren't too happy about freely handing out their "S" suffix. As would later be seen on the 924, 944 and 928, it takes a certain type of car to wear the sacred "S." For a start, a Porsche motor was required, and the 914 2.0 certainly didn't have that. Porsche may also have taken umbrage at the 914 2.0's success. While their own 914/6 gathered dust on showroom floors, its Vee Dub–motivated replacement was going gangbusters. It was a bitter pill to swallow.

Those who try to downplay the credibility of VW-powered Porsches should note that while the 1.7 and 1.8 motors used in the 914/4 and 914 1.8 were very close to their VW Type 4 counterparts, the 914 2.0's engine showed some fine touches. The 2.0's casing was both stronger and better finished, and its crankshaft had wider-spaced journals and had received treatment to make it harder. The 914 2.0 had better-flowing heads, superior quality pistons and sodium-filled valves. This last item was useful for any owner wishing to turbo their car. Even the Bosch D-jet injectors had extra capacity compared to the units used in the 411/412. So the injected 2-liter VW flat four was certainly fit for a Porsche, and its power rating matched the most powerful 356 Super 90 motor in spite of the change to SAE net ratings by 1973.

The Fourteener had overcome its shaky start, and it became West Germany's best-selling sports car in 1972. The discontinuation of the Opel GT, the Fourteener's arch rival in the U.S. and Europe, at the end of 1973 signalled extra hope for the 914 in the 1974 model year, where revisions continued apace. Most noticeable was the arrival of the 1.8-liter 914, replacing the 1970–73 1.7 base model. This new powerplant was sourced from the VW 412, the new and improved update of the VW 411 luxury model.

The giant bug now had an upgunned 1,795 cc flat four with bore and stroke dimensions of 93 × 66 mm. Although the injected 412E was the top version for VW, the 914 1.8 switched from the 914 1.7's Bosch D-jet to carburetors in the interests of maximum performance. The

A 1974 914 1.8 in Olympic Blue Euroglow color. The VW 412's 1.8 was the new base motor, featuring Bosch L-Jetronic injection in the U.S. (courtesy Rev. C. Emerson Strain).

411/412E injection applications were emissions-compromised, as was the case for most fuel-injected motors of the time. So the European spec 914 1.8 featured dual 2-barrel Weber carbs and a raised 8.6 to one compression ratio. Power was up from 80 to 85 horses, with a useful 105 lbs./ft. of maximum torque. The 914 1.8 North America received used electronic fuel injection only, but had switched from Bosch D-jet to the second generation Bosch L-jet.

With tightening federal pollution laws, the Fourteener was never going to get by on carbs. The L-jet system offered greater reliability, in theory. Rather than intake-manifold pressure, the computer now sensed the amount of air aspirated, gauged by the position of a moving door in an airflow meter housing. The latter method should have been less troublesome, but in practice vacuum leaks from various places could trick the system and precipitate rough running. However, the new engine was for 50-state use. In 1973 there were the 80 bhp 49-state 914 1.7, and the special 914 1.7 for California with 72 horses. The new 1.8-liter split the difference between the two outgoing 1.7s by having 76 bhp, and it was emissions-cleared for the whole of America.

The time for dual and triple carbs was fading. The 1974 U.S. 914 1.8 was part of Porsche's learning curve towards the goal of using fuel injection to achieve performance parity between markets. For America Porsche+Audi separated the option packages into luxury and sport, placing the Pedrinni and Fuchs aluminum rims, Bilstein shocks and sway bars specifically into the sport grouping. The 914 2.0 continued on for 1974 without a power drop, and still used Bosch D-jet fuel injection.

Indeed, for the 1974 model year there was a Can-Am limited edition of the 914 2.0, with all the sport/luxury goodies and three color schemes: black with yellow trim, white with green trim or white with orange trim. Porsche had been Can-Am series champs in 1972 and 1973. Who could forget the late Mark Donohue pushing the Sunoco-liveried 917 replete with "Porsche+Audi" franchise decal? The commemorative Can-Am 1974 914 2.0s were created to celebrate the achievements of the previous two racing seasons.

The Incredible Shrinking Market

However, the celebrations were tainted by economics. Though improved for 1974 with a bigger-engined base model, and a 914 2.0 which maintained its 1973 power level, the Fourteener was losing ground. The energy-crisis-inspired recession was in full swing, and West Germany's floating exchange rate was doing the 914 range no competitive favors. In hard times the public concentrates its spending on necessities, and cuts back discretionary expenditure on fanciful items such as 2-seater sports cars. The Fourteener, also known as the square Porsche, may have had the rectangular edges of a box of cereal, but that didn't fool the consumer.

In truth the 914 had arrived onto a North American, and world, market, that was already quite full of sporty rides by the start of the seventies: English Triumph TR 250, MGB 2-seater, a 7-liter American muscle car, or perhaps one of the new sports sedans from Japan?

Looking down the road at a future mid-engined entry level Porsche, the 914 was the Boxster of its generation (courtesy Rev. C. Emerson Strain).

Right in the 914's neck of the woods was the 1968–73 Opel GT 2-seater, also known as the mini Vette. Produced in the heart of the 914's production run, this Opel sold 103,373 copies, with the lion's share going to America. And consider the fact that TV's favorite secret agent Maxwell Smart drove an Opel GT, whereas the 914 looked rather suspicious. An evil KAOS agent might have driven a 914!

In the U.S. the Opel GT could draw upon its General Motors parentage by being sold through upscale Buick showrooms across the country, which was handy. In contrast the shake-up of distribution arrangements that saw VW/Porsche outlets having to choose between staying with VW, or spending big to be Porsche+Audi dealers, resulted in the number of places selling Porsche in the U.S. dropping by a third! The Opel GT and Porsche 914 were duking it out over the same piece of the sales pie. One can also speculate how much better the 914 could have done if Porsche hadn't been pressured by VW on the price of Fourteener bodies. A lower-priced 914 flat four, available from the same number of U.S. showrooms that offered VWs and Porsches prior to 1970, could have helped the mid-engined VW-Porsche exceed the projected 30,000 sales per year.

Even the Opel GT's departure was of little comfort, because its place in the U.S. was taken by the hot-selling Fiat X1/9 in 1974 — another mid-engined rival for a Fourteener that seemed to be running out of gas. As one door opened, another seemed to slam shut for the 914. It is surprising to see the sheer volume and variety of foreign sports cars sold in the U.S. up to the mid–1980s. Following the lead of the British after World War II, America became the number-one export market for speedy, curve-hugging coupes. And if one added up the

It's back, the four-cylinder 912! The 1976 912E was for North America only, and tided Porsche over until the new 924 could surface (courtesy David L. Lovato).

production runs of the various models from England, Italy, France and West Germany, they came to a sizable figure.

VW wasn't really interested in these recent developments. In the Beetle's heyday they were used to people buying Karmann Ghias come rain or shine. So if Porsche came to VW with worries about the congested and deflated market they would have pooh-poohed those concerns, or words to that effect in German. The VG was a partnership, the 914 was using VW parts and VW flat fours. VW weren't too pleased with the flagging Fourteener. They wanted more 914s sold, more cars using VW hardware supplied under contract, just like in the days of the Karmann Ghia.

It wasn't just the Fourteener that was bugging Wolfsburg. In 1973/74 they were in the midst of generational change away from a rear-engined, air-cooled past that had seen them become the best-known quality economy brand in the world. Porsche's partner in the VG garage was getting restless, and the 914 had an air-cooled motor positioned aft of the passenger compartment. Dr. Ferdinand Porsche may have created the immortal Bug, but the Porsche-VW partnership was about to get squished! At the behest of VW, the two groups parted company on May 8, 1974.

The agreement to disagree involved Porsche's taking ownership of VW's share of VW-Porsche VG GmbH; the 914 would be exclusively their baby from now on. To this end Porsche's sales people moved into the VG's headquarters in Ludwigsburg and plotted the 914's course for its final two production years. The tightening choke of emissions regulations saw air injection for the 914 1.8 and 2.0, with selective use of exhaust-gas recirculation on 49-state cars. California's 914s now had a catalytic converter, implying the compulsory use of no-lead gas.

Using a very similar powerplant to the outgoing 914 2.0, the VW-powered 912E had nearly the same outright performance as the earlier Porsche-powered 912 (courtesy David L. Lovato).

The 914 2.0 lost 5 SAE net horses compared to 1973/74, and all 914s picked up 5-mph, insurance-friendly impact bumpers, plus a steadily rising price. Porsche took the decision to sell the Fourteener in America alone for the 1976 model year. It was down to just one version now that the VW Type 2 van had ditched the 1.8 flat four to match the 914's 2 liters. The 411/412 family was history, the Beetle was barely hanging on in the U.S. and Europe, the last vestiges of the VW air-cooled empire were vanishing! To keep the 914 2.0 company in America during the 1976 model year, Porsche introduced the 912E.

The 912E shared its 2-liter VW flat four with the 914 2.0, except that it offered 86 horses and Bosch L-Jetronic, rather than the 914 2.0's D-jet. It was a junior version of the current 911, in the same manner the 912 had been in 1965–69. It also exactly matched the performance figures of the Super 90–powered 912. Only 2,099 examples of the 912E were sold in America for 1976. Like the 1976 914 2.0, it was a USA-export-only model, and was priced midway between the final 914 2.0 and the 911. The trickle of final U.S. Fourteener sales helped to take the 914 total close to 120,000 units produced. Not a small total, but below the 180,000 originally projected for the Fourteener over the 1970–76 production period.

A Boxster in Another Place and Time

The Fourteener was an unlucky machine. It was in effect the Porsche Boxster of its day: a design connection across the decades that is hard to ignore, especially with the 914/6 and 916 cars. It was quite simply the little brother of the 911, just as the Boxster has been since 1996. Of course the Fourteener never reached its sales potential for two reasons: high price, and the fact it didn't look like a 911. Had Porsche cleverly clothed the 914 to resemble the 911, it would have had the showroom magnetism of a latter-day Boxster — that is, a 911 that one could more easily afford.

The 914's high price was due to economic factors, and its joint venture relationship with Wolfsburg. This wasn't due to any shortcomings concerning VW machinery, but more to the business constraints of having a party looking over your shoulder and laying down some onerous ground rules. In addition there was the practical reality that VW supplied a lot of Fourteener parts, especially the large-capacity 1.7–2.0 flat-four boxer motors. When your big

Porsche was preparing us for the high cost of 21st century living as far back as the 1970s (cartoon by author).

buddy starts creating tension, or stops production of models that provide parts/engines to complete your cars, there isn't much you can do. Recall the difficulty Canadian entrepreneur Malcolm Bricklin was placed in when American Motors couldn't maintain regular supply of the 360 c.i., 4-barrel V8 for his SV-1 gullwing coupe.

It isn't easy being small. Porsche would have to tread cautiously. The 914 could have been the Miata of the early seventies, if it had entered a vacant market like the small Mazda did in 1989. However, close isn't good enough, and soon after the commencement of the 1976 model year, Porsche announced a successor to the beleaguered 914 — the 924. A sequel with a similar sounding name, but Fourteener II was a whole different animal. For Porsche's sake it would have to be.

Chapter 2

924—The New Littlest Porsche

The Decade of the Anti-Hero

It was difficult to be a car in the 1970s. This was the follow-up decade, when esteemed manufacturers had to replace their designs from the fifties and sixties, designs that were considered classics even in their lifetime. More often than not the sequel wasn't as well received. Maserati Quattroporte II wasn't up to the standards set by Quattroporte I, and the public didn't warm to the Dino 308 GT4 as much as they had to the previous 206/246. The Jaguar XJ-S always lived in the shadow of the immortal E-type, and very few enthusiasts were willing to extol the virtues of the Triumph TR7 compared to the TR2–6 dynasty.

Sharp, chiseled models gave way to dumpy-looking successors that were usually slower, and had strange glowing devices warning about seatbelt usage. It was a bitter pill to swallow, not so much for the average buyers of family cars as for the buyers of sporting cars, especially sports cars. This was an endangered species, and the choice was fast becoming limited to aging models from yesteryear as design requirements of safety, emissions control and convenience equipment saw car makers give up on this segment.

In the decade that gave us the bean bag chair and Barry Manilow, the challenge was put to Porsche to come up with something capable of going beyond this decade, and possibly into the next century. Naturally it would have to be a timeless design, one that avoided the contemporary clichés of a wedge plated with matte black plastic and adorned with cubed taillights arranged to create the illusion of rocket afterburners. Porsche had such a vehicle. It was going to be called the 928, and work on it commenced in 1971. The powers that be at Volkswagen knew of this plan, and were eager to have a knock-off to serve their image in the way the Fiat Dino bridged the gap between Fiat and Ferrari ownership.

Volkswagen had acquired an upscale marque when they purchased DKW. Under the banner of four circular rings, the reborn Audi brand had been successful for the VW group, giving it a way to move upmarket, gain factory space and fine engineering minds. Audi had made a good start, and a sports coupe bearing the four-ring logo would have been a nice image car for the Ingolstadt manufacturer as it moved beyond merely worthy sedans. Ferry Porsche's nephew Ferdinand Piech, formerly at Porsche and now with VW-Audi, thought it was a good idea for Porsche to design this sports car for VW-Audi. The finished coupe would use as many family VW parts as possible, but draw on the sports car experience of Zuffenhausen regarding the design blueprint.

All seemed to bode well for the sporty newcomer. Although VW boss Rudolf Leiding had canned plans for the Porsche-designed EA-266 Beetle replacement, VW were now wedded to front-engined/front-drive Audi & NSU thinking for their future. The EA-425 sports car received approval on Leiding's watch. Porsche were formally given the task of designing

On the track and in the showroom, the 924 was carrying the weight of history on its shoulders (courtesy John Gacioch).

the new Audi coupe in January 1972, and things would be different with this second joint venture. Unlike the arrangement with VG for the 914, Porsche would be staying in the background. The new car would be badged as an Audi, and apart from being a second attempt to replace the Karmann Ghia, would also take over from the early–'70s Audi 100S coupe, which was also going to wrap up by the mid–'70s.

It seemed like another scheme that couldn't lose, although the same had been felt about the 914. However, during the course of 1974 VW's interest in EA-425 dwindled. Mighty Volkswagen were in trouble from the fuel-crisis-triggered recession, strong deutschmark, pressure from Opel and over-reliance on the Beetle. Apart from the economic problems that were affecting all car makers, VW had a special problem with their Beetle-based range. For the past decade Wolfsburg had tried to come up with the next Beetle, and had failed to find it. VW tried the Type 3, Type 4 and even the K70 that they had won by buying out NSU, but these cars were stopgaps, fillers until a real Beetle replacement could be found.

In 1974 VW made its first loss ever, and Beetle sales slumped to half their normal figure. The Love Bug that had taken VW to third-largest car maker in the world was running out of gas. Indeed, staff that worked at VW during these hard times were against the idea of reviving the steel insect 20-plus years later as the Golf-based VW New Beetle, prompted by bitter memories of job losses and pay cuts and management inertia in coming up with a new VW small car. They didn't wish to be reminded of those days of forced restructuring. Casualties of the 1974 storm were EA-425 and Rudolf Leiding; altered culture at VW meant that neither had a place at VW by the close of 1974.

Leiding's replacement at VW was Toni Schmücker, and the Beetle's European replacement

A 1972 924 prototype, looking not unlike a plump three-fourth-scale early '70s Ferrari 365 GTC/4 (courtesy Porsche).

was the VW Golf. The 1973 European Car of the Year was the Audi 80, and it was this model, through the closely related VW Passat, and the Golf, that paved the path for VW's recovery. From this new family of front-drive, water-cooled inline four-cylinder cars with tremendous engineering commonality would first come the VW Scirocco coupe, and after a lag of four years the Audi 80–based GT first seen as the glamorous 1980 Quattro. All of this meant that the VW group had all the coupes they needed, making EA-425 unnecessary.

EA-425 may have been surplus to VW's requirements, but it was certainly of value to Porsche. They had the 928 set up to completely replace the 911 by 1980, but still needed a junior model to maintain sales volume. While the 914 2.0 and 912E were both 1976 model year choices, the latter replaced the former because the 914 was out of stock during the spring of 1976. A four-cylinder 912 would be cheaper than a 911, but wasn't the budget model Porsche needed to take over from the moderately successful 914. The answer was EA-425, or Type 924 as Porsche referred to it internally. However, VW had spent 180 million deutschmarks on the intended Audi sports car; if Porsche wanted to reclaim their work it was going to cost them.

It could still have been a bargain. The 914 was sold as a VW-Porsche outside the U.S., so Porsche had yet to capitalize on the effect its name might have on a true junior Porsche. A Porsche is what the new car would be, according to the deal Porsche formalized with VW by January 1975. It would be sold exclusively with the Porsche shield, but the deal didn't end there. Apart from having to pay to get their own work back, Porsche were locked into buying major parts and components for the Type 924 from the VW empire. This wasn't a problem initially because the new coupe was designed by Porsche to use such parts, but, by insisting

The 924's steering wheel logo featured a furry animal against the background of Wolfsburg Castle; after all, EA-425 was a project for VW/Audi (courtesy Porsche).

on a 2-year course of continual purchasing, there would be a delay before Porsche could start using their own components and thereby take the 924 away from its initial state.

This was so much added cake icing for VW, because the new Golf/Rabbit and all their other new water-cooled front-drivers had turned out to be hot sellers, allowing VW Beetle sedan production to close out in 1978. That said, if Porsche was going to send a few deutschmarks VW's way, Toni Schmücker wasn't going to refuse. Indeed, recent developments marked great change in the relationship between VW and Porsche. The Beetle EA-266 from Porsche had been elbowed out, the 914 VG operation was over, and Porsche's racing exploits were of little interest to VW in 1975. In the fifties and sixties, Porsche victory on the track was all to VW's good, because Porsche was increasingly one of the few companies showcasing the road-to-race-car rear-engined-air-cooled format. This enhanced Beetle sales, so VW showed their appreciation. Now VW had passed on Porsche's designs and found a new future with the Golf. Porsche were buying those parts for the 924, beyond that it seemed like VW had forgotten their friends at Zuffenhausen.

924—What Porsche Is This?

Entering the mid '70s it was interesting to see the approach Porsche would take as a long-time exponent of rear-engined automobiles. Part of the design criteria laid out for the 924 was that it would generally resemble the expensive 928, but Porsche also wanted the 924 to

In the wind tunnel in 1975, the 924 recorded a creditable 0.36 Cd (courtesy Porsche).

adopt the 928's front-engined transaxle layout. As the seventies gathered pace designers were falling out of love with the mid-engined layout, as seen on the 914. At one time the mid-engined location was seen as indispensable for perfect handling. Formula One cars made a rather retrogressive step by going back to front-engines after World War II. The few front-engined chassis left by the start of the '60s, like the Scarab, were easily outpaced by those putting the motor amidships.

The problem with having all the weight up front was major understeer: the front wheels turned, but the nose kept going straight on. Rear-engined cars threatened to bite back with mad oversteer, where the tail could overtake the nose given sufficient chance. The mid-engined layout promised a perfect middle ground, easy directional change with greater neutrality than rear-engined racers. For a time this all held true; mid-engined cars came onto the market, and there was always the rumor that even the Corvette would go mid-engined. The problem is that mid-engined cars have a low polar moment: they like to change direction because they are relatively easy to spin.*

Easy to spin, but also easy to stop spinning. Even so, the part about "easy to spin" could catch out the unwary, so designers tried to defuse the situation with slow steering and dialed-in understeer. Numbing the reflexes seemed to defeat the very reason for mid-engined cars in the first place. In the search for another middle ground, Porsche went the front-engined transaxle route. This avoided the ponderous understeer through spreading out the weight, by having the engine at the front and gearbox at the rear. Plus, by having these two masses at the car's outer ends, the finished design would have a high polar moment, making it hard to spin. Although great strides had been taken to limit the rear-end waywardness of the 911, Porsche thought a clean sheet would get them safer handling faster. Since the mid '70s the theory has developed that there is more to handling behavior than the placement of engine and gearbox masses. By playing with other chassis factors it's possible to make the rear-engined formula a safe one, proof of which is the continuance of the 911 into the 21st century.

**Thoroughbred & Classic Cars,* Vol. 16, no. 12, September 1989, p. 133.

The benefits of the front-engine/transaxle layout extended to safety and noise pollution. For crash protection it made sense to spread the car's machinery along its length for more effective crumple zones and energy absorption, indeed the transaxle chassis itself could take some load with the torque tube at its center. Spreading the machinery was also good news for drive-by noise pollution tests: having a front engine allowed noise to be dissipated using a car-length-long exhaust system. This was more easily achieved than when all the cacophony-making hardware was located in the tail.

With tighter safety and noise pollution regulations already reality, the path the 924/928 took was very necessary.

From the showroom perspective Type 924 would be much more appealing in terms of packaging, that is, the business of combining mechanical and passenger/luggage accommodation components into a vehicle of modest dimensions. Make it small on the outside, but big on the inside. The new boxy VW Golf/Rabbit was very good at this. The VW Beetle, even in Super Beetle MacPherson strut front suspension configuration, was not. Rear-engined and mid-engined cars are intrinsically space inefficient. It confined the 914 family to 2-seater status, and put off heaven knows how many customers due to the absence of those token rear seats. The 924 wasn't going to make that mistake. The third requirement for EA-425 insisted upon by VW was that the new car have at least as much accommodation as the 2+2 911.

Thus, the 924 joined its contemporaries by adhering to that 1970s phenomenon known as — the liftback! The 1974 Mustang II fastback went this route, as did the 1974 second series Mercury Capri and the 1976 Toyota Celica, as well as the 1974 Volkswagen Scirocco. The long-

Out of love with the mid-engine, in love with pop-up lamps and a hatchback! The 924 was a contemporary mid-seventies vehicle (courtesy Porsche).

dormant hatchback/liftback concept was so much more practical than the tiny notchback trunklids that used to be the only choice for such cars. In the mid '70s people wanted practicality in their sports cars, and it was even better if fold down rear seats were included. The 924 had fold down rear seats, and very useful they were too. With the seats in the upright position the 924 boasted 10.4 cu. ft. of trunk capacity, rising to 18.3 cu. ft. with the +2 seats folded flat. Up or down that was more trunk capacity than was normally associated with a sport compact. And just compare that against the Corvette of the day, which was 15 inches longer and whose only storage area was a tiny compartment behind the seats.

The drawback was a high load floor, a consequence of the transaxle layout, but this was still a Porsche a couple could shop for groceries in. Purchases could also be concealed by pulling a roller blind cover that extended from the top of the rear seats. Behind the rear wheels in the trunk were useful covered compartments deep enough to store a couple of years' worth of scrunched up speeding tickets. The orderly minds at Zuffenhausen obviously didn't want 924 owners to litter! The 924 was for pragmatic Porsche owners mindful of contemporary gasoline prices and wanting storage space greater than that necessary to flick their cigar ash into — but how did it all *look*?

Styling of the 924, like the 928 which was being done concurrently, was the preserve of a styling team headed by Porsche's Anthony Lapine, which included a young Harm Lagaay. Compared to the 914 the new car had a very harmonious, easy-to-like shape. It was smooth and flowing; when light levels were low and just the 924's silhouette was visible it resembled

The 924 combined the yet-to-arrive 928's transaxle layout with many VW empire hardware items (courtesy Porsche).

an early–'70s Ferrari 365 GTC/4 thanks to the accentuated dip in the windowsill near the door post. This was a simple, pretty shape that wasn't as strongly in the wedge mold as cars of the day. The 924 did have the then-fashionable pop-up headlights, but this characteristic seemed to work in its favor.

Interestingly, 8 prototypes were built during 1973/74, and these early drafts looked decidedly dumpy. They resembled an early–'70s safety-design-vehicle study, or a baked potato. Wisely, Team Porsche removed the heaviness from the basic shape. That said, the 924's rear 3/4 area has been considered rather noticeable from some angles, like a generous set of female hips. Renault seemed to like it, though, since the later French Fuego coupe mimicked the high-waisted style. Overall, though, this was the first Porsche road car released that was styled for looks. Going way back to the days of the 356, it's unlikely that appearance was a high priority for Ferry Porsche, as he tried to get his car roadworthy and Werk production off the ground. The upside-down-bathtub shape served those early Porsches well enough, its aerodynamic form allowing the little car to attain enough velocity to justify the nameplate Speedster. At a time when a full windshield was considered a frivolity, enthusiasts seemed content.

One generation on, Butzi Porsche's 911 body's main goal was to conceal the workings of the amazing new flat 6. Stylewise it was still within shouting distance of Doctor Porsche's original Beetle. Observing the dual tailpipes of a late–'60s 911 and the dual pipes of a Beetle Bug, one can clearly see the evolution from the 1930s. Now in the slick seventies buyers eschewed detachable side screens in favor of weather-tight glass, but it wasn't enough for the 924 to be simply functional. In spite of a likeable customer clinic shape, the 924 notched up a drag coefficient of 0.36: a most respectable figure at a time when such matters were little discussed, and largely responsible for the littlest Porsche's meeting its claimed terminal velocity of 125 mph.

Stylistic faux pas really came down to the class of car at hand and people's expectations. The standard 924 came with 14 × 5.5-inch pressed steel rims that somewhat resembled those from the Citroen Visa economy car. Step into the racing cockpit and the dashboard was a simple molding with HVAC housing center console. Lots of plastic, lots of Golf Mk1-sourced VW switches, as one would have expected under the EA-425 design proposal. The left hand circular dial housing colored idiot warning lights and the water temp/gas gauge was extremely Dasher/Passat-like, and the 924's 2-spoke steering wheel was very much the equivalent of the 2-spoker in a Rabbit, with the exception of having the Porsche shield embossed in its center.

Quality was good, everything was screwed together nicely, but the nature of the materials and the '70s color scheme of browns/beiges mixed with tartan seat inlays was unusual for a Porsche. If the 924 had been badged as an Audi such things wouldn't have raised a Roger Moore-esque James Bond eyebrow, but with the Porsche crest such cute eccentricities were hard to excuse. Low priced for a Porsche the 924 might have been, but its interior/exterior style seemed to place it in the Triumph TR7, Mazda RX7 zone, and it was a lot pricier than those two cars. This was a Porsche in the era of the 930, a Porsche wasn't meant to be cute!

Mother Nature, an Insect and a Monster!

The parts bin nomenclature directed at the 924 was due to the new coupe's heavy reliance upon mechanical components from within the VW family. As part of the initial deal struck between VW and Porsche, the 924 used items from the Golf/Scirocco (an ocean current and

The integrated dash molding and center console were a generation past the 911, but at least Porsche kept the counterclockwise tach (courtesy Porsche).

wind respectively), the Super Beetle (our insect) and the VW Type 181 cross-country vehicle also known as "The Thing" (the monster component). The good Doctor had given Volkswagen "strength through joy," as it were, via the original Beetle, so it was only right that Wolfsburg return the favor by supplying components for the new 924.

It may have originated under a directive to cut costs, and suit Volkswagen, but the 924 was getting components from legends of the past and future: the Beetle, the world's most popular car of all time and the car that introduced America to the concept of a subcompact with bullet-proof reliability, and the Golf/Rabbit, *Consumer Reports*' highest rated 1975 modern subcompact and Europe's number-one quality family car for the next 25 years.* Even outside these facts was the historical legacy of the 356, a car that made great use of Beetle mechanicals and the hardy flat four before Porsche hit the big time and could afford to specialize its designs.

Did not the revered MG marque stand for Morris Garages, and can't the reborn Maserati 3200GT trace ventilation grilles and switchgear from within the Fiat group? After years of the rising cost of Porsche ownership, Porsche were just trying to beat the high cost of living by going back to basics and making a cheaper car that embodied Porsche values, values related to integrity of design rather than slavish adherence to the dictates of rear-engined air cooling. The 924's journey would have been much easier had the 928 come out first. A V8 luxury car would have been a much easier sell to the public, easing acceptance of a water-cooled front-engined Porsche. But the fuel crisis and financial concerns delayed the 928, and it fell to the humble 924 to bring on Porsche's new wave at the 1975 Frankfurt motor show.

**Consumer Reports*, Vol. 40, no. 7, July, 1975, p. 406.

Porsche lays down a new law with the 924. Zuffenhausen supplied special cars to the Police and other emergency services. If it's a life or death matter, one can rely on Porsche quality (courtesy Porsche).

With 914 production about to cease, it was of much greater concern to get the volume 924 into showrooms earlier than the 928 supercar. Image-wise it was a mistake, because buyers would have loved the idea of getting a budget 928, had the big car existed — the 924 might have glowed in its halo effect. And the public were getting a smaller version of the 928: at the core of the car was a similar torque tube transaxle chassis of front water-cooled engine/rear gearbox. The downside was that a car retailing around $10,000 couldn't have the same high-end components as a car with a $30,000 price sticker. So the 924's disk/drum brakes came courtesy of the by-now-defunct NSU/VW K70 sedan. The MacPherson strut front suspension was derived from the VW Golf, with lower A-arms and rack & pinion steering both supplied by the VW Scirocco. At the rear the semi-trailing-arm transverse torsion bar suspension came from the VW Super Beetle.

The regular Beetle featured the infamous swing axle. In theory, the switch to semi-trailing-arm suspension meant that the Super Beetle and 924 were unlikely to flip over in trying circumstances. As part of the 924's sturdy make-up, Porsche selected the 924's driveshafts from the go-anywhere VW Type 181 cross-country buggy, of all things. Part of the deal between VW and Porsche was that the 924 draw on the hardware VW had at its disposal. No problem in the 914 days when the Beetle was still king, but more difficult now that VW as a modern company had gone front-drive. The 924 was a rear-drive machine, as per real sports car practice. The only vehicles listed above that were rear drive were the original Type 1-descended Super Beetle/Thing.

Porsche had selected well considering the range of cars open to them, and Porsche were ahead of their time marketing this multipart-sourced 924. In the modern era of platform-

Top: **The original Porsche 924 alloy wheel, measuring 14 × 6 inches, served on into 1985 (courtesy Benny Proot).** ***Bottom:*** **A European spec 1978 924 in action in Belgium. The new four-cylinder coupe was a clean sheet design by Zuffenhausen (courtesy Benny Proot).**

sharing and V12 Aston Martin engines based on joined Ford V6s, the 924's parts inventory would be normal. Indeed, the 924 was an original idea that just happened to use off-the-shelf parts, as a platform it was unique. Next to the 924, the Porsche Cayenne-to-VW Touareg interface resembles a verbatim exchange program. However, in 1975 the idea of drawing on the VW parts bin was hard to take, as was the idea that all 924s would be built at the old NSU Neckarsulm factory, not the Porsche Werks.

The assembly point was geographically close to Porsche's factory, but a world away in the mind of critics. How could it be a Porsche, if Porsche didn't build it? But the 924 was made in Germany, practically walking distance from Porsche. In addition, the NSU factory had assembled the complex rotary-engined NSU Ro80, so it had pedigree as a production concern. Why are there no qualms expressed over the BMW Z4's being U.S.-built? Answer: a lot fewer auto enthusiasts in 2005/6! Given that the 924 would take over from the 914, it was impossible for the Porsche Werks to build the projected/actual 924 sales volume. The 924 wasn't on the same level as the 911, that was the job of the yet-to-arrive 928. Thus, it was unfair to compare an early 924 with steel wheels to an exclusive 911. Under agreement with VW the 924 would be assembled at Neckarsulm, just as the large-selling 914 had been made at Osnabruck. In fact Porsche only took over production of the 944, also made at the NSU factory, once sales had slowed to a snail's pace.

But one wouldn't be travelling at a snail's pace around corners, or in the treacherous wet, when driving a 924. Whether 928 or 924, it made no difference, either car had better handling than a 911 could deliver. Based on the technology available at the time, the 924 offered

The steel monocoque structure of the 924 offered superior crush protection as compared to Porsche's rear-engined cars (courtesy Porsche).

much safer, more predictable handling than the much improved, but still "pray & hope," 911. It was a question of balance, and thinking; Porsche avoided the pitfalls so far experienced by others that tried the transaxle in a front-engined vehicle. Pontiac put forward a bent driveshaft in their 1961 transaxle Tempest, partly to elicit as much passenger space as possible, but also because a rotating shaft tends to whip awkwardly when straight.

A good idea to have the shaft bent, but in practice only the automatic Tempest seemed able to mask the vibration, which defeated the raison d'être for the bent shaft in the first place. Transaxles also tend to be associated with slow, awkward manual shifts. There's the mechanical inertia of a heavy driveshaft straining the match-up job of the synchromesh. So Porsche slimmed down the driveshaft and ran it on four sealed bearings inside the torque tube that formed a rigid connection between the motor at the front and transaxle at the rear. The 924's

A quality check on the 924 assembly line at the Neckarsulm NSU factory, where 924s were assembled to a very high standard (courtesy Porsche).

clutch was at the forward (engine end) bell housing. The stick shifter was conveniently mounted on top of the tube, with the shift rod taking a straight path back directly along the torque tube to relay shift selection to the transaxle via an aperture in the empty rear bell housing.

Porsche had replaced the nightmarish remote shift linkage of the 914 with a model of simplicity. The 914's linkage mechanism was the very definition of indirect, prone to maladjustment and subsequently the vaguest shift action anyone would wish to encounter. On the 924, gear changes were accompanied by a weighty precise action. It made little difference that the changes were relayed to an Audi 4-speed box. The design of the shift mechanism was shared with the 928 as well. Indeed, the two big differences between the transaxle systems on the 924 and 928 were limited to the number of support bearings for the driveshaft and the gearbox placement. The 928's shaft ran in just 2 bearings thanks to the smoother behavior of the V8 engine. The 928's gearbox was placed in front of the final drive, in the 924 it was placed behind due to space constraints.

It was more desirable to have the gearbox ahead of the final drive, because it was a bonus for rear passenger accommodation and handling. The improvement in the latter was because it kept the mechanicals ahead of the rear axle line, making for a better compromise between having a low and high polar moment. The 928 was more akin to the mid-engined style of keeping the mechanicals in a concentrated space. In contrast, the 924 had more in common with the 911 by having its gearbox behind the rear axle line. However, in spite of gearbox placement and the absence of the 928's Weissach axle, the 924/944 family turned out to be Porsche's best-handling package of the modern era. Having the gearbox way out back didn't make it oversteer wildly when at the limit like the 911.

With a hatchback and fold-down rear seats the 924's utility quotient was immense (courtesy Benny Proot).

Fold down the exquisitely trimmed rear buckets and luggage capacity rose to 18.3 cu. ft. (courtesy Porsche)

The 924 didn't possess the 928's fancy wishbone suspension, either, but in the spirit of "less is more" the smaller car's weight advantage seemed to account for its ultimate advantage in the Porsche clan. Weight is always the enemy of a sports car. Lightness was the reason 911-based cars blitzed the opposition in racing, and it was the secret of the 924's success. If anything, at least the torque tube/transaxle complex was a handy place to suspend the exhaust system from. As different as the 911 and 924 were at first glance, it's surprising how much they had in common. Porsche threw the 911's distinctive high-backed bucket seats into the little 924, and the special touches didn't stop there.

The 924 had a partially galvanized monocoque structure even from the earliest times. The rear fenders, floor section and rocker panels were galvanized. It allowed the 924 to sport a full 6-year anti-corrosion warranty at a time when Lancia Betas were dissolving before their disgruntled owners' eyes. An optional high-capacity, 911-style headlamp-cleaning system was available for the 924. With this item the standard container was replaced by a huge water tank, and high-pressure jets would keep the 924's pop-up lights bright and shining. The 924's instrument cluster featured a typically Porsche racing style offset tachometer, permitting easier sighting of the needle at high rpm.

The informed will know that VW and Porsche flat fours and sixes rely on both air and engine oil to prevent overheating. As a result, an oil temperature gauge was a regular Porsche

Testing the 924's integrity. Even the earliest 924s carried a 6-year antirust warranty thanks to galvanized steel (courtesy Porsche).

fixture, and this tradition continued with the 924 — even though it was water-cooled! On the center console there were two circular gauges flanking either a clock, or the air conditioning switch on cars so equipped. The left gauge gave oil pressure readings, and the right gauge oil temperature. For 1977 this quaint holdover was replaced with a boring voltmeter. To complement the experience, the 924 could eventually have its VW-like 2-spoke steering wheel replaced with a genuine leather-wrapped 911 three spoke tiller. Even better news came in 1978 when Porsche made available its own 911-sourced, close-ratio 5-speed manual gearbox for the 924.

The Getrag 5-speeder was the usual dogleg racing shift (1st located out of the H pattern) and marked the first appearance of Porsche-patent synchromesh on the 924. Two years from the initial VW/Porsche agreement Zuffenhausen could start moving away from the VW connection. By accident or design the 924 was always following in the 911's tire tracks. Both cars had MacPherson strut front and semi-trailing-arm rear suspension, and as a comparison of 2-liter machinery separated by a dozen years the results were startlingly close. The very first 911 of 1964 had a 130-bhp, 2-liter flat six that pushed the car to 130 mph. In 1976 the early 924 2-liter straight four had 125 horses that took the new coupe up to a solid 125 mph.

On the one hand the progress of 12 years might excuse the performance similarity, but the younger car didn't have everything its own way. The old 911 could rely on gurgling carburetion, not emissions-compromised mechanical fuel injection. The old 911 didn't have such a great appetite for passengers or cargo, but it had a greater hunger for gasoline than the thrifty 924. As a comparison in speed and efficiency it was a wash, and the 924 was quicker out of the box than the 914/6, all thanks to a relatively unloved 1,984 cc I4 engine.

Powered by Mercedes-Benz

The 924's 2-liter, 4-cylinder engine is often referred to as the VW LT van motor. This modern squared-up van replaced the long-lived air-cooled VW Type 2 Transporter. In truth this engine was derived from the 1.9-liter unit used in the final first-generation Audi 100 sedan/coupe, but its history goes much deeper than that, back to the 1950s and a Grand Prix designer. It was all related to the acquisitions VW made during the sixties. To expand and diversify, VW eventually formed Audi-NSU Auto Union AG when it bought the financially comatose rotary specialist in 1969. In joining NSU to Audi, VW had assembled its own early equivalent of a Lexus division.

In the Audi-NSU company, VW had bought the Audi part in 1964, and they had purchased it from Daimler-Benz. Actually VW hadn't bought Audi in 1964, they had bought two-stroke, front-drive guru DKW. DKW was effectively the sole surviving member of the once glorious Auto Union combine, the only one that had continued to manufacture motor cars after the disastrous effect on German industry brought by the Second World War. Auto Union's legacy lives on through the continued use of its badge on Audi automobiles. The familiar four interlocking rings represented the conglomeration of four manufacturers which had combined to guard against the tough times of the 1930s.

The four-ring logo represents the makers DKW, Audi, Horch and Wanderer. When VW bought DKW they chose to bring back the Audi name as part of an upmarket makeover. DKW was associated with thrifty small cars, and it was felt that use of the Audi name would better conjure up images of Auto Union's 1930s Grand Prix-winning V16 racer driven by the elder Hans Stuck and Bernd Rosemeyer. Indeed the V16 racer was a Porsche design. However, prior to VW's purchase DKW had spent some time under the guidance of Daimler-Benz. DKW had been doing well in the 1950s and Mercedes had bought them in 1958. In the works for DKW was a new larger family car, and with it a new four-cylinder engine.

The new car was the DKW F102, and its intended engine was the work of Mercedes' Ludwig Kraus. Kraus had done the chassis design of Mercedes' dominant W196 Formula One machine of the mid–1950s. For DKW's F102 Kraus brought Mercedes' concept of a super-high-compression "middle pressure" overhead valve I4, but it was all too late for poor DKW. The 1960s marked the company's decline; their two-stroke mainstay motor had overstayed its welcome in the German market. The by-now-more-affluent public wanted something along the lines of the 4-stroke BMW 1500 sedan. As things stood, the DKW F102 came out with an enlarged version of the two-stroke on the eve of VW's purchase of DKW from Daimler-Benz.

As the new DKW F102 two-stroke finished up in 1966, Audi was using the same design to good effect. They combined a revised F102 body with the new middle-pressure, high-compression-ratio motor to create the 1965 1.7-liter Audi 60. This front-wheel-drive car was a hit, and they weren't joking about the CR — it was 11.2 to one! Continuing with the Audi F102 body, Audi went through the 70 to the Super 90, and then the all-new Audi 100. The bigger 100 used a 1.8-liter version of the middle-pressure engine. It was this fresh front-driver that came out for 1970 in America, with its super-high-output 107 c.i. I4 knocking out more than 1 horsepower per cubic inch. It wasn't the smoothest of I4s; *Consumer Reports* thought it sounded like a diesel at low rpm.*

It may not have been the most refined four, but it was hardy, efficient and destined for

**Consumer Reports*, Vol. 35, no. 7, September 1970, p. 439.

The 1977 AMC Gremlin and Porsche 924 could have the same engine, albeit with detail differences. Strange bedfellows does a fuel crisis make (courtesy Donnie Solomon and www.gremlinx.com).

the Porsche 924! But not before Audi had reworked the overhead-valve I4 into a single-overhead-cam I4, for their second-generation Audi 100 of 1977–82. The bore was upped from 84 mm to 86.5 mm to get the new 2-liter engine size. As mentioned, the VW LT van would be a recipient of this revised 2-liter, and so too would the U.S. AMC Gremlin. Yes, as of mid–1977, America's first-ever domestic subcompact could be specified with a version of the VW/Audi/Porsche I4. In attempting to deal with the 1970s fuel crisis, American Motors needed a four-cylinder engine so that it could offer better fuel economy.

Having no inline four design of its own, AM chose to use the VW/Audi 2-liter I4 under license during 1977–79. The upshot was that it was possible to buy both a 1977 Porsche 924 and an AMC Gremlin with a 4-on-the-floor and the VW/Audi I4 engine. Strange bedfellows do a fuel crisis make! Detractors of the 924 engine should note that AMC wasn't buying cheap junk. This was a West German–designed overhead-cam I4 with aluminum crossflow cylinder head, and AMC had to pay for the privilege — so much so that it wasn't economically feasible to offer the 2-liter I4 as the base motor in the basic Gremlin.

The cost of the licensing agreement meant that the 4-cylinder was the base motor for the Gremlin Custom. This version of the 2-liter I4 was assembled by AMC in Richmond, Indiana; it used a single carb and made 80 bhp. The version Porsche used in the 924 had 95/110 SAE horses, and multi-point fuel injection. Cost was a serious issue in the seventies. AMC boss Gerald C. Meyer admitted what a relief it was when they switched from using the VW/Audi I4 to the GM 2.5 Iron Duke 4-cylinder during 1980–83. Using the GM I4 saved American Motors a lot of cash, and if using the German I4 was expensive for America's fourth-largest automaker, then consider what the cost was to Porsche.

Porsche weren't making the 2.0 I4 like AMC was, VW were making the engine on Zuffenhausen's behalf. The 924's 2.0 was built at the VW Salzgitter plant, formerly the new factory chosen to build the Volkswagen K70. VW were not averse to charging hefty prices to companies like AMC or Porsche, making up for those lean Beetle years, so the financial impact of using the VW/Audi engine wasn't light. Go to 1979 and place the $4,000 AMC Gremlin/Spirit 2.0 next to the $14,000 924 2.0: the 924 doesn't sound like such a bad deal. The 924's 2.0 made 30 bhp extra, it had fuel injection and higher CR, both the car and engine were fully imported from West Germany, and it could exceed 100 mph.

Has it also been forgotten that the more expensive car is a Porsche? Even though the Gremlin/Spirit and 924 used the same basic powerplant, there is the issue of badge cachet to consider. The valet parking attendant might have thought your new Porsche sounded suspiciously like a Gremlin, but he would not have dared to say so. All of which makes the value

AMC built the VW/Audi four-cylinder engine under license in Indiana; Porsche got its version from the West German Salzgitter VW factory. This particular 1974 Gremlin X has a 304 V8, however (courtesy Donnie Solomon and www.gremlinx.com).

of the Porsche key fob simply priceless! Porsche, being a small company, would naturally charge more for a car like the 924 than Datsun would for a 280Z.

When fewer cars are sold, more has to be charged for each to make business worthwhile. Far from showing greed, the Gremlin-versus-924 comparison shows where the money went for two like-engined cars. So often the complaint is made that imported upscale German marques offer poor value for money, but this example shows the reverse. For an extra 10 grand over and above the price of a domestic subcompact, the fiscally aware buyer got a fully imported Porsche sports car with obvious upgrades. Factor in tuned-port fuel injection, independent rear suspension, galvanized bodywork, and the need for Porsche to make a profit, and the price level doesn't seem out of line.

Gremlin owners were less amused. The idea of having to go up a trim level to get a smaller, less-powerful engine than the standard I6 didn't make much sense. After the fuel crisis, people were paying more for well-trimmed small cars with smaller engines. Instead of getting a well-specified intermediate, the same money bought a Gremlin Custom I4 with power accessories. Rather than buying a fire-breathing V8 Mustang, buyers were expending more dollars on a Porsche 924. It seemed that the fuel crisis and inflation had focused the public's mind on making considered, responsible choices. The age of the gas guzzler was at an end, the people had seen through the lie. AMC's George Romney was right after all!

In European specification the 924's engine seemed well up to the mark on paper. Cast-iron block, alloy SOHC head, 125 DIN bhp at 5,800 rpm, and 121.5 lbs./ft. torque at 3,500

The seemingly Salvador Dalí–inspired Porsche Pasha trim graced the 924's interior as well as the 928's (courtesy Porsche).

rpm from 1,984 cc. The BMW 320i/520i's 2-liter I4 also had 125 bhp, and like the Porsche 924 engine also used Bosch mechanical K-jet fuel injection with one injector per cylinder. Indeed Porsche's — ahem, Audi's — four-pot had the added modern touch of a camshaft belt rather than the BMW's chain. Using a cambelt is supposed to reduce engine noise and aid refinement, which was ironic because the major failing of the 924 engine was refinement.

If a greater contrast to the free-revving flat six than the 924's hydraulic-lifter I4 exists, it has yet to announce its presence with untimely valve clatter. The 924 didn't have the smoothness of the BMW 2002 engine, nor the musical sound of Italian twin-cam units. The offset tach, nicely spaced footwell pedals and precise gearchange encouraged full redline exploitation, but the engine didn't. It wasn't that the 924 I4 couldn't sustain high rpm, or that it would disintegrate at 125 mph, far from it. This was one of the sturdiest, most reliable four-cylinder motors anywhere, it just wasn't an endearing one.

The 924's engine was very true to its Daimler-Benz origins: efficient, durable, but rather coarse. Mercedes have long been the masters of worthy sedan I4s, and the Porsche 924 motor was certainly in that ballpark. Its middle-pressure origin also meant that it was the only engine family sold by Porsche in the late '70s that couldn't meet Porsche's market plan of being able to run on low-octane gasoline. Thus, where the 928 and 911 could get by on 91-octane gas, the European spec 924 needed 98-octane Superbenzin. Due to the middle-pressure I4's high–CR design, Porsche's cheapest car needed the same diet as the 911 Turbo! The 2-liter's nature also meant it wasn't happy about a CR drop to suit the U.S. market.

For Europe the 924's engine had 40 mm inlet and 33 mm exhaust valves, along with a 9.3 to one compression ratio. A couple of features common to all markets were fuel injection

An Australian right-hand-drive 1979 924. Unlike the earlier 914, the 924 was readily available in right and left hand drive from the factory (courtesy Peter Barnett).

and a modification for the hydraulic lifters. Bosch K-jet mechanical injection was chosen instead of the electronic L-jet. Porsche probably took pity on its customers, and even though the U.S. VW Beetle was one of the cars using computer-controlled L-jet, the 911, 924 and 928 made do with the simpler K-jet. Another difference between the VW/Audi applications and the 924's 2.0 lay in rotating eccentric-wedge-style adjusters for valve clearance maintenance. This feature had been used, and dumped, on the Chevrolet Vega's I4 engine. Zuffenhausen wasn't bothered by this; the concept had merit and Porsche would make it work for the 924.

For the U.S. the 924 slipped behind somewhat, with its very early specification involving an output of just 95 SAE horses from the 2-liter. A good comparison for the car was the U.S. BMW 320i, which also had K-jet and 125 bhp in Europe. The 320i was a bit cheaper than the 924, came out around the same time, but had 110 bhp. Clearly Porsche hadn't done all their homework in getting their I4 emissions-ready. The U.S. 924 initially made do with smaller 38 mm intake valves and a CR of just 8.0 to one. The 49-state version was called XH and Californian 924s had the XF motor. Both versions had an air pump. The 49-state 2.0 had exhaust gas recirculation (EGR), and the Californian 2.0 had EGR plus a 2-way catalytic converter!

A Time to Be Sensible—The Value of Thrift

The silver lining of this slumbering cloud was that all 924s had transistorized ignition. The 2.0 I4 used in the Gremlin had simple points, just another reason why the thinking person paid a few more dollars for a 924. Even with the asthma-inducing effects of the added clean-air apparatus, the 924 could reach its 6,500 rpm redline in the first three gears. Shift into the 4th slot and the 924 would reach approximately 110 mph, edging ahead of the more powerful, but boxier and heavier, 320i. That the 924 could accomplish these feats wasn't in doubt, whether the driver enjoyed the act was another matter. Reaching that final 1,000 rpm band or remaining top speed was something achieved grudgingly. Such was the lot of the emissions-controlled '70s engine, even the Mazda RX4's rotary wasn't spinning happily anymore.

The emissions/performance balance hadn't been achieved yet, it was very much one or the other. The end result of pumping in extra air and leaning out the fuel mix was a rough-running, lethargic motor prone to overheating. Drivers of average transport resorted to playing around with the fuel mixture and ignition timing to get their new cars to function properly. This wasn't necessary with a 924, whose injected I4 did the expected tasks of starting from cold and general running without fuss. However, this wasn't enough for a Porsche, not even for the basic 924, so Zuffenhausen made appropriate changes for the middle of the 1977 model year.

To add some sparkle to the competence, the new 49-state XG and Californian XE had the 40 mm intake valves of European 924s, plus the compression ratio raised to 8.5 to one using different pistons. Along with a sportier cam profile and more advanced ignition timing, from 10 degrees atdc to 3 degrees atdc, this brought maximum power up from 95 bhp at 5,500 rpm to a 320i-matching 110 SAE net bhp at a pokier 5,750 rpm. The 49-state 924 also had a catalytic converter now, but that was of less importance than the 1977–1/2 924's new-found zip. Why couldn't the 924 have started with this tuned-up 2.0? It was probably due to uncertainty over 1977 emissions standards.

The 95-horse U.S. 924 was configured to withstand all possible disasters, including disappearing down the San Andreas fault should the big quake strike. Porsche realized this was

Rudi Lins and Gerhard Plattner rely on the strength of steel rims to carry their 924 around the world in 28 days. Phileas Fogg would have been proud (courtesy Porsche).

RBR 21T

overkill, and with its new sensible setting the 924 could be called — amusing. Others were also biding their time to see how tight emissions restrictions would be. It wasn't as bad as expected; this fact, combined with rising interest in fast cars, saw the return of the Camaro Z/28 350 and the debut of the Trans Am W72 400 — but did one need that much car? *Road & Track* wrung 117 mph out of a revised 1977½ 924 4-speed. That's equal to the top speed of a 4-speed 1977 Vette with base 350 V8. The same terminal velocity, but on 2 rather than 5.7 liters. The 924 was a 2+2, not a pure 2-seater, so the prudent Porsche owner could do some judicious car pooling in the morning and stretch out those mpgs even further!

In Europe the 924 was also displaying the advantage of efficient design by outpacing 6-cylinder cars like the Ford Capri 3000S and Datsun 260Z on top speed, and matching or bettering their standing-start acceleration times. When *Motor* magazine tested one of the very early 4-speed, right-hand-drive 924s in 1977 they recorded 0–60 mph in 8.2 seconds. This was much better than Porsche's habitually conservative claim of 10.5 seconds for 0–62 mph. Normally a Euro spec 924 would take around 9 seconds. The 8.2-second time could be explained by the fact this was an especially well bolted together 924, with a better than average example of the 125 bhp 2-liter.

The other explanation for the fast acceleration by *Motor*'s 924 was that it was an early non-Lux-spec car with a very plain equipment list. No power windows, which weren't available at the time, no sunroof and certainly no air conditioning. The last feature was commonplace on U.S. 924s, including *Road & Track*'s 117-mph 924, but very rarely seen on 924s sold outside the U.S. The only toy *Motor*'s 924 came with was a radio/speaker set, it didn't even have a wiper for the rear window glass. As with any car, the 924 stacked on the comfort features with age. So the 8.2 seconds clocked wasn't likely to have been a misprint.

The downside to the outright performance figures was a lack of intermediate spryness. In contrast to gutsy British sports cars like the Austin-Healey or Triumph TR250, one couldn't floor the gas pedal in top and expect inspiring pick-up within speed ranges. The 924's 2-liter had a goodly amount of twist, and it was wise to exploit that pull quotient and change up early to avoid the I4's mechanical coarseness, but this was no 928. Compounding the problem was the Audi 4-speed box, whose tall intermediate gears showed the gearbox's sedan origins with an unpleasant chasm between second and third.

The 924 was a ground coverer, rather than a road burner. The smooth body, tall ratios and 4-cylinders were meant for maintaining high average speeds with the reward of a long cruising range: an easy 350–400 miles from the 16.4-gallon tank even on the low–CR U.S.-spec 924 manual. Owners needn't worry about being targeted as gas hogs, but the 924's transaxle chassis stopped them from being too relaxed. The entire I4/4-speed gearbox/torque tube complex was a rigid unit attached to the body via two rubber mounts at the front and two at the rear. Porsche had discreetly tested the transaxle complex disguised by the bodywork of a BMW 520 and Opel Manta, test mules in car-industry speak. All seemed fine at Weissach and on German roads, but all wasn't well in America.

U.S. freeway driving surfaces set off an uncomfortable ride sensation as the 924 passed over the joints between concrete sections. Even though much of the 924's suspension hardware had

Opposite, top: A very early 4-speed U.K. spec 924, bringing the competition right to the door of British Leyland's Triumph TR7 (courtesy Lee Furness). _Opposite, bottom:_ Thirst for well equipped versions of the popular 924 led to the arrival of the 924 Lux for 1978. By late 1979 the 924 Lux 5-speed was practically the default U.K. variant (courtesy Lee Furness).

After decades of the upside-down bathtub, the 924 was a modern art sculpture in steel, a clean example of industrial design (courtesy Lee Furness).

been seen before on other models, in this particular transaxle application passing over road ridges triggered a suspension movement that wasn't damped out. It was an oversight by Porsche engineers for this export market, and proof of the 924's uniqueness because the symptom was absent from VW's Rabbit or Super Beetle. It wasn't quite as simple as inadequate shock absorbers. Porsche solved the problem by tightening up the assembly tolerances of the torque tube/transaxle's body fitment.

The changes were introduced along with the improved U.S. 924 engine in February 1977. It didn't bring Cadillac comfort to the 924, but it did eradicate the oscillation. In other respects the 924 handled like any other Porsche. This involved a firm, objectively very firm, but compliant ride that got better at masking road imperfections with speed. Unfortunately, as with the 911 and 928, the 924 transmitted a lot of tire roar and produced an unendearing "thump" over low-speed bumps. Such foibles were emphasized by low wind noise and a quiet engine at cruising rpm, and were amplified by the 924's solid monocoque.

924 — User-Friendly Porsche

For those looking to buy the best-handling 924, the basic steel rims could be replaced by 14 × 6-inch cast alloys with 185/70 HR rated 14-inch tires. A natural accompaniment for the big wheels were 20 mm front and 18 mm rear anti-sway bars. Even without the sway bars, and using skinny 165-section radials, the 924 could still attain 0.78g on the skidpad; adding the wide-section aluminum rims and sway bars saw this figure rise to 0.81g, very good for 1976 and enough to earn the 924 a place at Camp Porsche. Unlike the 928, but in keeping with the 911, the 924's absence of power steering allowed the enthusiast to feel the road without undue roadshock. Having the gearbox at the back meant the steering was still light with 6-inch-wide rims.

There were also the modern advances that the 924 enjoyed over the 911, by virtue of being a younger design. Go beyond the Beetle's ancient controls placed on the floor and other mystery locations, and enjoy the Rabbit's water-valve heater and sensible center console, even if heat modulation wasn't very exact. To keep warm and avoid cluttering up the exterior styling with extra vents, Porsche devised a noteworthy method of getting rid of stale air. Extraction slots were placed at the leading edge of the rear hatch's interior; the stale air then went into the door area and exited through a hidden vent at the front of the door. With the 924 moving forward the rear hatch glass wouldn't mist up, and the doors would be warmed as the stale air escaped.

The 924's dashboard was set up for air conditioning from the start, making the 911's system look very add-on. Those 924s with a/c had a circular on/off dial switch placed where the clock would be on non-air-conditioned 924s, directly above the cigar lighter on the center console. By virtue of its conventional front-engined layout, it was easier to place such a/c hardware items like condenser/fan and route refrigerant lines.

As with any current car the 924 eschewed noise-provoking vent windows in favor of four fresh-air dash vents, fan-boosted ram air ventilation and distribution/blending via three slider controls above the radio. And as with most cars of the time, the 924 had the option of a conventional 3-speed torque-converter-style automatic. Beginning with the start of the 1977 model year, the 924 auto became the first Porsche to offer a normal fully automatic gearbox, beating the 928 to market by a few months. The 911 continued in 1977 with its efficient interactive semi-automatic "Sportomatic."

The VW Beetle 1500 was also fond of a semi-auto, but only a real autobox with cushioning torque converter would suffice for the 924/928. Whereas the 928 raided Mercedes' parts bin for its slushbox, the 924 made do with an Audi unit. Manual 924s used their front bell housing to contain the clutch, in automatic 924s this area was empty. The 924 auto's torque converter would be placed in the rear bell housing, but used the manual's 3.44 to one final drive. With a little more weight in the tail the 924 auto had a bit less understeer than a 4-speed 924, but its acceleration shortfall was a more significant loss. That said, the customer is always right.

Most 924s were manuals, but a number of automatic cars were sold too. Porsche wanted to satisfy consumer needs, and to expand the 924's appeal an undemanding air-conditioned automatic 924 for town use was no bad thing. Know the market, and what people are prepared to pay for. Buyers in the U.K. don't like to own plain vanilla versions of prestige brands. So, in the spirit of the earlier 914SC, Porsche GB came up with the very spiffy 924 Lux. The 924 Lux became available for 1978, and was so in tune with what U.K. buyers wanted from their junior Porsche that it just about became the default 924 for that market.

For an extra 450 pounds sterling, the Lux brought tinted glass, alloy wheels, rear glass hatch wiper and 911-design high-pressure headlamp washers. With the 6-inch-wide alloy wheels came the 185-section tires and front and rear anti-sway bars. In Europe it was possible to buy a simpler 924, but in most export markets extra goodies implied exclusivity, and

The 924's 2+2 seating, hatchback and choice of full automatic gave the new Porsche mass market appeal (courtesy Porsche).

that was certainly seen as part of the Porsche mystique. It also helped bridge the mental gap to the 911/928 class. In America 924 extras were grouped in the expected option packages.

Option Group I retailed at $345 and added 185-section tires/alloys, and radio antenna/speakers/interference suppression kit; Group II brought the high-jet headlight washers and both front and rear anti-sway bars. Where Porsche differed from everyone else was by making the various items available separately. Normally both domestic and imported brands had mandatory packages, where to get one worthwhile option, the buyer was also forced to take on a vanity mirror/decal pack or other unnecessary frippery. Wishing to make friends rather than enemies, Porsche chose not to go down that road.

Porsche were definitely making friends with the 924. The 914 got off to a slow start, but with the 924 there was actually a waiting list! Dealers that got stuck trying to move lethargic 914s saw a chance for revenge, and in the early days mark-ups on a 924 occurred as with other hot-selling '70s imports like the Honda Accord and VW Scirocco. The louder the critics and air-cooled devotees carped about the 924, the more the showroom bonanza continued. That was because the detractors and buyers were different groups. Just as Mercedes widened their catch with the 1990s A class, Porsche got a lot of first-time Porsche buyers.

By the middle of 1977 the presence of the 911 and 928 made owning a Porsche even more desirable. The 924 was a good-looking first rung on a ladder that might have led to a 911 in the garage one day, if Porsche resale value was anything to go by. Apart from image it seemed that major parties were noticing and following the 924's lead. Jack Turner, the boss of the returning Chevy Camaro Z/28 project, said that GM had purchased a Porsche 924 as an example of a very good road car to benchmark the new Z/28 against during its development.

In the 1980 sales brochure Ford put out for the Foxstang, the 0–50 mph acceleration time of the eco-warrior Mustang Turbo 2.3 I4 was compared to the figure recorded by the 924. Volvo ran an advertising campaign in Europe trying to promote the 1982 360 GLT as a

It was 1981 and Porsche made a toast to the 924's 100,000 sales (courtesy Porsche).

sporty hatchback with the slogan "It goes like a BMW, it corners like a Porsche, it stops—like a Volvo." The models Volvo had in mind were clearly the BMW 316 and the Porsche 924. Praise within the home market too, as the 924 scooped magazine *Auto Motor und Sport*'s "best sports car under 2 liters displacement" title four times between 1977 and 1980.

The curiously shaped 914 didn't engender much of a response from the general public. It was observed, considered, but didn't have a large public profile in the car world, and car makers were not as interested in its ways as they were in the Fiat X1/9. Comparing sales volume between the 914 and 924, 120,000 vs. 150,000 is misleading, because from 1981 much of the 924's demand was taken up by the new 944, itself a 924 development. The main point was that the 924 got Porsche noticed in the budget ranks.

For 1978 the 924's entire unibody was galvanized, power windows were available, the outside rear view mirror base and door handles were black rather than chrome, the rear chassis rubber mounts were redesigned and the optional dogleg Getrag 5-speed had eliminated that annoying ratio gap. The 5-speed now had closer ratios and an overdrive top of 0.71, combined with a much shorter final drive of 4.71. Originally the U.S. and Euro spec 924s had the same 4-speed ratios and final drive, but the former was shortened thereafter to enhance acceleration. First the final drive was shortened to 3.88 for the 1977½ 924, and when the Getrag 5-speed was chosen on the U.S. 924 that became a very tight 5.00 to one.

Chapter 3

924 Answers the Need for Speed

924 Meets the Turbo

It all looked very refined and nice, but in outright terms the 924 5-speed was no quicker than the very early 924 unveiled to the press at La Grande Motte resort in the South of France in November 1975. By 1979 the initial mandatory VW parts-purchase period had expired and Porsche had chosen to develop a turbocharged 924 variant that drew mechanically on the best parts Porsche had to offer. By the late '70s turbo cars, either from the factory or kit converted, were all the rage.

Small engine size and economy, but when on boost the power and torque of a large engine, and all from channeling waste exhaust gases to spin a turbine. Cars like the BMW 2002 Turbo, Saab 99 Turbo, Buick Turbo Regal and TVR Taimar Turbo V6 all showed that the theory worked. The turbo route was also very tempting for selling cars in America because a turbo car would mostly be off boost when recording an appealing EPA CAFE MPG figure, and in the era of the green/yellow/red econometer better mileage was worth virtual gold.

Much would be expected of Porsche in developing the coming 924 Turbo, due to their position in the field of forced induction. Zuffenhausen had many Can Am Turbo racing miles under its belt, and the 930 had been unveiled in 1974, but what had Porsche done for the blown enthusiast lately? Turbos were also amassing a reputation for turbine lag in performance delivery, and reliability concerns because of the thermal load of using hot exhaust gases. The world was looking to Stuttgart for solutions. In addition, the 930 was a hair-raising beast that added to the 911's reputation of chewing up and spitting out unsuspecting drivers. Surely the blown 924 wouldn't be like that?

Since the 924 Turbo was the first turbocharged road car since the 930, the younger car was afforded the design code Type 931. Showing Porsche's engineering expertise, they chose to retain and turbocharge the 924's VW/Audi 2-liter to bring about the model's first power hike, from 125 bhp to a sizzling 170 bhp, just 10 horses short of the 911's base 180-horse, 3-liter flat six. The 924's 2-liter was a tough little I4, well up to coping with forced induction, and Porsche felt the bottom end could be left alone. To reach 170 DIN bhp Porsche designed a fresh aluminum cylinder head.

The 931's special head had recessed valves, and exhaust valves larger than the normally aspirated 924's at 36 mm. Combustion chambers were redesigned, and to ward off detonation the 924's CR dropped from 9.3 to 7.5 to one. Compared to the normal 2-liter, the spark plugs were shifted to the intake side and had platinum electrodes. To create the boost Porsche chose the K26 turbo unit from KKK, and sited it in the usual turbo spot, low down on the

The KKK K26 turbocharger Porsche enlisted to give the 924 a boost (courtesy Hannes Deutsch and www.porscheclassic.at).

exhaust side of the block near the exhaust manifold. A fabricated pipe took the forced air up over the engine to meet the intake manifold.

Across the top of the pipe was the plaque "924 turbo," and on the intake manifold it said "PORSCHE," and so it should have, because the basic 2-liter motors went from the VW plant to Porsche's factory where they were transformed into turbo engines. However, the latter plaque had worked its way onto even the normally aspirated 924s by 1980. Porsche were getting more confident about their 924 range. Zuffenhausen could certainly be confident about their 924 Turbo; instead of being satisfied with just 45 extra bhp, they upgraded the entire 924 to remain in balance with turbo power.

Given the extra torque involved, the torque-tube driveshaft had its diameter increased from 20 to 25 mm, and now ran in three bearings rather than four. To handle the power the original 215 mm clutch was replaced with a 225 mm 911 unit. Porsche also called on their

928-design calipers to give the 924 Turbo better braking. Ventilated disks at all four corners gripped by the V8 car's floating calipers replaced the rudimentary K70 solid 10.1-inch front disks and 9.1-inch rear drums. The bigger brake rotors were now up to 11.1 inches front and 11.4 inches rear; they would be seen later on the upcoming 944.

Larger brakes were housed by larger rims on the 924 Turbo. Instead of the standard car's 14-inch, 4-stud rims and HR tires, the turbocharged variant used 5-stud, cast-alloy, 15-inch lattice spoke, or 16-inch, forged, flush design rims like the 928S. Both sets of wheels were 6 inches wide and their rotation was aided by 911SC-sourced wheel hubs and bearings. Other heavy duty items to cope with the onslaught of 180 lbs./ft. of torque were the main shaft of the Porsche 5-speed box, the differential and axle half shafts. Plus, every time the 924's pilot made a gear change, it would be achieved via hydraulic, rather than the standard car's cable, operation.

It was very easy to tell a 924 Turbo from a normal 924 based on appearance. The Turbo car had four very noticeable vent slots above the front bumper and between the front pop-up lamps. There was also an aerospace-inspired NACA duct on the right side of the hood, and a rather more restrained rear rubber-lip spoiler bonded to the rear glass hatch. All the above were functional, a very unusual occurrence by the standards of 1979, but the equivalent of the 930's whale tail air-admitting/downforce-creating rear wing. The four nose slots admitted more air, very important for the 924 Turbo's engine oil cooler.

The NACA hood duct was also handy for keeping things cool. Its job wasn't to take air in, its role was to allow heat to exit from the under-hood turbo inferno — an important item, because the 924 Turbo, like the Audi 200 Turbo and other blown cars of the era, didn't have an intercooler. There were also vertical slots in the front spoiler to deliver cooling air to the car's front brakes. The rear spoiler dropped the 924's drag coefficient from 0.36 to 0.35 and played its part in the new claimed top speed of 140 mph.

There was a theory going that Porsche attached the spoiler to the glass, not the sheet metal, because they didn't want people easily affixing it to lots of the 60,000+ 924s already sold. The fear was that the 924 would go beyond its 125 mph top end and into the red zone in top gear. This myth was busted when Porsche made the rear spoiler optional, then standard, on later 2-liter 924s.

Unusually for a German company, Porsche introduced the 924 Turbo with the option of a two-tone paint job, the sort one would find on a Pontiac Grand Am. It's possible that the new 1979 Mustang Turbo, with its two-tone Cobra appearance pack, influenced the 924 Turbo's look. U.S. market tastes could indeed have tipped the balance at Zuffenhausen. It was also a neat way to conceal the 924's impact bumpers. The 924's 5-mph federal bumper bars didn't protrude too badly, but the light clean look of the European version was still preferable. However, on a U.S. 924 Turbo with silver over black, black covering the lower sections of the car up to the door protector strip, the extended bumpers weren't even noticeable.

There was also the visual bonus of the darker lower half concealing the front fender amber side marker lights. The rear red side marker lights were above the level of the door rub strips, so they were still exposed, unfortunately. Inside the 924 Turbo there was sparingly little to distinguish the Turbo from the non-turbo, save for green instrument markings and a speedo that went up to 160 rather than 150 mph. Standard on the Turbo was the very inviting three spoke 911SC leather-wrapped steering wheel; optional was the new, smaller-diameter, 4-spoke 928S-style wheel that was standard issue on right-hand-drive U.K.-market 924 Turbos.

924 Turbo pilots had to master the vagaries of the racing shift pattern in changing from 1st to 2nd. It was all part of the charm of a genuine Porsche 5-speed box (courtesy Porsche).

Step into a Porsche 911SC and the interior is stark; it couldn't be described as luxurious at all. There wasn't really a center console, just a lower fascia section with assorted switches, and literally a "gearstick" to move around, very Saab 99, very 1960s. After that the 924 Turbo seemed posh and integrated, like a junior 928. Even though the 911 was supposed to be replaced by the 928, its natural enemy seemed to be the 924 Turbo, and the younger car might have been the better car. The 2-liter turbo had the outright "go" of the revered 3-liter flat six. *Autocar* magazine's 924 Turbo easily exceeded Porsche's claim of 0–60 in 7.8 seconds, by registering 6.9 seconds. The 142 mph recorded on the Autobahn was also better than Porsche's promised 140 mph.

The 911SC could edge out the 924 Turbo by a half second in zero to sixty, but the top-speed contest was a wash, and the little Turbo could travel a couple of miles further on each gallon of gas — a convenient circumstance considering the second gas crunch was coming to a gas station near you very soon! The astounding result was that all this acceleration and frugality had been achieved using the unloved VW/Audi I4, and it was still displacing 1,984 cc. The 924 Turbo's brakes were easily up to coping with all the speed, and handling wasn't a worry either. The stock 924 was a better-handling machine than any 911, so add on the Turbo's

With a top end of 140 mph and a miserly thirst for gas, the 924 Turbo left big engined coupes lining up jealously at gas stations around the world (courtesy Porsche).

bigger wheels/tires, 23 mm front/14 mm rear sway bars, along with Koni front/Bilstein rear shocks, and you really had a winner.

At 15 percent less than a 911, the 924 Turbo was an absolute steal to buy, offering swifter speed than a 4.5-liter 928 manual and better maneuverability. Porsche had only intended to bridge the gap between the 924 and the 911, in reality they had created something greater. Zuffenhausen showed its knowledge by making the first easy-to-drive turbo Porsche. Apart from the expected wastegate that kept boost pressure limited to 10 psi, the 924 Turbo made use of a blow-off valve. This latter device was first used on Mark Donohue's 917 Can Am racer. When the driver lifts off the gas pedal, closing the throttle body plate, this bypass valve recirculates the forced air back through the turbo to keep the turbine spooled up.

From the racetrack to the road, the bypass valve helped to overcome the dreaded turbo lag and promoted the 924 Turbo's even power delivery. Yes, the 924 Turbo was quiet up to 3,000 rpm, but the power didn't turn on like a light switch, and the penalty when trying to summon passing power at Autobahn speeds was minimal. The blown 924 was very progressive, so Porsche didn't bother to include a boost gauge because it was so refined. The adoption of turbocharging had also predictably quieted down the 924, and made the 2-liter seem almost, dare it be said—smooth? The 924 Turbo was the most exciting car Porsche didn't build for 1979.

The prospect of pushing a coupe with 911 speed without worrying about the rear overtaking the front was an exciting prospect, and one eagerly awaited in America, where the 924 needed more motor to take on the 280ZX, Corvette, Triumph TR8 and other big-engined cars. However, there was some preparation work necessary because Porsche wanted to tune the 924 Turbo for U.S. conditions, and that included a new Porsche pollution control strategy for 1980. To suit speed-limited America, and the liking for quick low-speed pickup, the U.S. 924 Turbo had a smaller turbo unit which was less lag prone. So the engineers at Weissach wanted the turbo to start blowing at 1,600 rpm rather than 1,800 rpm, with maximum boost at only 2,800 rpm. With the smaller blower the driver would only receive 7, not 10, psi.

The other half of the U.S. Turbo engine program was the use of a three-way catalytic converter with a Bosch Lambda Sond oxygen sensor that enabled the 2-liter Turbo to be a 50-state engine. The system allowed tight control of carbon monoxide, hydrocarbons, and nitrogen oxides. The sensor lived partly in the exhaust manifold, sensing differences in the oxygen content of the exhaust gases compared to the outside air. A difference in content created a voltage sent to a computer relaying a signal to change the air/fuel mixture set by the Bosch K-jet fuel injection. The goal was to keep the air/fuel mix at 14.6 to one.

This was a system being rapidly adopted by imported models in the U.S. The only slightly unusual element in Porsche's system was the use of mechanical fuel injection. This implied the use of a computer to relay the mixture change, whereas with Bosch L-jet the sensor signal would have been processed directly by the L-jet's ECU. At least the 3-way cat/oxygen sensor allowed the Turbo to dump the previous pollution controls that the 924 had used, and the Weissach Wizards were free to get the best power possible without pollution-control compromise. That power turned out to be 143 SAE bhp at 5,500 rpm and 147 lbs./ft. at 3,000 rpm.

Mission accomplished, Porsche had got the 924 Turbo to make its best at lower rpm. Initial impressions were also good as Porsche brought over 600 1979-spec 924 Turbos as a curtain raiser for the model's 1980 U.S. introduction. These early cars were easily distinguishable by their original 924-style exposed gas filler caps. The 1980 924 and 924 Turbos had the filler cap neatly concealed by a circular metal flap. *Road & Track* tried one of these early cars out at a wintery Weissach proving ground, garnering a most impressive 7.7-second 0–60 time in the process. *Car & Driver* went one better, running a limbo-low time of 7.5 seconds.

Within one second of the 911SC's 0–60 mph time at a saving of over 5 grand, and with the handling advantages of the 924's layout. This seemed more like it, but then a funny thing happened on the way to the drag strip. Emissions regulations for 1980 were much stricter than those of 1979, CAFE gas-mileage dictates were more burdensome too. The result was that the 1980 924 Turbo seemed rather flaccid. Its zero to sixty time had worsened by a huge 1.5 seconds. At the last minute Porsche retuned the U.S. 924 Turbo, even though there were no changes from the provisional quoted power and torque figures. In 1980 all the car makers were taking their knocks — the 5.0 was axed from the Mustang at the close of the 1979 MY, and Porsche canceled the 930, so the 924 Turbo wasn't alone.

A word also on the vagaries of car testing in those pollution-controlled times, with variability in the results discovered. *Consumer Reports* found zero difference between the ordinary 2.3-liter I4 Mustang and the turbo version. Less discrepancy existed where large-engined normally aspirated cars were tested, which explains why car makers went back to that approach when the price of oil eased in the mid-eighties. For the present any rivalry between the U.S. 924 Turbo and 911SC 3-liter seemed at an end. In Europe the two were within fractions, but in America the Turbo's worth seemed anchored to how well it went around corners. For those

The 924 Turbo wore a wild optional two tone paint job. U.S. 924S Turbos that featured the M471-associated "S" hood decal were a visual match for 1980 Mustang Turbo with the Cobra pack (courtesy Porsche).

retrospectively looking for rocket performance, the only hope is to search out one of those 600 introductory-offer 1979 924 Turbos. Only those early cars were the fast ones, the rest were "sheep in wolf's clothing."

The ultimate 924 Turbo in America could be found through judicious box-ticking on the car's order form. To keep the 924 Turbo under the magical $20,000 threshold, Porsche stripped down the model for the U.S. market. The U.S. 924 Turbo arrived at $19,880, but some noticeable mechanical items were absent. Most obvious were the 4-wheel ventilated disk brakes, in place of which were the 924's stock 10.1-inch solid front disks and 9.1-inch rear drum stoppers. And related to this were specified 15-inch, but 4-bolt, lattice-spoke rims, still with the Pirelli CN36 185/70 VR rated tires one would find on a Euro spec car.

Initially air conditioning wasn't standard equipment on the U.S. 924 Turbo, but the car's base spec was no sweat. Porsche had come up with a version that acknowledged the fact that many Turbos would be visiting Hardee's, and cruising freeways and turnpikes legally at 55 mph, during summer's vacation season. For most U.S. drivers the stock Turbo had enough brakes, for the rest Porsche had conveniently grouped all the serious hardware into the M471 Sport Pack, which could be purchased separately for $1,960. Batteries weren't included, but the enthusiast did receive 4-wheel ventilated disk brakes, 16-inch, flush-design, 5-bolt forged aluminum rims with Pirelli P7 tires of 205/55 VR size, and a rear 14 mm anti-sway bar to

Siegfried Köpke pushing his Group G 924 Turbo hard during 1984. Recording 11 wins and one second place from 12 starts, Köpke became the Valvoline Sprint Cup champ that year (Courtesy Porsche).

complement the front 23 mm item. Porsche also refitted the car with the Euro Koni/Bilstein front/rear shocks, and the finished result was called 924S Turbo.

Maybe it still made more sense to go with the standard 924 Turbo, or the much cheaper turbo installation offered by BAE of California on a regular 924. Overall, turbo trials on the 924 didn't seem that inspirational, since Porsche had passed the three-way cat/Lambda sensor onto the regular 924, along with a CR hike from 8.5 to 9 to one and cam/ignition changes, with sprightly results. The 1980 Turbo was only a bit over a second quicker to sixty than the revised U.S. 924 with VC-coded 2-liter. The disappointing aspect was that the 924 Turbo took over in 1980 as the sole turbo Porsche road car for America, now that the 930 had gone. It would be tempting to determine that originally planned 1979 Turbo setting, recalibrate a car privately, and regain that 7.5-second 0–60 time, but then one wouldn't pass the dreaded smog inspection.

Porsche continued alterations to the Turbo; in 1981 U.S. 924 Turbos received the Euro-spec 4-wheel disks as standard. There was also the adoption of the 924 Carrera GT's Siemens-Hartig computer-controlled ignition, and a CR rise to 8.5 to one. Both measures made the 1981 924 Turbo less lag-prone and more responsive. At this time the Turbo's 66-liter gas tank was replaced with an 84-liter unit, the green dash instrument markings were changed to white, and the smaller 360-mm 4-spoke steering wheel was standardized for all markets.

A positive spinoff from the Turbo was of benefit to the normal 924 and its exploits in SCCA category D-Production racing. The Turbo passed along its chassis upgrades and cylinder head to aid the standard 924. The M471 Sport Pack upgrades (brakes and suspension) were initially made available on a run of 100 non-turbo 924s. Soon a version of the M471 package was a formal option for the U.S. standard 924; it was priced at $1,575. The Sport Pack for the non-turbo 924 used the standard U.S. Turbo's 4-bolt, cast-alloy, 15-inch lattice rims, and Pirelli P6s instead of the 924S Turbo's pricier P7s.

The 924 racers that competed in SCCA racing were built at Porsche's Weissach facility. Porsche built 16 special 924s with bored-out 2,039 cc, 175-bhp versions of the moderately loved VW/Audi I4. These engines used dry sump lubrication to ward off oil starvation in tight turns, plus facilitate lower ride height. The engineers also reached onto the parts shelf for the 924 Turbo's head, because that liberated a few extra ponies. Quite a sight the finished engine bay was, with its honed, polished inline four and suspension tower strut brace that enhanced torsional rigidity.

The D-Production racer looked very purposeful on its Goodyear racing slicks wrapped around 5-bolt BBS alloys, and housed by slightly flared body arches. The rear glass hatch wiper/motor was deep sixed, and in came a welded roll cage. The roll cage helped the 924's monocoque work with the 924 Turbo–borrowed vented disks/sway bars, even though special aluminum shocks and titanium alloy coil springs replaced stock turbo items. Many was the spectator that wished all 924s could look like that! How SCCA racing had changed from just 10 years earlier when pony cars supported by domestic automakers were battling in front of big crowds.

After the 924's 1980 and 1981 triumphs in the D-Production category, the SCCA axed that grouping, causing several cars to be upgraded to GT-3 specs and raced in that category. This is Don Meluzio competing in GT-3 at Road Atlanta in October 1989 (courtesy Porsche).

This particular racer was converted to GT-3 specs with much input from David Finch, a GT-2 winner in his 944. 924 D-Production champ Tom Brennan mentioned the speed benefit brought by the 944 bodywork (courtesy Porsche).

Now in 1979/80, in the aftermath of the second fuel crisis, a lot of interest was in the sub-2-liter class where Datsuns, Sciroccos and TR7s were duking it out using I4 power. Porsche were rewarded when Doc Bundy and Tom Brennan won the 1980 and 1981 SCCA D-Production titles. In addition, Ken Williams took the 1980 Showroom Stock A title and Tom Brennan added to the 924 trophy collection with the GT-3 category win in 1985. Along more privateer lines, the Carlsen Racing 944 claimed the 1986 SCCA Showroom Stock GT title in that year's Escort Endurance series. Freddy Baker won the 1987 and 1988 SCCA Showroom Stock GT titles with a 944 Turbo.

Carrera—The Third Coming

The 924/944 family had made an impression on SCCA racing. The end of the factory-backed 924 effort in SCCA D-Production at the close of 1981 came because the 944 was going to arrive soon in the U.S. to replace the 924. The new wave Porsche had proven its durability and carried the Porsche shield to victory using largely stock cars. However, Dr. Ernst Fuhrmann had grander things in mind when he spoke of bringing Porsche racing cars closer to their road cars. In mathematical formula: 924 + Le Mans = 924 Carrera GT. This startling 924 was revealed at the 1979 Frankfurt Show, and was the best indicator yet that the 924 was evolving in Porsche fashion.

Revealed at the 1979 Frankfurt Show, the 924 Carrera GT soon became a folk hero of the West German public (courtesy Hannes Deutsch and www.porscheclassic.at).

The surprising thing about the 924 Carrera GT was how close it was to the ordinary 924/924 Turbo, and yet for the time this was one of the best sports cars money could buy anywhere in the world. It quickly became a superstar in its homeland and its basic wide-body look would be reprised by the 1981 Porsche 944. It was certainly the sportiest front-engined car Zuffenhausen had made, even if the also-new 928S shaded it out slightly in acceleration and top speed. Porsche had a lot at stake in giving the 924 the Carrera name, such was the reverence with which the nameplate was held. There had been a Carrera version of the 356 in the 1950s, and the lightweight 1973 911 Carrera RS 2.7 was so esteemed that many regarded it as quicker than even the later 3.3 Turbo 911 around any circuit with a few twists.

So this new 924 had a great deal to live up to. However, in keeping with Porsche's nature in 1971–1981, they didn't feel overburdened by a sense of their own history. Zuffenhausen felt it was better to take the work seriously, than themselves seriously. As a result the 924 Carrera GT persisted with the VW/Audi middle-pressure 2-liter I4. This latest iteration of the gruff four made 210 DIN bhp, exactly the same horsepower as the 911 Carrera RS. That's what Porsche meant about taking the work seriously. The 924 Carrera's powerplant was one of the most efficient motors on the planet for power production and gas mileage.

Cruise along at 55 mph and the 924 Carrera would do nearly 40 mpg, and yet floor the accelerator and the car would go on to a claimed 150 mph. Porsche also claimed 0–62 mph in 6.9 seconds, although 0–60 was an easy 6.5 seconds and there was one report of 5.8 seconds recorded by former Le Mans winner Paul Frère. And yet, all the above was achieved with just a few tweaks to the original 1979 924 Turbo engine. It was still a cast-iron block, alloy

The 924 Carrera GT was as plushly trimmed as any 924 Turbo, and also used the tough Porsche 5-speed dogleg box (courtesy Porsche).

head 1,984 cc motor with Bosch K-jet injection, but benefited from an air-to-air intercooler and a CR rise from 7.5 to 8.5 to one. It also featured Siemens-Hartig digital ignition.

The 924 Carrera would bestow the CR rise and computer-controlled ignition system on the normal 924 Turbo in 1981, but the intercooler was a unique feature in the 924 clan. It was essential for packing cool dense air down the throat of the blown I4. Rising air temp implies a falling away in horsepower production as the ignition timing is automatically retarded. The use of the intercooler, a sort of radiator or heat exchanger, implied staying on the ragged edge for longer. Porsche were forcing in more boost pressure in this application, a 1.5 psi increase over the 924 Turbo, so keeping detonation at bay was even more important. Along with the higher CR it made the fine control offered by computer-controlled ignition essential.

Even with the smaller turbo, 8.5 CR and digital ignition given to the 1981 177-bhp 924 Turbo, the 924 Carrera was still the most driveable and progressive of the blown 924s. The revised 924 Turbo had 184 lbs./ft. of torque at 3,500 rpm, but the 924 Carrera had 203 lbs./ft. at the same rpm. That kind of efficiency called for 98 octane gas, and that, plus the cost of federalization and the Carrera's niche nature, sealed its fate as a Europe/U.K.–only

Opposite, top: **Note the "Carrera" front fender decal — Porsche was invoking the 356 spirit with this modern 210 bhp 2 liter turbo puff! (courtesy Hannes Deutsch and www.porscheclassic.at)** ***Opposite, bottom:*** **Another surprise from Porsche was the choice to retain the 924's VW/Audi I4 as the basis for the new Carrera supercar. It worked thanks to the addition of an intercooler (courtesy Hannes Deutsch and www.porscheclassic.at).**

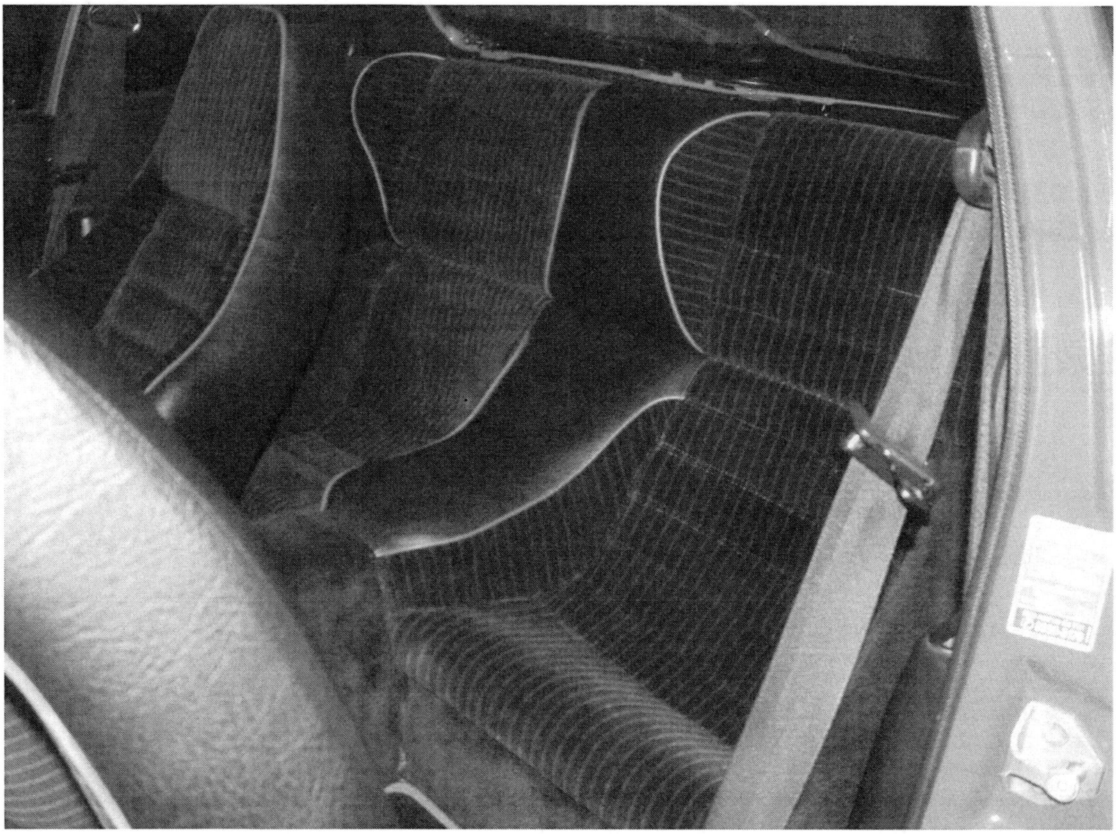

Even in the 1980s Porsche maintained the tradition of the Sunday racer. Drive the Carrera GT to work during the week, and on any given Sunday it was time for play! (courtesy Hannes Deutsch and www.porscheclassic.at)

model. This wasn't a concern for Porsche, the 924 Carrera was an homologation racing special, and as a result they only had to make and offer 400 cars for sale. Two hundred were earmarked for the home market, and 75 of the 400 were right-hand-drive cars for the U.K.

The left-hand-drive cars came with the usual 3-spoke 911SC tiller, but the U.K. cars had the optional, smaller 4-spoker. In all, Zuffenhausen made 406 924 Carrera GTs, and don't think that these were race-car stark. The cars were as plushly trimmed as any high-spec 924 Turbo, and a fair number of Carreras even had air conditioning! So the third Carrera was not the lightweight the 911RS 2.7 was, but technical advances since 1973 resulted in the 2-liter turbo car's having the same outright performance in comfortable surroundings. Indeed, the 924 Carrera used normal 924 body panels, and included the same 6-year anti-corrosion warranty.

Differences from stock 924 concerned what was bolted onto the Carrera's body. There was a mean-looking, functional, forward-facing hood scoop, just about where the 924 Turbo's NACA duct would be. The scoop supplied air to the Carrera's intercooler. There were fender flares to cover the bigger wheels. These flares, plus the scoop and front spoiler, were made of "Bayflex" polyurethane, the same stuff used on the 928's deformable nose and tail casings.

No need to fear that the Carrera's wide-body look would wreck the 924's drag factor; thoughtful design of the frontal area, a 10 mm front/15 mm rear lowering job and flush-fitting

Top: One could take a few tools along for a race weekend thanks to the 924 Carrera GT's luggage area. It was shallow because of the transaxle configuration, but then a Volvo wagon couldn't do 150 mph at the dawn of the eighties! (courtesy Hannes Deutsch and www.porscheclassic.at) *Bottom:* The Carrera GT's hood scoop was functional, admitting air directly to the turbo's intercooler at the point where the 924 Turbo's NACA duct was normally sited (courtesy Porsche).

windshield allowed the 924 Carrera to have a coefficient of drag lower than the 924 Turbo's 0.35: it was now 0.34. The Carrera also had a rear spoiler attached to the glass hatch like the Turbo, but this unit was much larger and very "Fast & Furious" tray-like. Other changes under the skin were less dramatic. Apart from the lowering job, the suspension was like a 924 Turbo, with the addition of a bigger rear anti-sway bar and the option of gas-filled shocks.

Brakes were once again what one would find on a 924 Turbo, except the front rotors were larger at 11.5 inches. However, the dual-circuit brakes were now split front & rear as opposed to diagonally, due to the change to positive scrub radius concerning the Carrera's steering. Unfortunately, that's the only thing Porsche changed with the steering, still a non-assisted rack and pinion system, but too slow. The 924 Turbo's 3.8 turns lock-to-lock was good for calm lane changing on the Autobahn, but lazy when applied to the Carrera. Pressing on in damp conditions with the Carrera, using all the gears and searching for the 203 lbs./ft. of torque, required quicker reactions from the helm to fight off oversteer once traction ran out.

Modern high-performance tires gripped to insanely high levels before letting go. In a car with as much rubber as the 924 Carrera, that implied a fair speed, even in the wet. In dry conditions the latest Carrera had as much contact with the pavement as anyone could ask for. Standard wheels and tires were 15 × 7–inch forged Fuchs all around wearing Pirelli P7s of

Just five years after the original 930 Turbo, Porsche had developed the 2 liter VW/Audi motor to within exactly 50 bhp and 50 lbs./ft. of the 930's blown 3 liter (courtesy Porsche).

With 245 horses, light alloy rear suspension castings and 911 Turbo brakes, the 924 Carrera GTS was the version directed at rallying (courtesy Porsche).

215/60 VR nature. Or one could choose to go large, with the 911 Turbo's asymmetric Fuchs combination of 16 × 7 front wheels with 205/55 VR tires, and 16 × 8 steamrollers out back with VR rated Pirelli P7s in a 225/50 size.

Transmitting the power from the intercooled 2-liter to the monster truck tires was a slightly modified 924 Turbo driveline, with stronger cogs for the Porsche dogleg 5-speed box, and beefed-up transaxle housing and driveshafts. There was the finished road missile: the fastest 924 known to mankind, around 600–700 lbs. heftier than a 1973 911 Carrera RS, and equally loud in looks. Apart from the hood scoop and bodykit, Porsche were happy to drop a "Carrera" stencil decal over just the passenger side front fender. Like Napoleon's concealed palm, or Michael Jackson's single white glove, both the great and the infamous seem to share a most peculiar sense of style.

Sadly, all this I4 turbo excitement cost money, over $40,000 worth of folding paper back in 1980. Porsche sold each and every car, no problem. In contrast there was a surplus stock of Lancia Stratos hanging around by 1980. The Stratos sold out around the same time as Carrera III, but Lancia had a 6-year head start! For its racing customers, Porsche had a more specialized, and therefore expensive, 924 Carrera, but still with the VW/Audi I4. Directed at rallying, the 1981 924 Carrera GTS had an 8 to one CR to accommodate extra turbo boost so that its 2-liter could reach 245 bhp.

The GTS had a fiberglass nose section/hood, and the headlight covers and side and rear windows were all made from plexiglass. By racing standards the interior looked almost passenger car-like and comfortable with its 935 bucket seats; only the racing harness and roll cage hinted at the GTS's true purpose. To help it achieve that end, the GTS was among the first models in the 924/944 family to use light-alloy rear suspension castings. Wheels and tires

Porsche built 59 Carrera GTS cars. They were surprisingly well trimmed inside for racers and had supportive 935 bucket seats. A 40 percent limited slip differential was employed (courtesy Porsche).

were the Carrera GT's optional 16-inch pack, whereas the wheel hubs, calipers and brake rotors all came from the 911 Turbo. The transaxle had an oil cooler, and a 40 percent limited-slip differential was used too.

Porsche constructed 59 Carrera GTSs, but only 17 1981 Carrera GTRs. The GTR was an even more powerful 924 Carrera, it was what a privateer would buy from Porsche to compete in Group 4 sports car racing. Sitting on whopping 16 × 11.5–inch Porsche 936 turbine-blade-pattern dished rims, these Carreras had 917 and 911 Turbo braking components. The 2-liter engine had its CR dropped to 7 to one, so that it could be boosted up to 375 horsepower. Top speed was over 180 mph, and if that looked or sounded wild, it really wasn't. The FIA was rewriting the rulebook for 1982 so that production-based sports car racing would become slower and cheaper.

A similar situation would take place with rally cars, when the Group B fire-breathers were given their marching orders in 1986. With the Porsche 936 temporarily mothballed it was part of Dr. Fuhrmann's strategy to launch a 924-based works campaign on Le Mans for 1980 using a car similar to the GTR; or, rather, the GTR was patterned after the successful 1980 Le Mans racer called 924 Carrera GTP. In this transitional rulebook period the humble 924 would be up against the big-gun prototypes, with little or no chance of outright victory, but there was a point to be proved.

The Le Mans–campaigned 1980 924 Carrera GTP had an uprated version of the 2 liter VW/Audi I4 making 320 bhp, with the reliability required for an endurance race. The car weighed 2,046 lbs. (courtesy Porsche).

The 924 was a popular cocktail coupe, but could it survive an endurance event like Le Mans? Porsche believed that it could, and in Fuhrmann's mind the "win on Sunday, sell on Monday" effect of a glowing outing would do no harm to sales of the visually similar 924 Turbo. And the racing car wasn't a million miles from the Carrera GT road car, and even used elements from the works 924 SCCA D-Production racers. This earlier incarnation of the GTR had plastic fender flares, doors, hood, and spoilers, and made use of weight-saving plexiglass windows. Brakes were from the 917, the gearbox simply a stronger version of the dogleg 5-speed box one could get in a pre–1980 924.

Suspension was basically 924 struts at the front, semi-trailing arms at the back, but with the SCCA D-Production rear coil-overs. Wheels were BBS 16-inch rims, 11.75 inches wide and using big Dunlop slicks. At this stage of the game the VW/Audi turbo 2-liter was producing 320 bhp at 7,000 rpm and 282 lbs./ft. at 4,500 rpm, using a 6.8 to one CR. As with the later GTS/GTR, the fuel injection was a mix of Bosch and racing mechanical Kugelfisher injection and the cars used a dry sump. The 1980 Le Mans 924 racer tipped the scales at a not-too-light 2,046 lbs.

True to the objective in spite of the differences compared to the vin ordinaire 924, this was no tube-frame racer with a special racing engine. The 924 structure was there, so too were the basic suspension and 2-liter I4. Porsche took a 3-car works effort to Le Mans in 1980. The three cars would each have a different flag to signify the nationality of the driver pairing. So there was the West German number 4 car of Manfred Schurti and Jürgen Barth, the U.K. number 2 car of Andy Rouse and Tony Dron, and the number 3 U.S. car of Derek

Top: **A three-car clan was taken to Le Mans in 1980 by Porsche, with West German, U.K. and U.S. driver pairings. The number 4 West German car of Schurti/Barth came in 6th overall. The U.S. driver pairing car pictured finished 13th (courtesy Porsche).** ***Bottom:*** **The 1981 924 GTP raced at Le Mans was more of a curtain raiser for the new 944 model range. The 924 GTP used a 2.5 liter four-cylinder, whereas the 924 GTRs continued with the old 2-liter (courtesy Porsche).**

Whether it was a 924 GTP or 944 GTP, it still brought home the bacon for Zuffenhausen when Barth/Rohrl achieved 7th place outright at Le Mans in 1981 (courtesy Porsche).

Bell and Al Holbert. The U.S. car was originally going to feature Peter Gregg and Holbert, but English Le Mans legend Derek Bell had to take Gregg's place at short notice.

The final outcome was a seriously creditable 6th, 12th and 13th place in the overall standings. The German driver pairing achieved the 6th place, the U.K. pairing came 12th and the quasi–U.S. combination made 13th. The only endurance failing that could be blamed on the car was a burnt exhaust valve on the 12th-placed car, and British sedan champ Tony Dron had experienced this earlier when endurance testing the 924 Carrera GTP at the Paul Ricard circuit. Porsche had proven that a water-cooled, front-engined car could at the very least complete the 24 hours. That the 924 could have managed such an excellent Le Mans debut with a clean-sheet design was testimony to the integrity of the 924 and Porsche's thoroughness.

There was a follow-up return to Le Mans in 1981, but this time the 924 GTP was a thinly disguised curtain-raiser for the new 944, and this racer used a 2,479 cc DOHC 16-valve turbo motor with counter-rotating balancer shafts. This 410-horsepower racer was driven by Jürgen Barth and rally ace Walter Rohrl to 7th place overall at Le Mans. The other works car Porsche brought along was piloted by Manfred Schurti and Andy Rouse. This was a tamer 2-liter 924 GTR and due to gearbox woes it didn't finish the race, but was still classified 11th overall. The same problem affected a privately entered 924 GTR driven by the Almeras brothers/Sivel, but this 2-liter car expired early.

Nineteen eighty-two saw further success at Le Mans for a 924 GTR — on road tires! Yes, BF Goodrich backed a two-car effort in the IMSA/GTO class, and one of the cars, driven by Jim Busby and Doc Bundy, was rewarded with first in class and 16th overall. Unfortunately

The playstation of the 1981 924 GTP. There were moves afoot by the FIA to reorient sports car racing closer to production cars, and the 924 was ready to oblige (courtesy Porsche).

car number 87's twin, number 86, the Miller/Bedard/Schurti–driven 924 GTR, didn't get far enough even to be classified. The cars did use over-the-counter BF Goodrich Comp T/A radials; the only concession to racing was that half the tread depth had been removed. A racer closely based on a road car with street radials, proof that the 924 had what it took to conquer the Automobile Club de l'Ouest.

The 924 had matched the achievement of the 914 at Le Mans, coming 6th overall on debut, but with the comeback of the 936 to record its final outright victory in 1981, and the new 956's win at Le Mans in 1982, the emphasis went back to the big bangers. Leave the racing to the "traditional" type Porsche, and let the 944 use the halo effect to get those sales numbers rocketing. As a result the 924 said goodbye to Le Mans in 1982. In rallying a similar pattern emerged concerning 924 support, except Porsche didn't put as much effort into the 924 for rallying as it did for sports car racing.

After a bit of a false start, Porsche got the 924 Turbo homologated for the 1979 Safari Rally, but both works cars expired. The following year Jürgen Barth took a works 924 Turbo to 19th overall in the Monte Carlo Rally. Better success occurred in 1981, when the more specialized 924 Carrera GTS driven by Walter Rohrl and Christian Geistdorfer won the Hessen Rally. This 924 GTS was factory backed. Things went a notch better at Porsche's favorite stomping ground, the Monte Carlo Rally, when Jürgen Barth and Porsche's head test driver Roland Kussmaul pushed their 924 Carrera GTS to 10th overall, but second in class B, behind a 911SC!

The 924 Carrera GTS of Barth/Kussmaul that managed an excellent 10th at the 1982 Monte Carlo Rally (courtesy Porsche).

With the arrival of the 944 in showrooms, Porsche switched their rally support back to the ancient 911SC, at least until their new high-tech all-wheel-drive 959 could be groomed up for the early-to mid–'80s Gruppe B super class. Little room for a 924 in all the above. With greater input it could have been a contender, but rallying was changing fast. Conventional rear-drive, front-engined cars like the Ford Escort were finished, even the Audi Quattro was soon eclipsed by specialist mid-engined designs, with little in common with the road cars that they took their general bodywork from. The 924 should have started rallying earlier, or after 1986; it came at the wrong time.

Life Goes On

Life was made easier for 924 patrons when Porsche replaced its own type 5-speed box on the normally aspirated model with an Audi 5-speeder for 1980. This gearbox didn't have enough capacity to cope with the Turbo's torque, so that model stayed with the old dogleg box. By going back to an Audi gearbox the driver had a conventional shift pattern, with the first four forward gears in the "H." This gearbox would also see service in the new 944.

A 1981 924 GTS raising a little hell in the Metz Rally. The 924 was a rear driver in a rally era moving towards all wheel drive and away from production based cars (courtesy Porsche).

Other changes were of the small but welcome variety. When the 924 Turbo got a bigger gas tank in 1981, the standard 924 received the Turbo's former 66-liter container as a hand-me-down. All 1981 924s were carrying a 7-year anti-rust warranty, and indicator lights on the front fenders, plus "Porsche" script on the interior door trims. Roll on to 1982, and the 924's roof was strengthened in keeping with what had been done with the 944. There was a Porsche badge on the glovebox, and at the very least a 911SC 3-spoke tiller.

By 1983 the 924 Turbo was history, and the plain 924 soldiered on as something of a toned-down price leader. The fancy "Porsche" script door trims were gone, but a Turbo-type rear spoiler was standard — the latter no doubt included with Porsche hopes that the middle-aged 924 would fly out of showrooms faster. Adoption of the 944's slightly more useful sunroof with power tilt function also aided the egress of stale air. However, little could change the fact that the 924 was fast becoming the forgotten one.

Top: A 1983 924, more refined and easier to use with its Audi sourced 5-speed, but was the 924 becoming the forgotten one? (courtesy Porsche) *Bottom:* This 1984 example features the smaller four-spoke wheel that helped to avoid the 924's dreaded "thigh rub" syndrome. However, more troubling was the VW/Audi four-cylinder engine. Sports fans wanted a change! (courtesy Porsche).

The Ghost & Herr Doctor Porsche

In the 1982–85 era the 924 was neatly stowed away in the corners of Porsche dealerships, that dark, out-of-the-way area where the office fern plant is placed. Raise a pop-up lamp and a cobweb would be found. Porsche weren't troubled, sales of other models were booming. However, there arose an opportunity to do something with the 924. For one, VW couldn't keep on indefinitely supplying the ancient I4 2-liter. It wasn't being used in current VW group offerings, so basically it was a dead duck, and not an especially tender one at that.

Porsche popularity, deutschmark strength, and the ever-rising price sticker of the 944 meant Porsche needed an entry-level machine, especially since the 924 had left America in 1982. The solution was to either offer a stripped-down 944 with the VW/Audi 2-liter, which was illogical given the engine supply problem, or to sell a 924 with the 944 mill. Porsche built a prototype 2-liter 944, but it wasn't very nice, so they decided to make the 924 with just the "Porsche" 2.5 I4. Thus, for 1986 the Porsche 924S was introduced with a detuned version of the Euro spec 944 2.5 I4, and selected 944 enhancements.

It didn't take a particularly observant visitor at the 1985 Frankfurt Show to realize that Porsche saved a few deutschmarks by keeping the 924's dashboard. The 924 was fitted these days with either a 911SC 3-spoke or 928S4 4-spoke wheel, depending on the market, and featured pastel interior hues, but it still had a steering wheel-to-seat squab clearance demanding well-toned thighs to squeeze in. The detuned 2.5-liter had also been seen before; it was

Say hello to the 1986 924S, a 944 engined 924—refinement at last! (courtesy Porsche).

The 924S took on the 944's balancer shaft 2.5 liter engine and "phone dial" aluminum wheels, but retained the pre–1985 924/944 dashboard (courtesy Todd Goranflo).

the 9.7 to one CR version introduced in the U.S. in 1986 for the 944. Whereas the Euro 944 had a 10.6-CR, 163-bhp 2.5, the 924S's 2.5 had 150 bhp, and so the Porsche hierarchy was preserved.

In South Africa the arrival of the 924S was seen as a chance to ditch the 2-valve 944, and if customers wanted something better the 16-valve 944S 2.5 was the new 944 entry point, leading on to the Turbo. Curiously Porsche didn't do this rationalization for Europe, U.K. or U.S. markets, where the 924S was offered alongside the 2-valve 944, but at a cost saving. Engine aside, the 924S took over the 944's 11.1-inch front and 11.4-inch rear vented disks, although these had come from the 924 Turbo in the first place. The 924S also incorporated the 944's aluminum front lower A arms and rear semi-trailing arms, although these items were left off the U.S. 924S 2.5 so that it could sport a base sticker price of $19,900 and still come with a/c, power windows and mirrors as standard equipment.

The 924S also started to look like the 944, because the long-serving 14-inch alloys had given way to 15 × 6–inch cast alloy Phone Dials with 195/65 VR footwear. Power steering was now available on the 924, and a worthwhile option — worthwhile and indeed necessary should the buyer have specified the optional 928S-style, flush, forged 16-inch hoops with 205/55 VR rubber. And the 924S would be burning rubber, because with the 2.5 all-Porsche-designed-and-built engine, 0–60 was 7.5 seconds and top speed easily over 130 mph, or a bit quicker than a 2.7-liter 911 from the mid–'70s. The response received by the 924S was along the lines of, "Hello there, I thought you were dead?"

With the 1987 924S, the 924 was back in the U.S. for the first time since 1982, and with a price tag under $20,000 (courtesy Todd Goranflo).

In all the eighties excitement, most had forgotten the fact that the 924 had been in continuous production and on sale since late 1975, except in America. In the U.S. the 924 had been unavailable since 1982, and the new 924S 2.5 was an early 1987 MY entrant. No need to get a secondhand ride, the 924S appealed to buyers on a modest budget. Even if the 1975 dash did look a bit dated, it was widely felt that the 924 had finally arrived in a suitable refined manner with its genuine "half a 928" motor. Also appreciated was its old-world solidity.

A hood that wouldn't flex under waxing, a door closing with a pleasant whump, such quality required heft, and the 924S had that. By late–'80s tinny front-drive standards, the 924S possessed build quality akin to a Panzer tank, and even more importantly it was rear drive. No torque steer distractions, just balanced handling and hang the space efficiency! It's often more expensive to do things cheaply, and the 924S wasn't cheap. On the nose of the 924S was Porsche's shield, and shields are known for being knock-resistant. So it was that with the 924S' arrival came Porsche's 10-year anti-rust warranty.

Even at this late stage Porsche were still making their improvements. For 1988 the 924S got faster, with Porsche's new all-market, 2–valve, 10.2 to one CR, 160 DIN bhp 2.5, which was used by the 944 as well. With a drag factor of 0.33, the slipperiest 924 of all was now faster than the like-engined but heavier 944. The 1988 924S also featured power steering as standard equipment. Right at the end of production of the '88 models the 924S received a cleaner, if more bulbous, front spoiler and a rear apron. It mattered little, for the 924 was finally at an end. Its 13th year was to be its last.

Top: The U.S. 924S may have lacked the European version's aluminum suspension pieces, but it was faster than the like-engined 147 bhp (SAE) 944. However, the $3,050 list price difference was partly nullified by the 924S's stark interior (courtesy Todd Goranflo). ***Bottom:*** In 1988, the 924's final year, the 924S was upgraded with a 160 bhp (DIN) version of Porsche's 2.5 I4. It also came with power steering as standard equipment (courtesy Porsche).

Somehow the light incisiveness of early 924s had been lost by the late 1980s; blame it on too much padding and fat rubber (courtesy Benny Proot).

Porsche couldn't keep the 924S' price down any longer, and its sales grew less impressive as its price rose. There were newer cars on the market that could go as fast for less money, even if they lacked the cachet of the Porsche badge and the 924S' bank-vault build quality. After a hard sales year in 1987–88, Porsche had a refreshed I4 lineup for 1989, but the 924 wasn't there. If there was one criticism of the 924S, it was its lost incisiveness. Like the 944, age and refinement had dulled its sparkle. Power steering and 20 mm front/14 mm rear sway bars made it seem a tad detached and soft. For a sharper feel try a 1979 non-power-assisted 924 with 20/18 mm front/rear bars, plus Porsche's own dogleg 5-speed, less portly and more confidence inspiring.

Collector Edition 924s—The Best Paint and Tape Money Can Buy

The popularity of the 924 was underlined by the number of limited-edition models, and when a production run stretches over a decade and past 150,000 cars, a couple of hundred cars here or there truly are limited editions. It all started with the M426 1977 Championship Edition 924, a white car with white alloys and body-length colored "Martini" decals, built

Opposite, top: **Porsche released a number of special edition 924s, starting with this 1977 M426 Championship Edition (courtesy Donald Rowan).** ***Opposite, bottom:*** **The Championship Edition 924 commemorated Porsche's triumphs of the past and present. Like some of the other 924 special editions, M426 was available in Euro and U.S. spec (courtesy Donald Rowan).**

WELTMEISTER
WORLD CHAMPION
CHAMPION DU MONDE
CAMPIONE DEL MONDO

to commemorate Porsche's taking Le Mans, World Championship of Sports Cars, World Championship of Makes and the Trans Am Championship. The M426 was specified with sports suspension pack, sunroof and a specially trimmed interior with a plaque near the shifter to mark Porsche's triumph in the various series. Of the 3,000 cars made, 2,000 went to America, with the remaining number for the rest of the world.

As a follow-up Porsche released 1,800 special 1978 924s painted metallic Dolomite Grey, also coded M426, but reserved for the U.S. alone. One hundred almost identical cars were sent to France, same color but no 5-mph bumpers, and this one was called M427. And Switzerland received 100 metallic pearl 924s the same year. Roll on to 1979, and Porsche cooked up the U.S. M429 Guards Red "Sebring 79," 1,400 924s named after the famous U.S. track and yet another tribute to Porsche's success in the racing world. Then came the 924 "Cork," again in metallic pearl, but 300 cars were Porsche—err, Audi/NSU built this time around.

Italy was treated to 900 all-black 924s, and Britain had a unique allocation of 50 "Doubloon" 924s, predictably painted gold. To celebrate the 924's triumphant 3-car team debut and finish at 1980's Le Mans, 1,030 924 "Le Mans" were created, white exterior/black interior with coachwork decals and 4-stud, U.S. 924 Turbo, 15-inch rims with 205/60 HR tires, plus 924 Turbo rear hatch spoiler. For 1981's U.S. market, 400 924 "Weissach" cars with platinum metallic paint also had the U.S. Turbo's base 4-stud lattice rims and rear spoiler. The 1981 "50th Jubilee" 924 painted metallic pewter for Continental Europe added another 1,000 plus to the 924's tally.

Even into 1982 Porsche organized limited runs of special 924s for specific European markets. So far all limited edition 924s had been normally aspirated, 924s, but for 1983 Porsche commissioned 88 924 Turbos painted metallic Zermatt Silver to mark the Turbo's demise. And for the end to the end? There were 980 white or black 924 "Le Mans," another 924 special edition built just after Porsche's 12th Le Mans victory. It had sports suspension, 6-inch-wide rims at the front, but 7-inch-wide wheels at the back, with the 500 924 Le Mans II cars destined for the U.S. being black. Le Mans takes place in June; the 924 Le Mans II was announced after the victory, with 924 production ceasing in July, so perhaps that was funeral black?

Chapter 4

A Four-Cylinder to Be Proud Of—944 under the Skin

Doctor Porsche Gives the 924 a Heart Transplant

Success can be measured in many ways. It would be correct to say that the Pininfarina-styled Ferrari 400/412i family was one of the best-selling Ferraris of all time. It would also be true to say that relatively few people know what a 400/412i looks like. Numbers aren't everything, not for a company like Porsche. The 924 was successful by 1981, having notched up an impressive number of sales over half a decade. In its turbocharged forms the 924 could be called a fast car, and it was always a good handler, but was it a success?

The 924 had achieved success in motorsport, most noticeably at Le Mans, but just as performance is more than mere figures, success means more for a hallowed marque. A good Audi that never was, a first-rate coupe in the Celica/RX7/TR7 mold, by 1980/81 the 924 was the king of left-handed praise. It was a first-rate coupe, but not an affordable coupe. The 924 was cheap for a Porsche, but it was never a cheap car. As the competition closed in and the performance/dollar equation was examined, it was time Porsche made a move.

Sales of the 924 were somewhat soft in the aftermath of the second-fuel-crisis-sparked recession, and Porsche needed to transition from a car that merely defended its existence, to one that could attack the opposition. Zuffenhausen had been busily working away at the drawing board on just such a car, and the fruit of their labor was exhibited at Le Mans in 1981. The car in question was the 400+ hp 924 GTP 2.5-liter turbo; driven by Jürgen Barth and Walter Rohrl, the racer finished 7th at the Sarthe track. That said, the 924 GTP didn't give the public much of a clue. It was denoted 924, looked much like any 924 works-prepared racer that had rolled out of the Zuffenhausen speed works to that point, and, disguised by Hugo Boss decals and racing-body add-ons, it resembled yet one more high-speed blur.

The confusingly named 924 GTP would give rise to the first front-engined Porsche that could be considered a substitute for an unblown 911. More importantly for Porsche's bean counters, they would have the antidote to weak U.S. 924 sales. Porsche's R&D chief Helmutt Bott did eventually admit that Porsche needed a 4-cylinder coupe more attuned to American tastes. It was, after all, Zuffenhausen's largest export market. To facilitate the improvement in market performance the new car needed a healthy image boost. Indeed, the latest four-cylinder chapter brought two obvious changes that rectified the 924 image issue, one involved looks and the other involved what was under the hood.

The first bad thing anyone had to say about the 924 concerned its engine. It made respectable power, was economical and reliable, but as four-pots went it was unrefined, and,

It was 1980, and designers in Zuffenhausen's Styling Studio were hard at work on the new 944 (courtesy Porsche).

more alarmingly, it wasn't a Porsche engine. Neither was the flat four in early 356s, the 914 or the 912 2.0, but by 1981 the lack of Porsche input for motivation was very bad for marketing. Porsche needed to put distance between itself and the VW/Audi 2.0, if for no other reason than, like the 2-liter flat four of the '70s, the 924's 2-liter I4 was being phased out in the VW/Audi empire. Naturally contractual supply obligations would keep 924 engine bays filled for the immediate future, but Porsche needed to look elsewhere.

Realizing the VW/Audi 2.0's shortcomings and its stopgap nature, and not being one to procrastinate, Porsche started looking for a replacement very early on. A car of the 924's ilk

Opposite: **In spite of the 944's wide body look, its drag coefficient had slightly improved to 0.35 Cd (courtesy Porsche).**

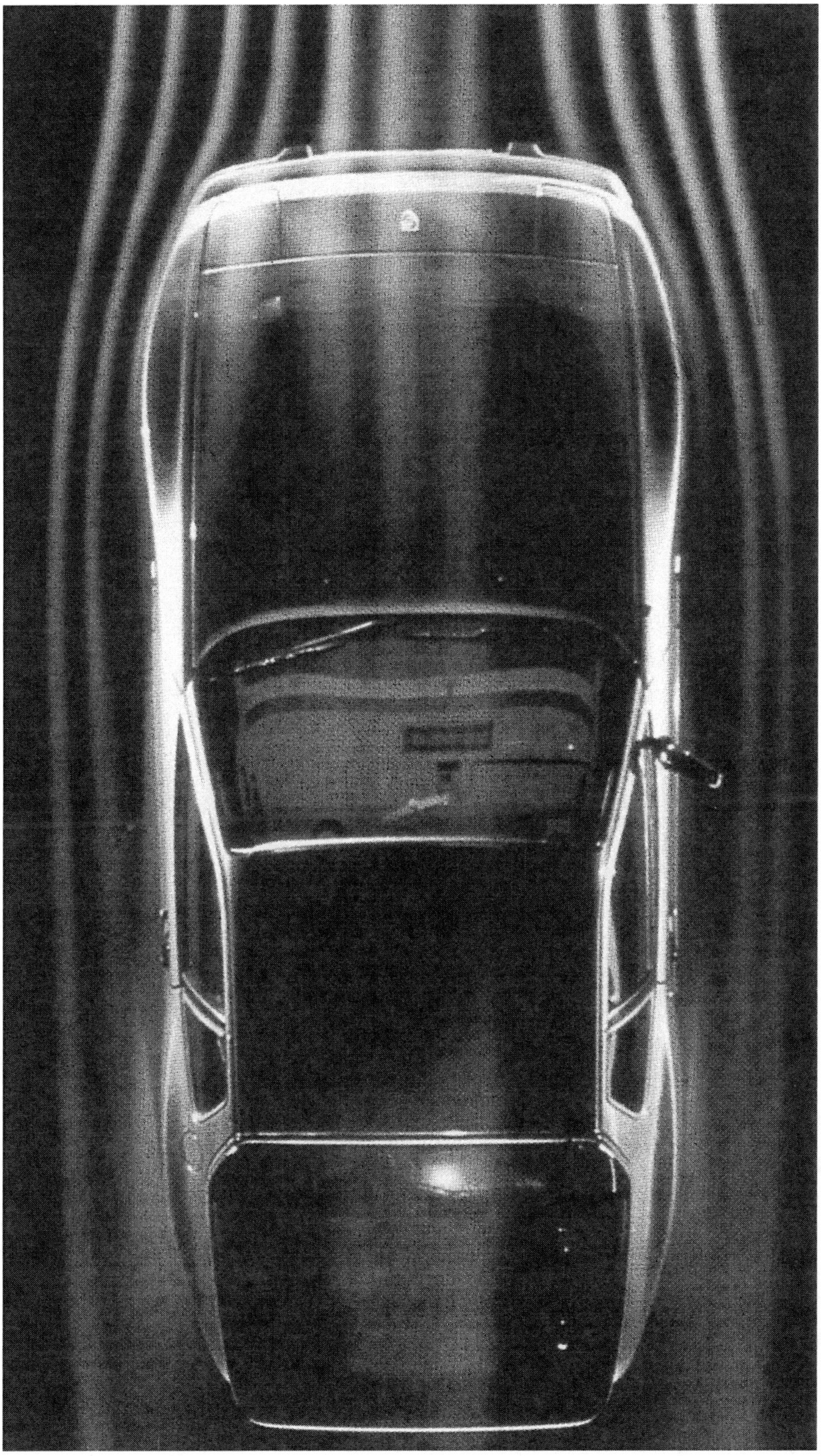

and price suggested a six-cylinder engine. Small-capacity sixes were considered desirable even in moderately priced German sedans, due to the refinement, power and prestige they brought compared to I4s and V4s of similar displacement. Plus, the 911 had gotten sports car fans used to the idea of six cylinders for years. A flat six for the 924's successor was out of the question. Porsche hadn't made the flat six in a sub-3-liter capacity since 1977, and there would still have been bitter lingering memories of the commercial failure of the 914/6 2.0.

In the search for more punch and refinement, Porsche engineers created a 924 powered by the Peugeot/Renault/Volvo V6 in 1976. That engine was successfully used in the Alpine A310, and would be used in the subsequent GTA and A610. The PRV V6 was also planned for, and would be used in, the 1980–82 DeLorean. This 924 V6 worked well, but not that well. Refinement and economy were not up to Porsche standards. Porsche decided to try something else. Perhaps the marketing department had a crystal ball gazer that could foresee an early–'80s *Road & Track* comparison test featuring PRV V6–powered Alpine, DeLorean and Porsche 924 getting whipped by a downsized Chevy 305–powered F-body costing half the price?!

However good or bad the PRV V6 was, it still wasn't a Porsche motor. That wouldn't look good in the sales brochure, and Porsche would still be dealing with an outsider for engine supply. Concerning the commemorative Ferrari F40, the great Enzo Ferrari said that the best gifts we receive, are the ones we give ourselves. Following that reasoning Porsche looked at its own 928 V8 as the basis for a new engine family. To be specific, a 3.5-liter derived from the all-alloy V8. Unfortunately this plan didn't yield an engine of great refinement either, and

The 944 retained the 924's pop-up headlights at a time when the GM F-body Firebird was getting the feature for the first time (courtesy Jako J. Koel).

at 3.5 liters it was too big. Not big next to a Triumph TR8, but too large and thirsty for a mainstay engine in Europe. It was also too close to the base 928 which was still at 4.5 liters.

Production and efficiency constraints also sounded the end for a V6. Thus far I4 Porsche junior had been constructed on the assembly line with its 2.0 engine, driveshaft and transaxle installed as one item meeting up with the monocoque body from below. In assembly jargon the joining of engine and gearbox is called a "wedding," and would be possible for a V6 only if the motor was dropped into the car's engine bay from above. So it was that Porsche turned to the idea of another four-cylinder, one that could be derived from the 928's V8. I4s had been derived from V8s before, as with the 1961 Pontiac Tempest, just as V8s had been formed by joining 2 fours at the crankshaft, as with the 1988 Audi V8.

Porsche could take advantage of common production tooling, shared development costs and, most obviously, interchangeable parts. A four-cylinder would also give the right displacement for Europe, while allowing capacity rises over time. The penalties were obvious, though: still nothing more exotic than a humble four in a Porsche, sorry 356 owners, and the noise, vibration and harshness (NVH) issues of a big, powerful four-cylinder. The need to overcome these problems was the reason that the new I4 was based on, rather than just being half of, the V8's mighty motor. It contained unique features and specification differences to make it an engine in its own right.

The most obvious difference concerned the use of counter-rotating balancer shafts running at twice engine speed. Porsche settled on a 2.5-liter displacement, the same 2,479 cc as the 924 GTP Le Mans racer, as the ideal starter size for a baby Porsche engine. A half-liter up on the 924 2.0 permitted more power and torque from an equal state of tune. This 2.5 size also tied in with the 928's stroke, allowing the crankcase to be made with 928 V8 tooling. It all sounded like a good fit, but four-cylinder motors over 2 liters tend to be rough devices.

It was a question of overcoming the vibration associated with inertia, trying to balance primary and secondary forces. A V8 is balanced, so is an I6, a V6 has only its primary forces balanced, and in an I5 or I4 neither primary nor secondary forces are balanced. Manufacturers normally get around this problem by cheating, using special engine mounts and cam profiles to minimize vibration. The counter-rotating balancer shafts were a more elaborate solution, but Porsche wasn't the first to use it, not even the second. The balance-shaft trick originated from Englishman Frederick Lanchester way back in 1911 for his Lanchester automobile. More recently than that, Japanese car maker Mitsubishi had successfully used Lanchester's idea to smooth out its own four-cylinder engines.

Porsche experimented with the balancer shaft concept to try and come up with a version that would allow Zuffenhausen to avoid paying a royalty to Mitsubishi for using their patented design. During the drawing board phase, Porsche engineers even cobbled together a 924 2.0 with balance shafts placed outside the engine block, trying to discern optimal placement for the shafts. Porsche ultimately relented and adhered to the Mitsubishi principle of using two counterweights, one near the shaft's central bearing, the second at the end of the shaft. Thus, Porsche paid Mitsubishi $8 for each and every car made utilizing the balancer shafts.

In the finished 2.5, the two balancer shafts were placed within the engine's alloy block: a low-mounted shaft and a high-mounted one, in close proximity to the four-cylinder's stout 5-bearing, forged steel crankshaft. The low shaft rotated with the crankshaft, the high shaft in the opposite direction, all thanks to a single, double-sided Gilmer belt. Their position in

Counter rotating balancer shafts solved the NVH hassles usually encountered with inline four-cylinder engines over 2 liters in size, but it wasn't new tech. The idea was pioneered by Dr. Frederick Lanchester. Dr. Porsche had sought a second opinion on taming big I4s (courtesy Porsche).

the block was discernible from two cone-shaped protrusions in the four-cylinder's timing belt cover. The Porsche V8 didn't have all that — it didn't need it — but there was another feature unique to the new 4-cylinder that the 928 would get later.

In the interests of scavenging that last ounce of efficiency from lower-octane gasoline, Porsche developed the TOP (Thermodynamically Optimized Porsche) concept on their new four-cylinder. A wedge-shaped combustion chamber with carefully located quench zones placed the heart of the air fuel mixture around the spark plug during combustion. In this high-turbulence environment, a high compression ratio can be used while avoiding detonation or misfiring. It's an engine design in the spirit of Honda's stratified CVCC, and the revised May "Fireball" Jaguar V12, maximum power and economy even with a weak fuel/air mix.

A third key point of difference between Porsche's V8 and the four-cylinder for its new mystery car was an ingeniously simple oil/water engine intercooler. Nothing to do with a turbo and cooling intake air, it was to get the four-cylinder up to speed faster, and keep it safe once it got there. Located on the exhaust manifold side, the intercooler was surrounded by coolant. The coolant helped to bring the engine up to operating temperature by heat transfer to the

Porsche continued to provide vehicles for the special services; here its 944 is decked out in the white and green colors of the West German Police (courtesy Porsche).

circulating oil. In hard driving the heat from the engine oil could be passed to the car's cooling system via the interface of the intercooler.

The 2.5 four-cylinder shared its 78.9 mm stroke with the 928's V8, but not its bore. Porsche didn't have a 5-liter edition of the V8 yet, so the 2.5's 100 mm bore was bigger than the V8 4.5's 95 mm and the 4.7's 97 mm. Weight of these large cast pistons was kept down to 720 grams, even with rings and pin assemblies. Apart from that, the four-cylinder relied on the construction principles of the 1977 V8. All-aluminum construction for head and block, utilizing Reynolds 390 aluminum, and linerless cylinder bores. The lower part of the 4-pot used the V8's ladder-frame construction, bringing the caps of the crank's 5 main bearings into a unified casting to aid rigidity and strength.

The four-cylinder motor featured 2 valves per cylinder and a single cam, like one bank of the Porsche's V8, but there were the differences permitting the I4's TOP system. As with the V8, the 2.5-liter also had maintenance-free hydraulic lifters, and a rubber cambelt between the crank and the camshaft. Sitting on a stand, the 2.5 obviously resembled half of Porsche's water-cooled V8, and because of that the new four had something the VW/Audi I4 couldn't have, the three-dimensional "PORSCHE" script embossed on the cam cover. It was a powerplant fit for a Porsche, the first four-cylinder Porsche motor to be fitted to a car wearing the Stuttgart shield since the old 1600 912 got pensioned off in the sixties.

A new engine bristling with features to help Porsche fight the 1980s, a cylinder count of four, it all hinted at the new name for Porsche's 924 development. The straight four was fitted to a 2+2 front-engined transaxle coupe denoted by the three digits—944! Zuffenhausen had multiplied the middle number by two, suggesting that the new car was twice as good. In light

The new 2.5 liter four-cylinder silenced critics that hoped for a six cylinder motor. The Porsche built 2.5 I4 had the refinement to match 6 and 8 cylinder rivals (courtesy Porsche).

of the other changes and refinements worked in by the wizards of Weissach, that just might have been the case. Before getting carried away, it must be realized that this was Porsche's idea of a new car.

Porsche Development—Waste Not, Want Not

The 944 was the son of 924, and their similarities and differences proved that Porsche is the master of making a good thing better, or, in the case of the 924-to-944 transition, critics might call it "making an okay thing superb." At 5 years old, the 924 platform was just getting warmed up by Porsche standards. Just fix the things that needed fixing. The weakest spot—the motor—had been done, so the remaining order of business was styling. The 924 wasn't a bad looker, just a little on the bland side and a bit bulbous about the rear haunches. Lucky for Porsche they already had the solution with their 924 Carrera body shape. The Carrera had a no-nonsense macho look, so Porsche merely adapted that car's appearance for volume production.

The 944 didn't have the Carrera hood scoop, nor the 924 Turbo's air intakes in the nose; it didn't need them, the 944 wasn't turbocharged—yet. However, the 944 did have Bayerflex bumpers and the Carrera's aggressive fender flares. This time the flares were no longer homologation plastic add-ons; for the new 944 its w-i-d-e body look was achieved using the real stuff, steel. The 924 Carrera's rear spoiler was also a standard 944 feature that each and every new 2.5-liter car would get in 1981. Apart from slight molding differences necessary for volume-producing the Carrera's look, the 944 seemed just like that older limited-run special. In Guards Red the resemblance was uncanny. The mild "offend no one" ways of the 924 had given way to something any boy racer would have been proud to call his own!

The 944 was different in detail from the 924 starter pack. Beyond the looks and new engine lay a host of upgrades, putting further distance between a basic 924 and the new 944. The "Dual 4" inherited the four-wheel ventilated disk brakes found standard on the European spec 924 Turbo, that is, 11.1- and 11.4-inch rotors front and rear. They were necessary to haul a 944 down in flight, good enough to arrest a 944 traveling at 62 mph in 3.3 seconds, according to Porsche data. Similarly, because the 944 driveline would be absorbing more torque than a 125-bhp 924, the larger 924 Turbo 1-inch-diameter driveshaft was used

It may have utilized the 924 Turbo's 4-wheel ventilated disks, but the 944 eschewed the Turbo's Porsche 5-speed in favor of a beefed up version of the Audi 5-speed gearbox the 924 had been using since 1980 (courtesy John Gacioch).

on the 944. However, the 924 Turbo's Porsche 5-speed dogleg gearbox wasn't required, so the new 944 used a stronger version of the regular 924's Audi 5-speed.

The transaxle layout had proven to be well balanced, so alterations for the 944 were directed at smoothing the rough edges off the 924 performance envelope. Sturdier rear semi-trailing arms increased the new car's wheelbase by 1.8 inches over the 924. In addition, Porsche weren't going to rely on Frederick Lanchester's balancer shafts for reducing the NVH associated with a big inline four. A further refinement over the 924 was to have the 2.5 engine supported by a crossmember, where its movements were soothed by hydraulic engine mounts. At the rear, the driveshaft and transaxle assembly was supported by rubber mounts, so the mechanical package's connection to the 944 shell was damped at four points. Plus there were rubber bushings to locate the rack and pinion steering to the crossmember.

So many changes to the skin, and under the skin, but not much to the four-cylinder coupe's interior. Porsche had blown the budget on the body and mechanicals, and the interior of the 944 was largely a 924 carry-over. Trim materials like carpeting were improved where possible, the color selections were toned down compared to what the 924 was wearing in the mid–'70s, but here was the same dash molding familiar to all owners of water-cooled four-cylinder Porsches. In spite of its 1970s VW "next generation" style, the flat dash with square center console and raised binnacle with three large circular faces was still sporty.

The 944's control station was imbued with more class than the 924's from the better trim and the mechanical refinements the 944 had brought. Plus, there were "Porsche" style touches to remind the owners they were part of the Zuffenhausen fold: the offset rev counter,

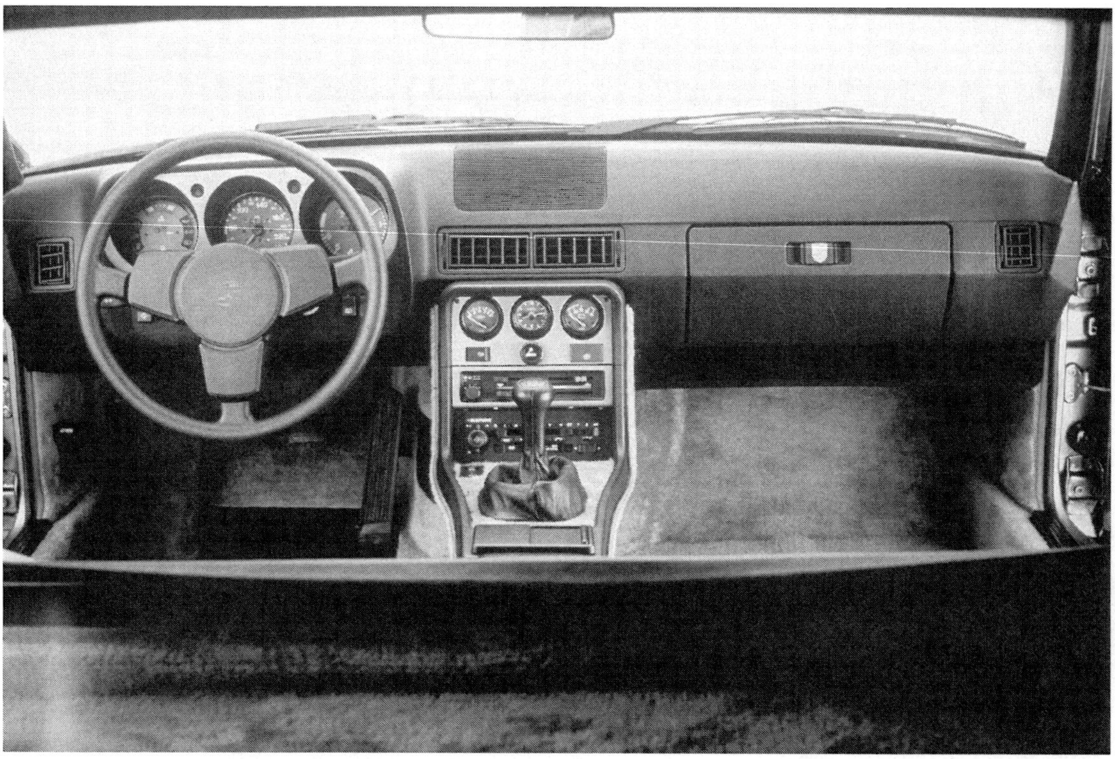

To start with Porsche carried over the 924's interior to the 944 practically unchanged. Strangely enough, Porsche was now using yellow markings for the 944's instruments (courtesy Porsche).

already present on the 924, and a standard 3-spoke 911-style steering wheel to replace the simple-looking 2-spoker found on ordinary 924s. Oddly, yellow had replaced the previous white markings on the black background of the instrument pod's 3 circular faces.

Yellow markings may have been of questionable taste, as with the Pasha upholstery ready to go for the 944 from the start, but it made things lively. Fluorescent yellow numbers, checkered flag seating and sports car racing fender flares all pointed to a driving and ownership experience out of the ordinary. This is the reason for buying a sports car rather than a sedan. Indeed, the 944 brought enough to the table to be interesting and different in the same way that had attracted so many to the air-cooled-engine concept of the 911.

Porsche took the opportunity this time around to reinforce the Porsche/911 connection. Look to the 944's standard wheels and there lay 911-type "Cookie Cutter" 15 × 7 cast alloy rims. The Cookie Cutter rim is so readily associated with Porschedom, and yet it had never featured on the 924, not even as an option. And following on from this the 944 mimicked the 911's upgrade path of offering more expensive forged Fuchs rims to replace the base Cookie Cutters. With the exception of the rare Carrera, the 924 never really did the Fuchs style so positively associated with 911 motoring. It went the other way and adopted the 928S Disc rims for the 924 Turbo, feeling that was where the glamour lay. Porsche had rethought the situation.

Yes, there were better trim materials for the 944 era, but no, Porsche had yet to tackle the 924 problem of limited clearance under the steering wheel for the thighs (courtesy Porsche).

The realignment of Porsche thinking concerning style deployment for the four-cylinder coupe might have had something to do with the arrival of Peter Schutz. Coming in as chairman at the start of 1981, Schutz was committed to the idea of 911 revival. The 944 arrived in June of that year. Peter Schutz accepted that realistically Porsche needed the four-cylinder front-engined cars to survive, but in the new "save the 911" climate it was natural that the 944 become steeped in all things Porsche.

There was a move back from the breakaway radical thinking that got the 924 and 928 programs underway, a realization that engineering by itself wasn't enough to push Porsche along. The company would have to call on one quality not possessed by its ever-more-competitive Japanese rivals — tradition. The 944 heralded the transition to the theory that while what a car can do for one is vital, it's equally important how the driver feels about things while the car does its work.

The 944 owner was feeling very good about things when lifting a hood supported by hydraulic struts, rather than the 924's rudimentary steel prop, and casting a proud eye on the word Porsche embossed on the cam cover. There was the feeling that this was a quality four-cylinder coupe, and rather good value. The 944 came in very well equipped for just a bit more than a normal 924 in the U.S.; it was priced at $18,980, placing it midway between the 924 and 924 Turbo.

As far as performance and equipment were concerned, the 944 made the U.S. 924 Turbo just about redundant. Porsche certainly thought so, because the 944 sounded the end for the 924 in America, for the time being at least. A relief for North American dealers, they had a fresh model, and the 924 said goodbye early on in the 1982 model year. The 924 did continue for the rest of the world, and the 924 Turbo trickled on to accommodate some markets with bothersome taxes on vehicles with over 2 liters of displacement. Would anyone care for an Italian-market Ferrari 208 Turbo? However, for the most part the Turbo wasn't needed anymore, the 944 introduced a new efficiency threshold.

The 924 was one of the new type of sports cars that could achieve impressive figures using a relatively small engine. It achieved this through aerodynamic efficiency and being quite light at 2,380 lbs. in its early form. Now, for the early '80s, the 944 raised the bar, thanks largely to its new engine. It weighed much more in its equivalent early, manual-transmission form, a portly 2,600 lbs., but its extra half-liter of displacement was used to good effect. Its official Porsche figures suggested a top speed of 137 mph, and on some occasions its 0.35 drag factor helped it go a few mph faster in independent testing. Acceleration was remarkable, Porsche claimed 0–62 mph in 8.4 seconds, but the car's true 0–60 range fell in the 7- to 7.5-second bracket.

The new 2.5-liter was making a lot more power than the old Vee Dub & Audi four-banger, making the 944 a genuinely quick car by 1981 standards. Its engine had moved on from the 924's Bosch K-Jetronic mechanical injection, to computer-controlled electronic L-Jetronic. This system calculated air/fuel mix based on aspirated airflow entering a vanemeter, relaying the information to the ECU via a potentiometer. Even better still, the 944's engine featured Bosch electronic ignition, and could rightly proclaim a choice of 256 ignition advance angles. Working with the L-jet's computer, 32 advance angles were programed into the ECU, taking into account engine revs and intake manifold vacuum.

Bosch Motronic helped the 2.5 to class-leading power and torque numbers. Try 163 bhp at 5,800 rpm and 151 lbs./ft. at 3,000 rpm, almost 40 horses up on the 924's 2.0 I4. Thank Porsche's TOP combustion chamber design, and the 10.6 to one compression ratio that was

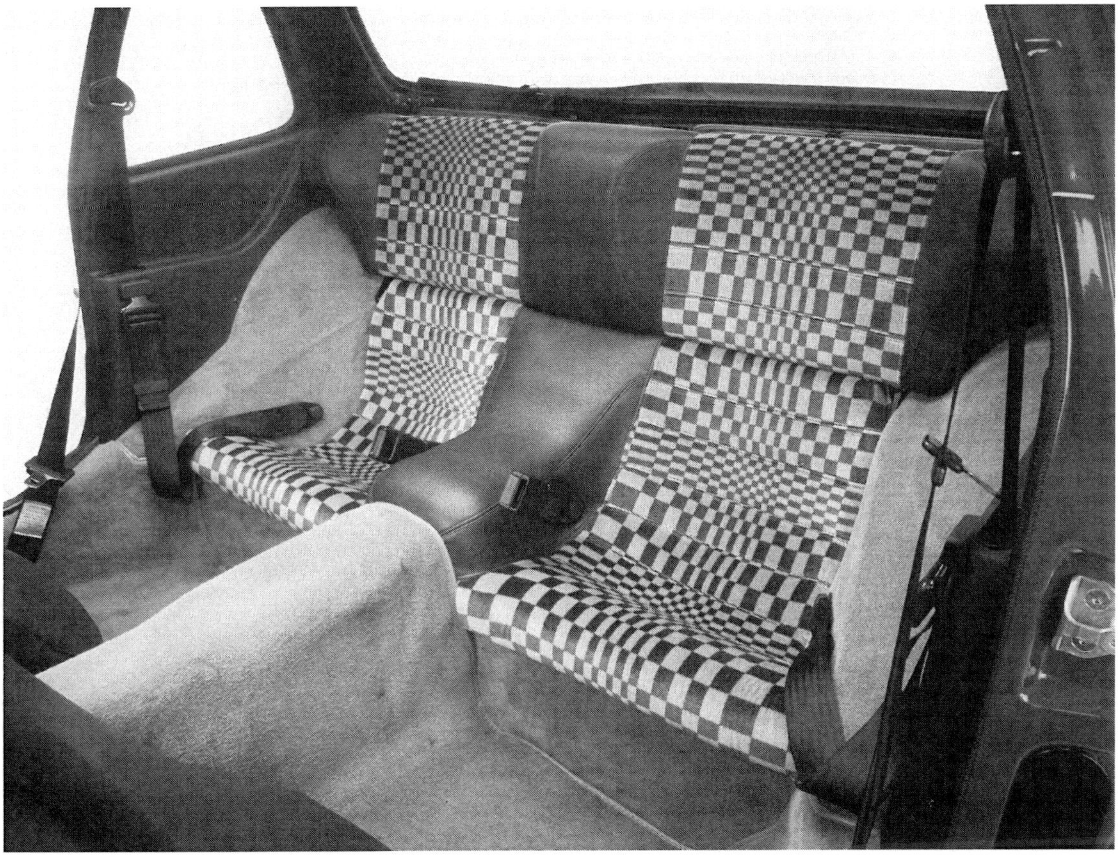

However, Porsche still offered the checkered Pasha upholstery, so the 944's overall progress was still all to the good (courtesy Porsche).

part of it. It seemed that the 4 bhp loss Porsche had allowed for the effect of belt-driven contra-rotating balancer shafts had brought very little harm. This was a good time to be an I4; the lower cylinder count compared to rivals made for reduced frictional losses, and fuel economy that a 6-cylinder Datsun Z-car or gas-guzzling Mazda rotary were deeply envious of. In Europe the 944 gave an average fuel consumption in the mid-to high-20s, and 35 mpg with gentle driving. With a 66-liter gas tank one was looking at a range of 380 to 400 miles.

How worryingly close the 944 was to the outgoing 924 Turbo: the blown car 5 mph faster, a half second swifter to sixty in sprinting. It should have come as little surprise, given both weighed 2,600 lbs. and the 944 was only 7 horses shy of the blown 924's early 170 bhp output. Porsche were nothing if not consistent, but the tide was turning against the turbocharged concept by the early 1980s. While originally seeing it as the only way to get around economy and emissions without having mind-numbingly slow transport, the world had now fallen out of love with the turbo. It added mechanical complexity, necessitated more exact and frequent servicing, and its driving characteristics were not enjoyed by everyone.

Avoiding going into reverse, due to the 924 Turbo's racing shift pattern, wasn't the only bother banished with 944 living. It may have had similar power and outright speed to the Turbo, but the performance was achieved with such ease. The blown 924 wasn't a car overtly afflicted with lag, but a turbo car will never match the response of a normally aspirated engine.

U.S. 944 performance, as with this 1983 model, wasn't far removed from the excellent results of the European spec cars. However, the 944's 5 mph bumpers were more noticeable than those used on 944s in other countries. That said, the 944 had nicer U.S. side marker lights than the 924 (courtesy John Breen).

Note the early transition of Juan Pablo Montoya from turbocharged Indy racing to normally aspirated Formula One. In the early days he was invoking throttle-induced oversteer, from not being used to the immediate reply when the throttle is depressed in an "atmo" car.

It was the same on the Porsche 934 Turbo, get on the gas early, and wait, and wait—and wait. There was no lag on the 944, because there was no turbo, and there was no turbo because the performance and economy were already very good. And if the 924 Turbo suddenly didn't seem relevant, neither did much of the coupe opposition. The 944 had achieved the kind of speed that would have required a V8 or V12 coupe only a few years earlier, and those cars didn't enjoy the practical advantages of compact dimensions, four-cylinder economy and the convenience of a rear tailgate hatch. It was also easy to believe in this new-age, post-fuel-crisis performance car, because the 2.5 four-cylinder provided a real alternative to sixes and eights.

Porsche's previous method of dealing with turbo 2 liters may have been to bolt everything down as tightly as possible, but half a V8 seemed to bring twice the refinement. The contra-rotating balancer shafts really did their job, providing a level of smoothness that was unbelievable. Was this really a 2.5-liter engine, was it really a four-cylinder? Doubts could be had if the Porsche 2.5-liter was compared to the GM 2.5-liter four-cylinder "Iron Duke," another fuel-injected I4 derived from a V8 engine. Comparing the Iron Duke with the 944 motor in U.S. spec, the four-pot from the house of GM was 51 SAE horses short and the gulf in harshness was even greater. It seems that not all I4s are created equal, and buyers had no reason to feel shortchanged because their 944 was powered by a mere four.

There was no need for the 944's 2.5 to use the contemporary Iron Duke as the only punching bag. Sit in those high-backed 911-style seats and the smooth hum of the four-pot from the house of Zuffenhausen made it hard to tell how many cylinders there were. Porsche said it was as good as a six, and there was no reason to doubt their word. The 944 had a much taller final drive ratio than the 5-speed 924, 3.89 compared to 4.71, but the gain in refinement wasn't down to keeping the engine ticking over more slowly. Although both cars made use of an Audi-sourced 5-speed, all 5 of the 944's ratios were shorter compared to those in the 924's box.

Little disappointment in the handling department either. The 944's chassis was very safe, and took over from the 924 family as Porsche's best-handling car—sorry, 911! This was a set-up that made great use of understeer, with a well-sized window of neutrality, and ultimately oversteer could be induced through determined use of the throttle, or by very ragged backing off in mid-turn. The 944 was an easy car to drive fast. It felt lithe, even though it wasn't that light, and was extremely easy to place. Its steering may have lacked that final layer of polish offered by Hethel, but by just about anybody else's standards the rack and pinion steering was accurate and had good feel.

With a June 1981 debut price of 38,900 deutschmarks the 944 was as sharply priced as any automotive bargain (courtesy Porsche).

The 944's appetite for both road and track may have made its suspension and wheels seem surprising: humble 924-style MacPherson struts and semi-trailing arms, and there wasn't any monster truck footwear to be found either. The standard Cookie Cutter cast alloy 15 × 7 rims were shod with 185/70 or 215/60 radials, the package was designated M104. M104 could be upgraded to M458's 16 × 7–inch Fuchs rims wearing 205/55 Pirelli P7s, at extra cost of course. All the tires mentioned were serious VR-rated equipment, but they exploded the myth that fat fenders need fat tires to keep one glued to the track.

That 185-section, 70-profile tires should be used by this time on a cutting-edge sports car might have raised an eyebrow or two; the reality was that they were the best choice. For a start the buyer didn't have to pay extra to get them, secondly the 944 didn't have power steering at this stage. The 185-section rubber on a 7-inch-wide rim was on the limit of pleasant for low-speed maneuvers like parking. The skinny tires also cut down on the road roar common to all kinds of Porsche. Working with the 944 suspension upgrades and 185/70 tires, the new car had noticeably better ride comfort than the early 924s.

Indeed, a suspension sport pack, containing 21.5 mm/14 mm front and rear sway bars, that were standard equipment in most export markets, was available for that extra bit of fine fettling. That aside, the 944's chassis and structure were well up to speed, and even the roof had been beefed up over 924 days. And the 944, in base unadorned form, might have been the best value Porsche of all time. The 924 was cheaper, but then its abilities and hardware dictated that it should be. The 356 and 911 were excellent, but at the price one should have expected no less. The same could be stated for later 944s, the 968 and the giant 928. More powerful, swifter and more able, but much pricier into the bargain.

The 1981 944 was a rare chance to get the goods without the inflated sticker. A chance to enjoy admiration during valet parking, and still have money left over for the rest of the evening. There was a conscious plan from Peter Schutz to move 944s out of Porsche showrooms, and it was keenly priced indeed, for a Porsche. Out the door for 38,900 deutschmarks, it was very tempting. The looks and much of the 924 Carrera's performance for just two-thirds the purchase price. In Guards Red the 944 was a wolf in wolf's clothing, and was either similarly or lower priced than rivals. That included the much-more-expensive, left-hand-drive-only Audi Quattro. The 944 could match the all-wheel-drive Audi's acceleration and speed, while greatly bettering its fuel economy.

944—Engineered to Excite

That a car based on the humble 924 could better a much vaunted, turbocharged rally champ for less money was good news for the enthusiast. The 944 arrived at a time in West Germany when manufacturers were concentrating on the technical side of their work. Much money had gone into weight saving and aerodynamic improvements. All of this needed to come after the second gas crunch. Mercedes replaced the W116 with the W126 S-class, and was preparing to launch its 190 as the 1980s' answer to its 200–280 compact range. Audi were on the verge of making big waves with the aero 100/5000, and BMW were paring down the pounds on their 5 and 3 series.

These revised, or new, models made much play of advanced technology. The public were very accepting of the claims and the idea of efficient '80s high tech. This period also coincided with German manufacturers' cementing their position in the luxury/sports category.

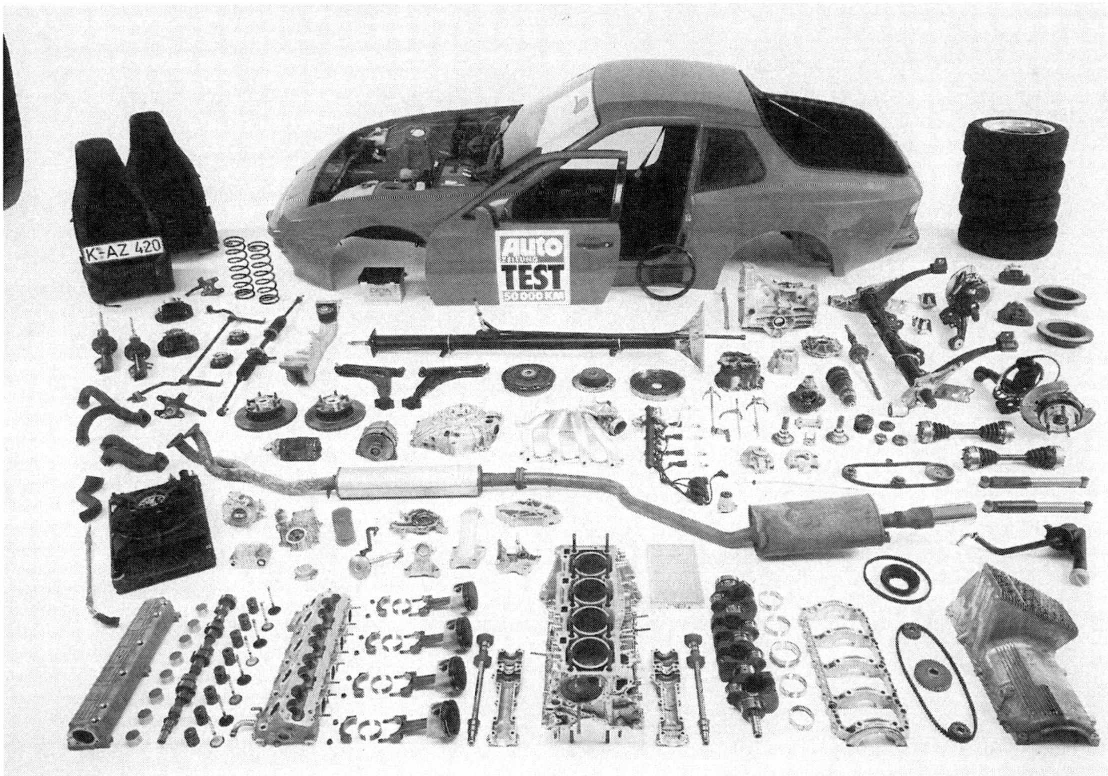

A stripdown of a 1984 944 by journal *Auto Zeitung* after 50,000 kms of usage. Solid materials and build quality at the old NSU plant ensured dependable service (courtesy Porsche).

Rival European and British automakers that had offered alternatives in the sixties and seventies had fallen away. The market was fast reaching the point where the German brands had the highest perceived quality and the most prestige.

So the 924/944 soon didn't have the Triumph TR7, Fiat Spider, etc., to kick around any more. As seen from the development of its engine, and detail improvements over the 924, Porsche saw the need to raise the game for the eighties, but their revised 944 placed the emphasis on fun. The 944 didn't boast electronic toys, and it was old-fashioned compared to new models. There was a new breed of hot front-drive hatchbacks in Europe. Models like the 1980 Ford Escort XR3, Opel Kadett GT/E, and latest 1.8-liter VW Golf GTi were using sub-2-liter engines and front-drive chassis to achieve things thought impossible for family transport just a few years earlier.

A car like an MGB didn't seem necessary when a go-faster version of the family shopping cart could do everything. Realizing the fast-improving acceleration, handling and braking of mainstream cars, Porsche wisely took the model they hoped would become their sales leader upscale from the 924. The 944 had a better profit margin, and closer rivals would be from a smaller pool. In this niche of near-extravagant grand tourers Porsche would find a few takers for an automatic 944, one with the Audi-derived 010 3-speeder, as used on the 924. Porsche claimed the same 137 mph maximum for the automatic 944 as for the manual, but the sprint to 100 kph was 1.2 seconds in arrears.

The 944 2.5 was better suited to handling an autobox than the 924 2.0, even if some

Back in the "image is everything '80s" the 944 was the right car for the times. It arrived in the U.S. at $18,980 and remained competitively priced until 1986 (courtesy Brian Joseph Webb, www.kiddoh.com/cars/porsche.htm).

felt that acceleration was still glacially slow compared to the stick shift editions. The shiftless 944 would find the most acceptance in the U.S., but the 944 already had the right ingredients to make it there. There was the previously mentioned $18,980 sticker price. No shock there, because for that money the 944 came with air conditioning, 924-type removable sunroof, power windows/mirrors, plus those neat Cookie Cutter alloys. Forget about the steel rims of early 924s, and the U.S. 944 even came standard with the one-size-up 215/60 VR-rated Pirelli CN36s as standard issue.

It was a good deal for those that had scrimped and saved for the Porsche experience. Even the side marker lights were more gracefully blended in this time around, and four-cylinder Porsches had always been one of the better imported models concerning the dreaded 5-mph bumpers. The only thing that could cause possible alarm, apart from the seatbelt warning buzzer, was the sight of a little plaque at the base of the instrument cluster, below the left dial face. It said those three very scary words—"Unleaded Fuel Only."

The sighting of "UFO" was usually the moment the bubble burst and the dream ended, since it suggested much-reduced engine performance compared to European editions. This had been the case with the 924, swift at home, yet tardy when made to cope with Federal pollution law and U.S. low-octane gasoline. However, no need to panic, Porsche's balancer shaft 2.5 was still manic! Power was 143 horses strong, only a couple shy of the 4-barrel, 5-liter Chevy V8 offered in the 1982 GM F-body sportsters. Half the displacement, half the cylinders, but the same power and smoothness thanks to Doktor Porsche.

A 1986 944 being tracked hard at Australia's Wakefield Park. The 944 chassis made the latest Porsche 4-cylinder coupe even easier to punt around a circuit (courtesy Bill Cagnacci).

The Euro-spec 944 2.5 made 20 horses more, but those were DIN not SAE horses, plus the U.S. 2.5's maximum power came in 300 rpm lower on the tach, even though peak torque still arrived at 3,000 rpm. This unleaded-gas, catalytic converter-equipped 2.5 wasn't all that different from the "good" version. It still had those smoothing balancer shafts, the TOP combustion chamber trick and a high compression ratio. Not the 10.6 CR of the Euro 2.5, but a still very creditable 9.5 to one. The 924's CR was so low one could practically slap on a blower without fear, but there was some hope for the new engine. Amazingly the U.S. 944 was only a half-second slower from rest to sixty mph than the European version, and 5 mph short on top speed.

What the 944 could do in America was less important than what it replaced, which was one of the biggest disappointments on four tires. That ride was the U.S. 924 Turbo, a car that promised so much and yet performed questionably. Something was lost in the U.S. emissions translation that saw the car relegated to the ranks of the expensive handlers. It and others relied on the infamous 0–50 mph statistic to look respectable during the bad days of 1979 to 1983. The 944 also used the 0–50 mph yardstick in early ads, but it didn't need to. The quoted time was 5.9 seconds. The 944 was at worst a low-16s car for the quarter-mile in America, too fast to make 0–50 meaningful, too quick to need to rely on it to look good.

That the U.S. 944 could be so swift and contain so many gewgaws was impressive. This version was loaded with convenience features, like a/c, that were normally absent in the home market, and those U.S. 5-mph bumper bars were doing the car no weight favors. It all pushed the 944 to a substantial 2,790 lbs., over 600 lbs. heftier than a Fiat X1/9 and over 300 lbs. porkier than the 924's old amigo, the RX7. No problem, the 944 could blast past both those

AGY 37Y

coupes with ease. It could also match the best Corvette around, the more expensive 1982 automatic Collector Edition Crossfire, with the ace of a stick shift.

Not everything was ideal for the latest Porsche import. Better gas mileage than the low 20s might have been expected from a four-cylinder model with a new Porsche motor. Then again, those four-cylinders were for performance, not part of some "gas miser" pack with super-tall rear gears. The Euro and U.S. 944s were the same for final drivc and the first 4 gears. The only concession to fuel economy and easy interstate cruising was a taller 0.73 fifth in the 016K 5-speed. The Euro spec 016J box had a 0.83 top gear. The 944 was also looking a bit out of step, considering that its weight was up there with the latest downsized, V6, mid-size front-drive family cars, that could seat 5 in comfort. But remember — Porsche doesn't downsize, it up-contents.

Many would gladly have a friend crouch in the 944's rear +2 accommodation on the drive down to McDonald's. With passenger wedged back in that automotive crawl space, the driver savors the admiring glances directed at the 944's swoopy lines. A Buick Century never received those. For Porsche the glass is always half full, and the driver is in the half-full part of the car. No need to worry, a Big Mac could always be passed between the front bucket seats to the starving rear passenger. Perhaps a Quarter Pounder; there may not have been enough space rearwards for a Big Mac. Next time the rear seat could be folded forward and the back-seat passenger could crouch in the luggage hold. They would have a bit more space and possibly enjoy the expansive view afforded by the glass hatch. If it was a clear sunny day they could even work on their tan. In a Porsche 944 one has options!

On the more serious side the good Doktor still hadn't done anything about the 924-style, low-set steering wheel. The 944 inherited this along with the 924's dash, and there wasn't much joy in steering a car from one's lap. The steering column wasn't adjustable, so the only avenue of relief was to specify the optional, slightly smaller 360-mm four-spoker. A pity, because then the nice-looking tiller that fueled the driver's 911 ambitions was lost; however, blood circulation to the lower legs was regained. Porsches are all about balance.

Unlike the homogenized, suit-all-tastes platform-sharers of the 21st century, the 944 was still from the era of the sports car with foibles, when engineering quirks made things interesting, even challenging. Italian cars were noted for their unique driving ergonomics, where short legs and long arms would have been handy. The 924/944 had their own unique wheel-to-seat-squab relationship, and that was not all. The windshield wiper pattern for right-hand-drive 944s was still in the same position as for left-hand-drive cars. As a small car maker, Porsche could not do otherwise.

A limited R&D budget meant there was no real updating of the 924/944 HVAC complex — a decent system when introduced in the mid–'70s, but only adequate by 1982. Porsche claimed some gains behind the dash that improved matters, but the claim hardly seemed credible since the dash molding stayed constant. No matter, the heater would keep the driver warm when visiting friends in Detroit, and the 944's bodywork had little to fear from a Michigan winter. Porsche continued its program of galvanized bodywork on the 944; it carried a 7-year

Opposite, top: **This 1986 5-speed Australian spec 944 represented the first year unleaded gasoline was introduced to Australia, bringing its 2.5 I4 into line with the U.S. spec 944 (courtesy Bill Cagnacci).** ***Opposite, bottom:*** **At 2,600+ lbs. the 944 was no lightweight; it was on a par with a 3.2 liter 911. On the positive side those extra pounds contributed to the four-cylinder coupe's solidity (courtesy Bill Cagnacci).**

By 1983 the 924 model range had been pruned, and the 944 had taken over as Porsche's volume selling model with 80 cars being built at Neckarsulm per day. The 944 was moving expediently (courtesy Robert Aponte).

anti-corrosion warranty, just like the pricier 911 and 928 and cheaper 924. The 944 was a Porsche among equals.

The complex galvanized treatment of the 944's steel panels was necessary for maintaining long service life. In Germany cars are subject to periodic inspections by the TUV organization. If a car displays structural rust it must either be repaired, or be taken off the road. The inspection's aim is to maintain the general roadworthiness of cars on German roads, and it covers more than just rust. Good build quality of Porsches contributes to their excellent resale value, and promotes repeat business because the owner doesn't have to come up with a lot of extra cash when trading in his car on a new Porsche.

Porsche and Peter Schutz certainly wanted the 944 to fly out of Zuffenhausen, or rather the Neckarsulm works. Porsche couldn't have produced the 944 itself, not if it was to sell in the volume required to take over from the 924, and this was achieved. By 1983, 80 944s were being assembled each day compared to 25 924s. And all those fresh 944s were contributing to Porsche's bottom line, and helping to fund development of the 911—excellent! The small independent car maker had risen to offering a full four-car range, from a budget Porsche (924) to a couple of the most expensive production cars in the world (911 Turbo and 928S).

Two companies that weren't liking Porsche's plan of dominance were Datsun and Mazda. Porsche and Datsun had traded places since the summer of 1970. Back in those days the 240Z was on its way to becoming the best-selling sportster of all time, while the Porsche 914 was dazed and confused. By the early '80s the Z was doing a passable impression of Las Vegas

Elvis, and in the 280/300ZX era the purists were looking to Porsche. Similarly, Mazda's RX7 had been blown out of the water. Like the 280ZX it was packing comfort features and an optional turbo, but it proved no match for a wide-fendered 924 with a VW Rabbit dashboard!

It was the 280ZX's turn to be confused, it didn't know if it was a Datsun or a Nissan. The Mazda's 12A rotary spun a tune as delightful as Vivaldi's Four Seasons, but when a driver is getting down to the serious business of challenging the road, Wagner is more appropriate. The RX7's image went down in flames. Porsche had a habit of creating icons, and it had now created the 944 class. In a dictionary, its definition would read: lithe, balanced coupe, not too much power, but enough comfort and accommodation to take a couple and their luggage on the longest of trips.

A Need for Self-Improvement

Not *too* much luggage, though, that independent rear suspension and transaxle arrangement made for a high loading floor. Porsche may have created a new standard with the 944, but that didn't stop the flow of improvements. Changes that had to be made concerned the innovative 2.5-liter engine. Not exactly a recall, they didn't really exist on European cars in those days, but modifications to improve durability. For 1983 attempts were made to lengthen the life of the counter-rotating balancer shaft's rubber belts via a design alteration to camshaft and balancer shaft drives.

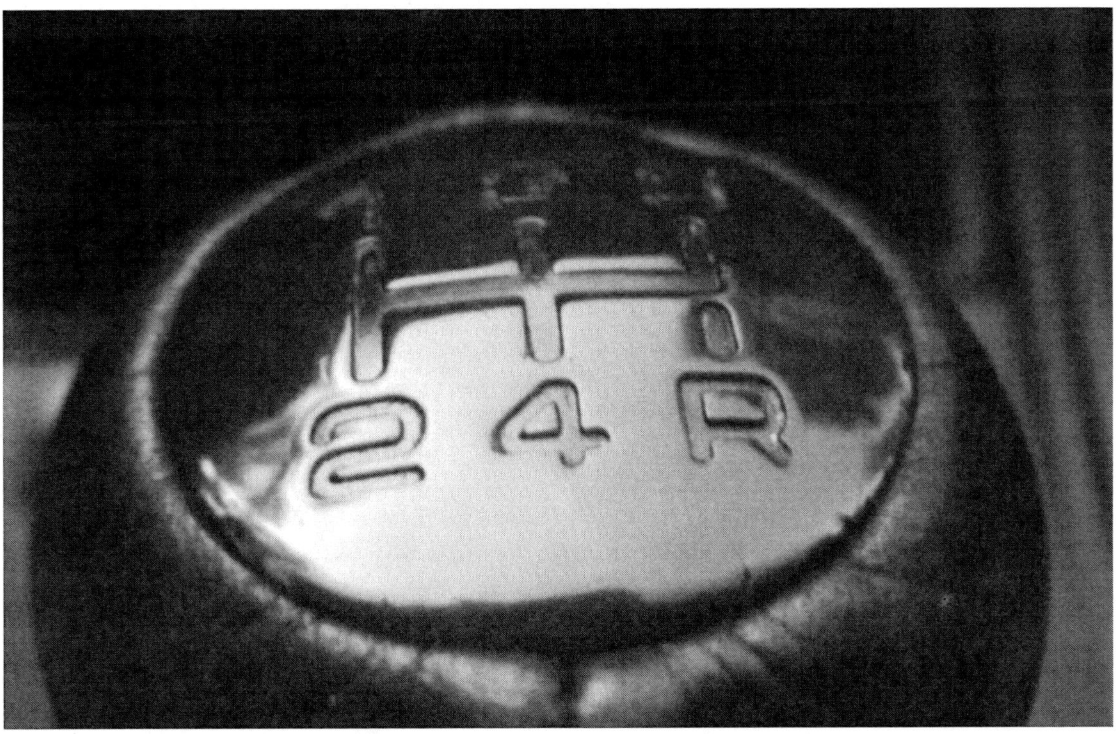

Shifting was a snap with the conventional shift pattern of the Audi 5-speed box. European spec 944s had an overdrive 0.83 fifth; U.S. 944s had a taller 0.73 top gear (courtesy Christopher Kotecha).

More seriously, heat from the exhaust manifold was cracking one of the special hydraulic engine mounts. To stop the driver from getting an unwanted massage, and extend the fluid-filled mount's life, different shielding to protect the mount was introduced in 1984. There were also reports of lubrication seeping out around the balance shafts, so these shafts got redesigned oil shields. Cylinder-block lubrication was improved at the same time. These service issues highlight the glitches experienced when introducing a new motor, even when it's based on an existing unit like the Porsche V8. It also shows the dependability of the 924 2-liter. Many had derisively called the VW/Audi I4 a nail of an engine, but nails are pretty tough!

A few convenience features wouldn't have gone astray either, like synchromesh on reverse gear in 1983 — shocking! Nineteen eighty-four saw the arrival of "Porsche" cloth as one of the interior trim choices: a marketing person's delight, the name "Porsche" in Porsche-style lettering repeated in endless parallel diagonal lines over the seats. If one has a great name in the auto business, why not flaunt it? Surprisingly, companies like Hyundai have yet to adopt such stylistic touches. It was the imminent arrival of Porsche cloth that probably goaded Zuffenhausen to introduce power steering on the 944 for 1984.

Teutonic thoroughness would have logically reasoned that the 944 owner couldn't sit smugly on the new "PORSCHE" cloth while beads of perspiration trickled down the brow from man-handling the 944's unassisted steering during parking. So it was that quicker-ratio 18.5-versus 22-to-one power steering was incorporated on the 944, with 3.2 rather than 3.8 turns lock to lock. Not the lightning quick response of the new 1984 Vette's scarcely more than 2 turns lock to lock, but quicker steering nonetheless. Porsche knew who would like the steering "lite" the most: they made it standard on 1984 automatic transmission-equipped 944s. Now it was possible to casually drive a 944 with one hand. Those ordering 5-speed 944s had to pay extra for this privilege.

U.S.-delivered 1984 944s came with power steering as standard equipment. However, the options list on both sides of the Atlantic now included cruise control and powered actuation for the sunroof. For convenience, the gadgets continued with an internal electric tailgate release. In keeping with Porsche's loose grasp of the concept of ergonomics, the release was located in the cabin footwell, and the 944's ignition had to be turned on.

There was another release to feature in 1984: the departing of Porsche from its association with luxury brand Audi in America. Yes, the concept of selling Porsches and Audis together in "Porsche+Audi" showrooms, and using the Porsche+Audi tag, had come to an end. This arrangement had been going since 1970 in association with Volkswagen, set up at the dawn of the 914's run. And there was another vestige of Volkswagen that was about to be tossed away, the 924/944 VW Dasher/Passat–inspired dashboard from yesteryear.

Another series of improvements were brought into place for the 944. Much of the work was related to a new and highly anticipated 944 variant that would take the family to the next level. Thus, from January 1985, the 944's interior received an elliptically themed dashboard, one that made great use of ovals, like the 1996 Ford Taurus. This new addition was said to

Opposite, top: **At last, the new 1985 944 interior with elliptical dash design, improved HVAC center and increased steering wheel to seat clearance (courtesy Porsche).** ***Opposite, bottom:*** **The 1985 944 featured white rather than yellow markings, in an oval themed instrument display and dash that was better designed but a bit blander than the pre–1985 control center (courtesy Christopher Kotecha).**

MILES

have imbued the 944's interior with "928-ness." The inside of a 944 was a classier, more up-to-date place now, but the dashboard comparison was odd because the 928's molding looked completely different, and the 944's instrument panel wasn't height-adjustable as on the 928.

However, relief lay in store for new 944 owners in terms of the infamous low-set steering wheel. With the steering wheel raised almost an inch, and the seat lowered 1-½ inches, here was relief for those who wanted to throttle steer, rather than thigh steer, their new 944. Ten years after the first 924, Zuffenhausen had given in. But just to show who was still boss, they scattered the 944's switches to the four corners of the interior. There must have been a mini-tornado in the Zuffenhausen design office, flinging assorted switchgear into nooks and crannies, where they might never be seen again.

To find those controls, and to use them proficiently, required careful study of the 944 handbook. Finally free from the constraints of the VW Dasher dash, Porsche let their imagination run wild, and the Easter-egg hunt for controls turned up some curious finds. If the driver wished to activate the hazard warning lights, the best thing to do was to ask the passenger, because they were on his side. If Batman owned a 944, that must be why he kept Robin around!

Switchgear foibles aside, the new dash had a more expensive look to its surfaces, and those huge moveable ventilation grilles were doing a lot more work. Porsche claimed a rise in

We are still waiting! The 924 Turbo was gone and the public were eagerly awaiting the blown 944, almost as much as the revised 944 interior (courtesy Vincent Roche).

Top: The Pasha was gone, but the 944 Turbo's 1985 debut ensured that the passion was still in the 944 range. A 1988 944 Turbo in France is displayed (courtesy Vincent Roche). *Bottom:* It made sense for tuner Strosek to customize the 944 once the Turbo arrived (note the retained Turbo front). Styled in the image of its special 928, the Strosek 944 pictured, simply referred to as Design-Programm 944/Turbo, kept its standard headlamps (Courtesy Strosek www.strosek.de)

A later Strosek, moving into the 944S2 era. A smoother bodykit than previous Strosek 944s, it avoided the earlier rear windowline buttress treatment that was reminiscent of the Jag XJ-S. (Courtesy Strosek www.strosek.de)

HVAC capacity of one third, and this time they were telling the truth. That the 944 no longer had a dash that seemed incongruous with the car's expensive leather seating option was a bonus, but there was sad news too in 1985: the Pasha was gone! The racing-flag upholstery so famous and loved was no more. It was last listed in 1984, so the new 944 interior featured just pinstripe or "Porsche cloth" fabric as the special 944 seat inlays from now on.

The pinstripe material went well with the upscale, Yuppie-mobile image the 944 was acquiring by this stage. It was the boom time of the '80s, a new Porsche was accepted currency if one worked on the stock market and in the world of high finance. And one hand washed the other, because Porsche was doing great business, with annual sales at the 50,000 units level. Ferry Porsche seemed to have made the right choice in selecting a chairman who knew the importance of sales and marketing. In business jargon Zuffenhausen was now a cash cow — it could afford to invest in the 944's improvements that filtered through global markets during the course of 1985.

Top: The early 924 prototypes would have been perfect for the film version of *A Clockwork Orange.* Note the red Opel Manta in the background used to test the Porsche torque tube/transaxle assembly. *Above:* A 1976 924 interior, pairing green paintwork with tan/brown trim — all in all rather funky (courtesy Porsche).

Top: **Porsche introduced the 2,380 pound 924 with comfy 911 front bucket seats and an oil temperature gauge (courtesy Benny Proot).** ***Above:*** **Technically the M471 code for the naturally aspirated U.S. 924 implied 4-bolt wheels and rear drums, but in reality most came with 5-bolt rims and 4-wheel disks like this 1982 S pack 924. During 1980–82 it was possible to have an "S" hood decal accompanying M471 (courtesy Eric Lynch and www.924.org).**

Top: The new for 1979 924 Turbo pictured outside Porsche's Weissach engineering HQ, with the Weissach Wizards and famous drivers that made it all possible. At extreme right is veteran chief race mechanic Hubert Mimler. Second and third from right *(front)* are Le Mans '77 winner Jürgen Barth and racing ace Manfred Schurti. Fourth from right *(front)* is race engineer Eberhard Braun; fifth is "turbo guru" Julius Weber; sixth, handling the champagne, is Andy Rouse. At extreme left is Porsche's styling boss Anatole Lapine; at the rear bumper in pale blue is Mr. Bäuerle of the racing department. ***Above:*** The 924 GTS of Walter Rohrl and Christian Geistdorfer on its way to winning the 1981 Hessen Rally, with factory backing from Porsche (courtesy Porsche).

PORSCHE
87
SCCA

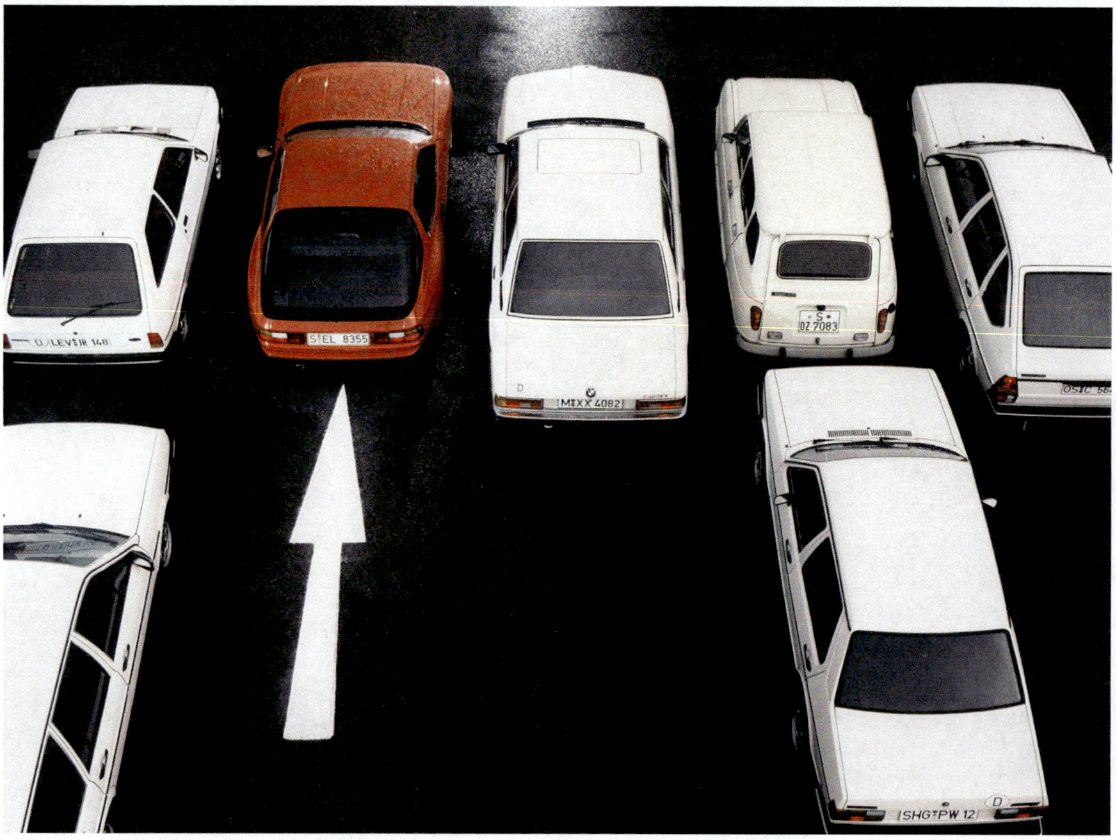
S EL 8355
M XX 4082
S DZ 7083
SHG PW 12

A 1982 944 in Guards Red was quite the image maker for Porsche in the early to mid 1980s. The 911 wasn't the only one in "Porsche World" now! (courtesy Porsche).

Opposite, top: With a bold presence that the relatively meek 924 lacked, the 944 also raised the bar as Porsche's best handling car (courtesy John Gacioch). *Opposite, bottom:* Porsche purposely pointing out a red 1982 944 in a field of bland white boxes (courtesy Porsche).

Built strong enough to withstand several Michigan or New York winters, the 944 started with a 7-year antirust warranty, boosted to 10 years in 1986 (courtesy Christopher Kotecha).

Top: Under the soon-to-be-retired Porsche+Audi banner, a preproduction 944 Turbo proved its mettle at 1984's Longest Day of Nelson Ledges 24-hour race with a 40 lap victory margin. *Bottom:* A 944 Turbo Cup entrant pictured at the West German Hockenheim circuit in 1987. By 1987 Turbo Cup cars were upgraded to 250 horses, and races took place in other European countries too (courtesy Porsche).

Top: Truly a Porsche among Porsches, the 1988 944 Silver Rose was a 250 bhp blown 944 derived from the 1987 Turbo Cup racers ... with luxury (courtesy Peter en Mijnte Remeijer). ***Above:*** Ferry Porsche with the new 968 coupe in 1991. Here was a Porsche engine in a car that was now assembled at Zuffenhausen (courtesy Porsche).

Top: In its new organic form, the 968's greenhouse was the only giveaway to its 924/944 DNA. This quality was absent from the Cabrio. ***Above:*** The stripped out 968CS is one of the finest cars Porsche has ever produced. Less was indeed more in this revival of 356 sense and sensibilities. No electronic aids, just driver and machine working as one (courtesy Porsche).

Left: The early 928 featured a brand new water-cooled 4.5 liter SOHC V8 of linerless design that relied on Reynolds 390 high silicon alloy in its construction (courtesy Porsche). *Below:* The early 928 became readily associated with the racing flag seat trim material known as "Pasha" (courtesy Chuck & Tina Zachman).

Right: **So expensive, so prestigious and luxurious. Ferry Porsche was happy to encounter this 1978 928!** ***Below:*** **The 928 was the first sports car to win the European Car of the Year title. The 928's holistic design gave it the edge over the usual practical, but dull, family cars associated with the competition (courtesy Porsche).**

As part of its luxurious orientation, all 928 models had air conditioning standard right from the start of production. The Behr A/C condenser and fan are visible at the front (courtesy Chuck & Tina Zachman).

Top: The ex–Al Holbert 928S4 being guided through Laguna Seca's Corkscrew (courtesy Mark Kibort, www.electricsupercharger.com). *Above:* Time for a group hug! The youngest, two 928 GTS 5.4s, with the oldest, an early 1978 928 4.5, pictured in fittingly opulent surroundings (courtesy Chuck & Tina Zachman).

Top: **The 928 GTS had a debut price of $89,092 and performance that towered far above the BMW 850i and latest Mercedes-Benz SL. To find something faster one had to visit Modena (courtesy Porsche).** ***Above:*** **Hidemi Aoki with a Gemballa 928 (courtesy www.nepoeht.com).**

Top: In standard form the space age 928 never had much to do with wood, but for an extra $6,000 Zuffenhausen would trim the GTS with mother nature's polished finest. *Above:* The 928 epitomized the rich person's toy for years. In speed, refinement and luxury it was a world away from the humble 356 Speedster (courtesy Chuck Zachman).

Top: Aftermarket converter Strosek offered its trademark mini projector headlamps, made by Bosch/PES, on its later 944s. ***Above:*** Apart from the regular ultra body package, Strosek also offered the "Ultra Wing." In 1993 this gullwing conversion would have set the purchaser back DM 29,000 and could only be performed at Strosek's home in Utting/Ammersee (courtesy Strosek www.strosek.de).

Chapter 5

A 944 for All Seasons—Turbo, S/S2, Convertible

Developments in the Engine Room

The world had experienced four years of the 944/944 Lux, and by 1985 there was room for a high-performance, 944-image car that would be the speed demon in an expanded range. That variant was the 944 Turbo. As expressed by *Motor* magazine, the public had been waiting patiently for the newcomer: "It has taken a long, long time coming, but this Autumn should see the arrival of Porsche's turbo version of its 944." This was said in a "Class of '84" write-up on what was going to be revealed before 1984 was over.*

In truth the wait had a while yet to go. *Motor*'s claim was made in May 1984 and it wasn't until February 1985 that the 944 Turbo had a press launch in the South of France. Fifteen prototypes were constructed with this in mind, with an extra 100 pre-production 944 Turbos made prior to the model's public release in July of that year at 74,000 deutschmarks. Doesn't price soar along with fun level? The 944's game plan was surprisingly similar to the earlier forced-induction 924 — that is, 911 performance from the four-cylinder/front-engine platform.

Of course, the turbo four-cylinder was now chasing a 3.2 rather than a 3-liter 911, but in other respects the story was much the same. This time around the turbo I4 had a slight edge in top speed, but lagged a little in standing-start acceleration as before. The elderly 911 had been improved too since the last encounter. However, the biggest reversal of fortune had been in price. Previously the 924 with 911 performance could be purchased with a handy saving over the classic one. Now, the 944 Turbo was one of the most expensive cars in its class, and even cost a smidgen more than the 911.

The 944 was up against it. The people had yawned long enough waiting for it to arrive, and the 911 was better than ever now Peter Schutz had turned its cash tap back on, so the 944 Turbo had some work to do. There was a question mark over why the 944 Turbo was chosen for the task. The V8 from which its I4 was derived had never been blown by Porsche, and critics had always been screaming for a six-pot 924/944. Even though the turbo era was on the slide, Porsche were still experts in the art of turbo, for both racing and production cars. Turbocharging the existing 2.5-liter was the quickest, most cost effective method of achieving the performance required.

The turn of speed needed was a level of performance to put the 944 in the junior supercar league. With that in mind, the 2.5 I4 was thoroughly reworked to endure the hardship

**Motor,* Vol. 166, no. 4253, May 16, 1984, p. 35.

Top: **Leave it to Porsche to come up with a thoroughly engineered turbo version of the 944 that extended beyond a mere bolt on blower. This 1985 cutaway drawing shows that the 944 packed an intercooler as standard equipment (courtesy Porsche).** ***Bottom:*** **Unfortunately the 944 Turbo cost more to purchase than the contemporary 911 Carrera 3.2 liter. This left the naturally aspirated 944 as the model range's volume seller (courtesy Jako J. Koel).**

of turbo life. It still had a single-overhead-cam, two-valve configuration, but at the heart of the installation was a KKK K26 turbo placed on the "wrong" side of the engine block. Usually ease of location results in turbo units being placed on the exhaust manifold side, where things get hot enough to incinerate a replacement turbo warranty claim. Porsche took the cooler, convoluted path of placing the K26 on the intake side.

Double-walled stainless steel tubing traced out the turbo system's path, with the turbo wastegate limiting boost pressure to a maximum of 11 psi. To keep the motor on the fine edge between maximum power development and destruction, the 944 Turbo used a knock sensor. At the center of the Turbo's fuel management system was Bosch L-jet combined with Bosch DME, and that knock sensor to ward off detonation regardless of the gasoline grade being used: detecting a misfire, it retarded the ignition timing for the cylinder in trouble. That didn't mean the 944 Turbo wasn't in for a CR descent, but it did minimise that descent.

The 944 Turbo's compression ratio dropped from 10.6 to one to 8 to one, using forged rather than the cast pistons of the atmospheric 944. Exhaust port inserts, cast-in ceramic liners, and water-cooled turbo bearings were further precautions taken to improve efficiency and durability. The problem of frying turbo bearings by shutting down an engine immediately after hard driving was solved. The Zuffenhausen wizards rigged up an electric pump, controlled by thermostat, that continued to circulate engine coolant after the engine was shut down. The turbo bearing was saved! The 1985 944 Turbo represented a generation change from the 1975 930.

With claimed and verified performance figures of 0–62 mph in 6.3 seconds and a terminal velocity of 153 mph, the 944 Turbo was closer to cartoon character Speedy Gonzales than Slowpoke Rodriguez! (courtesy Wayne Cowley).

Whereas the 930 was a racing-style turbo adapted for road use, the 944 Turbo was a 1980s-smooth operator. The younger car was about getting spectacular figures while maintaining driveability and not falling foul of emissions regulations. So, naturally, the 944 Turbo had an intercooler, and the location of the turbo implied cooler exhaust gases reaching the K26, and a shorter journey to the intake manifold. Thus, there was less lag, and with a water-cooled bearing even the thoughtless driver could shut the car down after a fast blast without harm. Porsche wanted the Turbo to be used like a normal car, so they kept on thinking, designing a new-style inlet manifold shape to help with low-end torque.

This engine was also going to be a star in America, so to avoid the speed gulf that occurred between the Euro and U.S. 924 Turbo, Porsche engineers became close friends with the catalytic converter. Engineers placed a small converter inline with the turbo wastegate, which spared the main converter from the excesses of hard turbo living. The reward for this, and for using a knock sensor, was the M44/51 turbo "world motor." Whether in Europe or the U.S., the 2.5 turbo I4 made the same output: 220 DIN horsepower was equivalent to 217 SAE in the U.S. There was the same 8 to one CR, the same final drive, and, most importantly, the same performance.

Porsche claimed zero to 100 kph in 6.3 seconds, and a top speed of 153 mph. In reality it could manage a few more mph, and was a fraction faster in sprinting. It was an explosively quick car, 57 horses up on the 944 and even more over the U.S. 944. The knock sensor, the Bosch DME, and the fact it was turbocharged, helped it create a level power playing field. Motronic magic also exerted influence over the level of boost pressure; the turbo was allowed

Even the best turbo motors have some lag, and despite water-cooled bearing, intercooler and unorthodox K26 turbo placement, the 944 Turbo 2.5 was no exception (courtesy Wayne Cowley).

off its leash a little more, which was enough to maintain peak horsepower parity with the Euro 944 Turbo, in spite of having to deal with unleaded gas.

Turbo motors have that tuning flexibility to bridge the emissions gap. To contain the extra urge given by the Turbo, the 944T sported an upgraded Audi 5-speed box called 083D, so there was no perplexing Porsche racing shift pattern. Braking hardware was also improved over the standard 944, with 11.7- and 11.8-inch vented discs front and rear, gripped by pads pushed by the four pistons of huge Brembo-brand fixed brake calipers. To help the Turbo's power get to the road, the 944 Turbo relied on asymmetric tires, 205/55 VR front and 225/50 VR rear. The Pirelli P7s fittingly covered 928-pattern Phone Dial 16-inch rims, seven inches wide at the front and eight inches wide at the back. Dunlop SP tires were an alternate choice.

The Turbo's standard Phone Dials were cast alloy, but more expensive 16-inch Fuchs rims could be substituted. Compared to the normal 944, the Turbo had its suspension amended by Koni, if the sports suspension pack was specified. So the 944 Turbo was no stranger to the occasional designer label for hardware, and it was only right that the stylists gave the Turbo a visual boost to distance it from the plebian 944. This was done most obviously with a new, smooth nosecone that was part of the drop from the 944's standard 0.35, to the Turbo's 0.33, drag coefficient. At the rear of the car an underbody diffuser panel was both an aerodynamic aid and a way to shoot some cool air to the transaxle complex. Between the two ends were rocker panel extensions.

The 944 Turbo was a great car by any measure. Every compensation necessary to cope with the additional power brought by turbocharging had been considered and put into effect by Porsche engineers. It was a cool-looking road car, with subtle body changes over a regular 944 that rightfully suggested high limits. Porsche could have left the "turbo" badge off the tail and most would have still suspected that this was indeed the long-promised turbo four four. To get an idea of the car's nature, compare its turbo tail script badge with that on the previous 924 Turbo. The 924's turbo badge was cartoonish, puffed up and toy-like, but the 944's badge had thinner, slimmer letters. This was a serious-minded machine, no fat letters, just fat tires.

Science says the 944 Turbo should be liked more than comparable cars, or even non-comparable cars. That such great speed and control could come from a vehicle with just 2.5 liters of displacement, and the same cylinder count as a base Pinto, was outstanding. Such efficiency demands respect, and yet among all that engineering there was some doubt and a little disappointment. Two cars were at the root of such worries. Two cars from a time when the world was a friendlier place, and living was simpler. The first was the 911 Carrera 3.2, no turbo, no hydraulic lifters — no problem.

The combination of rear-engine weight bias and normally aspirated motor meant that the 911 was going to get the drop on the 944 Turbo in zero-to-thirty, creating a gap that the 944T could never hope to close by sixty, regardless of the savage technique employed to "de-lag" the four four off the line. Time and time again the 911 would eke out a small, but noticeable, sprinting edge. You knew on paper that it would, once the 911's lightness and the four four's turbo recalcitrance were factored into the equation, but that didn't lessen the anguish. This battle had been lost, at least it had for Euro-spec cars.

It was bad enough to have an enemy in the 944 Turbo's own Porsche camp, but it had another spoiler that had arrived in 1985. It was the Chevy Corvette, with the spiced-up 230-horsepower L98 V8. The Corvette and V8 at hand may not have been as old as the 911, but the idea was. The V8 Corvette had a surplus of 13 SAE horses over the 944 Turbo. The great

Taking a page from the 928 and 944 Turbo's book, the "Phone Dial" became the 944's standard aluminum wheel style by 1986 (courtesy Christopher Kotecha).

plastic one drank unleaded, and cost noticeably less than the Porsche, even if it didn't quite match the 944 Turbo's ultimate figures. It rumbled, it creaked, it was only a matter of time before you had your first argument with the Chevy dealer service manager, but this car had something that the 911 had, and the 944 Turbo did not.

Call it "the carefree performance quotient," the "let's go now, worry about the slide rule later" kind of performance. The 944 Turbo didn't have this old-school quality, its major was competence. Turbos have a soothing effect on engines, and this took the already good 2.5 I4 to a new soothing level. The additional power pushed the Turbo version closer to being a neutral handler than the regular 944. If it was a competition over how to cover ground quickly with ease, the 944 Turbo would beat the 911 any day of the week, especially if it was wet.

Proof of this competence came at the Longest Day of Nelson Ledges 24-hour Showroom Stock showdown, where a pre-production 944 Turbo claimed victory by a forty-lap margin. The blown 2.5 I4 had also proven its worth by allowing a 1981 924 GTP to come 7th in that other 24-hour race called Le Mans. The 944 Turbo was the new main attraction for four-cylinder cars, and brought a number of benefits that it unselfishly shared with the humble 944. Porsche were never going to build a 944 Turbo fitted with the 924 dash, so it's obvious they had the new Turbo in mind when designing the revised dashboard and interior.

The 944 Turbo also introduced the Phone Dial rim to the 944 line. This 928-only feature took over from the Cookie Cutter as the base rim on the 944. The standard 944 now rolled around on 15 × 7–inch Phone Dials with 195/65 VR tires. The larger section of the standard tire was no problem because all 944s received power steering from 1985 onwards. Your everyday 944 was also traveling further on a tank of gas. The 944 Turbo had seen the introduction of a bigger 80-liter gas tank, and this plastic unit replaced the 66-liter steel tank on previous 944s.

It was possible to get 911 Turbo handling and body upgrades on a standard 911, so Porsche continued family tradition with the 944. The normal 944 was also available with the 944 Turbo's optional 16-inch forged Fuchs, 7 inches wide at the front, 8 inches at the rear, and shod with 205/55, 225/50 VR tires. It was also more than just for show, because all 944s were now using the lighter 944 Turbo–design cast alloy front lower wishbones and semi-trailing arms. Combined with the bigger Fuchs, the lighter alloy suspension pieces provided a level of roadholding for the atmospheric 944 fit for, well, a Porsche!

Porsche also wanted the normal 944 to perform more satisfactorily, so a makeover was in store for the non-turbo 2.5 I4. Revisions were made to combustion chamber shape, pistons and valves, and the engine CPU was tweaked too. The altered 2.5 sat on 944 Turbo–style engine mounts, benefiting from their greater durability. With the changes came some new engine codes. The Euro M44/01 and U.S. M44/02 manual transmission versions gave way to

Restyle-shy Porsche reworked the 944's appearance for the turbo model, cutting the drag coefficient to 0.33 in the process (courtesy Porsche).

Porsche revised the naturally aspirated 2.5 I4 several times. In its final year all non-turbo 2.5 liter cars for all markets, like this 1988 U.S. 944, were using a 160 bhp (DIN) edition (courtesy Christopher Kotecha).

M44/05 and M44/07 respectively. Similarly, the Euro M44/03 and U.S. M44/04 engines of automatic cars were now called M44/06 and M44/08 respectively. However, in all the alterations Euro engine output stayed at 163 DIN bhp, but the SAE rating of U.S. 944s climbed from 143 to 147 horses for 1986 — the latter re-rating possibly to trump the new Mazda RX7's 146 bhp in America.

By 1986 the whole 944 range had adopted the Turbo's flush bonded windshield, and that model's absence of rain gutters. There were a new radiator, increased sump capacity from 5.5 to 6 liters, and the comfort options of power door locks and heated seats with power height adjustment. Baby steps along the path of Porsche evolution. Porsche had even swapped over the windshield wipers for an appropriate wiper pattern on right-hand-drive cars in 1985. All these changes filtered through, and were ready and present in all world markets by 1986. If all the minor failings of the 1981 944 were listed, then Porsche had checked off every concern by 1986, even the infamous "thighsteer" tiller!

Here was the modern sports car of the 1980s: fast, frugal and carrying a fair amount of comfort-oriented amenities. Driving along on open roads, or in the solitude of a track setting, it might have seemed that things couldn't get better than this. However, even though the 944 had gained so many logically good things over the years, it had lost something too. *Autocar* magazine was aware of the mystery: "Generally, then, the 944 Lux is something of a

In 1986 Porsche started a single model racing series featuring the 220 bhp 944 Turbo. The Turbo Cup was initially contested on West German tracks, and the inaugural season was won by Joachim Winkelhock (courtesy Porsche).

conundrum, for although it has become more of a driver's car thanks to the improved seating position and 928 style instrumentation, it has lost some 'edge.'"*

Porsche hadn't refined the 944 to the point of being inert, but the addition of the power steering and other accessories with no increase in power made the whole thing seem like one was running on the spot, rather than forward. Weight was part of what separated the 1986 944 from its scalpel-sharp 1981 equivalent. Comparing U.K. Lux against Lux, the 944 had risen from 2,632 lbs. to 2,815 lbs. It seemed like the 944 was suffering weight creep like its big brother the 928. Lotus's founder Colin Chapman was right, it seems that all cars put on weight. In the 944's case that implied a top speed lower by a couple of miles per hour, and a zero to sixty time a half-second slower.

The other challenge for Porsche was the availability of faster and faster hot hatchbacks. Cars like the 16-valve VW Golf/Scirocco, 1.9-liter Peugeot 205/309 GTi, Fiat Uno Turbo and Renault 5 GT Turbo were delivering a lot of go and show for attainable money. Even something like the diminutive Lancia Y10 Turbo showed what could be achieved with a very-small-engined small car, with the latest in aerodynamics, weight saving and engine technology. So Porsche had to make their volume seller more interesting to justify their high asking prices.

Porsche already had the recent Turbo; now it needed a cheaper model with a better turn of speed than the base 944. The solution was shown once more on the 1981 924 GTP Le Mans racer. That car not only had a turbo and counter-rotating balancer shafts, it also had

**Autocar, Road Test Yearbook 1986*, p. 44.

a double-overhead-camshaft, 4-valves-per-cylinder arrangement. The DOHC 16-valve quality would be the main difference separating the starter 944 and the latest addition to the 944 family, the 16-valve 944S. Porsche had joined the 16-valve brigade in the nick of time.

944S 16 Ventiler—Better Breathing

Earlier in the decade the 928 received a helping hand from the little 944 in terms of the TOP combustion chamber design, now it was time for big brother to return the favor. The 16-valve, dual-camshaft heads already existed, not just on the 1981 924 GTP, but also on the 1986 U.S. spec 928S3 5-liter. Porsche had already put the design in production, and in the game of Porsche V8/I4 interchange, the 944 would be the winner. Now the Porsche V8 and I4 were getting super close: same bore and stroke measurements, since the 928S3/S4 were at 5 liters and the 944 was still at 2.5 liters displacement, and the cylinder layout was shared from SOHC to DOHC.

Porsche was building all these engines, and it made life easier given that the cylinder heads for both V8 and I4 cars could be cast using the same machinery, whereupon they channeled off downstream to their respective 928 and 944 areas. Porsche's recipe for DOHC/16 valves was also straightforward. The 2.5 SOHC's single cam remained exactly where it had always been, and continued to be driven by a rubber belt off the crankshaft. This camshaft now became the exhaust cam in the new DOHC arrangement and drove the additional intake

Pressing competition and a noticeable performance gulf between the standard and turbo 944 models prompted Porsche to introduce the 16-valve DOHC 2.5 liter 944S for 1987 (courtesy Porsche).

camshaft, sitting inwards of the exhaust cam, via a short chain. To combat the mechanical rigors and strain of the new arrangement, the 16-valve 2.5-liter used a wider rubber cambelt of stouter construction than that found on the normal 8-valve 944.

Head work continued along in an evolved TOP manner, with central spark plug location permitting more equal flame distribution and helping the 944 to run a huge 10.9 to one CR. Sixteen valves in a pent-roof combustion chamber, and Porsche still managed to find space to include hydraulic lifters. This was just as well, double the valve gear meant double the cost for setting those valve clearances at service time, thankfully this wasn't necessary. However, given the sky-high CR, knock-sensor control would be very necessary. The 944 Turbo had one sensor, the 944S trumped that with 3 knock-control sensors.

The 944S would be using its three sensors and Bosch DME to run close to the razor's edge of efficiency, because the 16-valve brigade was multiplying in the high end of the performance market, not just among the hot hatchbacks. The three knock sensors had three rivals that were building up a high profile reputation in touring car racing. They were the BMW M3, Daimler-Benz 190E 2.3–16 and the fire-breathing Ford Sierra RS Cosworth: All four-cylinder, high-powered '80s rockets using 16-valve technology. Porsche wasn't formally racing its 944S like the other manufacturers, and as a production car the 944S was the most expensive. However, out of this group the Porsche marque still carried the highest street cred for the sports car aficionado.

Speed is one criterion, but style is another, and there is no way a Ford with a sizeable tea-tray spoiler and a trash-can-sized turbo can compete with a Porsche on style. There is something intrinsically desperate and sweaty about production-car racing, and it seems the best image that can be gleaned from its association is "king of the boy racers." The 944S steered

It was expected that the 944S would be the new base 944, but Porsche retained the services of the 8-valve SOHC 944 for most countries and the 8-valve model continued to be the sales leader (courtesy Jako J. Koel).

away from that crowd; it was the Gucci loafers of the 16-valve world, and look, it even carried its own designer label. There was a neat "16 Ventiler" script adorning the side of the front fenders next to the turn-signal lights and on the engine's air filter box. This and the 944S chrome rear deck badge were the only visual giveaways that extra had been paid for better 16-valve breathing, courtesy of better Porsche breeding.

Even those "16 Ventiler" fender badges were body-colored. Gucci doesn't make neon, glow-in-the-dark shoes, and similarly, Porsche doesn't use garish badging or signs to show off its tech features. Such sign writing is best read in a car park, not on the racetrack, the cars are moving too quickly, and Porsche was all about moving quickly. It didn't matter that the new M44/40's intake-tract magnesium passages and smaller 1.38-inch valves were concealed from view. Porsche could be relied upon to put everything together properly and include what was needed. This included a pressure regulator, originally from the 944 Turbo in pre–ABS days, that fought rear brake lock-up.

Porsche had done really well, but if only they hadn't screwed things together so tightly with the 944S. As can usually happen in these cases, the 944S invited everyone to play "hunt the performance gain." Porsche put forward claimed top speed and zero to 100 kph figures of 142 mph and 7.9 seconds, 5 mph up and a half-second better than what the regular 944 was supposed to do. A handy improvement, considering the new car's weight was 2,866 lbs., and in that hefty load was a goodly amount of convenience options from the 944's options list.

Those seeking serious punch from a 944 still had to knock on the door of the 944 Turbo. The 16-valve 944S felt closer to the plain 8-valve 944 in terms of swiftness (courtesy Wayne Greham).

Porsche put the weight gain over the equivalent 944 at 88 pounds, enough to warrant different suspension settings involving stiffer springs and shock absorbers. Wheels and tires varied depending on the market. Home-market issue were the 944's ordinary 195/65 VRs on 15-inch Phone Dials. The U.S. 944S, as usual, had the one-size-up 215/60 tire so that it wouldn't embarrass itself on the skidpad. The buyer could go all the way and choose the 16-inch Disc type 944 Turbo rims with asymmetric 205/55 and 225/50 VR tires. There was a home-market option of sports suspension and the even more serious club sports package available, as with the 944 Turbo, that jettisoned many comfort features.

Getting rid of a/c and power goodies may have helped the 944S establish a real-world speed gain over the plain 944. It was similar to the situation a few years earlier when Saab brought out the 16-valve 900 Turbo. For some of the in-gear incremental acceleration times, there was little or no improvement over the 8-valve edition. It was the same for the 944S, and it soon became clear that the 16-valve 2.5 needed to be revved to make the 944S fly. And it was happy to rev, all the way to its 6,800 rpm redline, 300 rpm up on the 8-valve, and it would have been happier still if it had some break-in miles under its belt before the performance envelope was explored.

As said above, Porsche likes to make things tight. It seems that the traditions set by the gnomes of Gmund were safe, because lab tests showed that a well-run-in 944S could do 0 to 60 mph in 6.5 seconds, only 0.5 slower than a 944 Turbo. So the chances were that by the time the 944S was like a comfortable pair of worn slippers, and some of the synchros started to slip, its owner would be moving like a meteor. However, independent testers didn't have the luxury of time, for them the 944S seemed adequate and somewhat flaccid unless

It may have had only one knock sensor compared to the 944S's three, but the 944T had one turbo and that was enough hardware to differentiate the men from the boys! (courtesy Wayne Greham).

With sufficient break-in miles the 944S could get within 0.5 of the 944 Turbo for 0–60 mph, but in a world where time is money a half-second is an eternity (courtesy Wayne Greham).

the 5-speed stick was rowed along enthusiastically. Would a Porsche be driven any other way?

The extra that the 16 Ventiler would afford its owner was 190 DIN bhp at 6,000 rpm and 170 lbs./ft. of torque at 4,300 rpm. Noticeable improvements over the 8-valve, albeit at higher, pokier rpm. This made the 944S closer to the outputs of the 944 rather than the Turbo. Maybe the 944S was the new 944? The thought of the 944S becoming the new four four default standard was a considered thought. The "S" seemed to have the added go that this type of car needed at this price level. In addition, the recent arrival of the 2.5-liter-powered 924 seemed to look after matters in the bargain basement area.

Porsche doesn't like to get rid of things, and so the 944 stayed between the 924S and 944S. Three choices of 2.5-liter Porsche, and of the three it seemed customers felt the 944S offered the least value. Only 12,831 944S cars were produced, with 8,703 going to North America. Not enough bang for the buck it would seem. The 8-valve 944 would live on as the family's sales leader. And it was a time to celebrate a few things with the 944. To mark the 100,000th 944 sold, 930 limited-edition 944 cars were offered in September 1987, either in Zermatt Silver or Satin Black metallic.

In addition, one 944, bearing the license plate LU-NA 944, was driven 500,000 kms, or the distance to the moon and back; hence the special license plate. This feat was accomplished inside a year by Gerhard Plattner, Porsche's public relations man in Austria. The car's bodywork

A 944 has the reliability to get one to the moon ... and back! PR man Gerhard Plattner drove this 944 with license plate LU-NA 944 500,000 kms in under one year (courtesy Porsche).

was then signed by Ferry Porsche. It wasn't the end of 944 sales, but Porsche's sales bubble was about to burst. There was a business downturn on the horizon, with the 1987 Wall Street stock market crash as a sign that Porsche would be traversing rough terrain over the next few years.

Even if high-flyers fell from being heroes to villains Porsche was still there. Its cars were just as worthy as ever, and it continued to make its amendments, such as windshield wipers that resisted lifting off the glass at high speed, in 1987. There was also yet another revised version of the 2.5-liter standard engine. This world-market 2.5 would be used by all 2.5-liter non-turbo Porsches, both 924 and 944, and it would be used by the U.S. too. For Europe this unleaded special represented less, 3 bhp less at 160 horses and a CR fall from the original 10.6 down to 10.2 to one. For the U.S. and 924, the new motor represented a lot more: the highest CR used by a U.S. 8-valve 2.5 Porsche. Previously the U.S. 944 was at 147 bhp and 9.7 to one, now it was up to 158 SAE bhp, the same as 160 DIN bhp.

As stock market prices fell, Porsche unleaded CR rose. That's what a sports car company had to do to survive, and Porsche were in the survival business. It was also in their interest to entice buyers, very important in troubled economic times. Porsche achieved this closer to home with a one-model racing series that revolved around the 944 Turbo. For Germany only initially, the Turbo Cup series kicked off in 1986, featuring 40 almost-standard 944 Turbos. Ace touring car driver Joachim "Smokin' Jo" Winkelhock won the 1986 series, it was a success, so Porsche continued with the racing format into 1987.

In tough economic times, how could Zuffenhausen convince the Iron Yuppie that the 944 was still a blue chip investment? (courtesy Christopher Kotecha).

The Turbo Cup gave way to the 911 focused Carrera Cup in 1990, but not before the Turbo Cup runners could inspire the desirable 944 Silver Rose road car (courtesy Porsche).

Apart from the expected pared-down interior fittings and roll cage, the 1987 series turbos had hardware upgrades over the stock 220 bhp 944 Turbo. Most obviously, power for all cars in the series was now at 250 horses, and there was heavier duty suspension plus anti-lock brakes. Devoid of climate control and power accessories, the 1987 racers were flying faster and further. Further because the series extended onto European tracks, and the format was adopted in France and Canada. However, all good things must come to an end, and in 1990 the Turbo Cup became the Carrera Cup. With some symbolic meaning for Porsche fans, the 911 had replaced the 944 Turbo as the chosen model for the series.

Silver Rose — Mr. Big Has Arrived

Fans of the 944 were not leaving empty-handed from the Turbo Cup. In 1988 the U.K.-market 16 Ventiler 944S received the Turbo's rear underbody diffuser panel, but there was bigger news for the year. The news was a rather nifty 944 Turbo, patterned after the Turbo Cup racer mechanically, and known as "Silver Rose." As with the racers, this limited run of turbo projectiles had 250 horses from a tweaked version of the 2.5 I4 turbo. It's always easy to get a bit more from turbo motors, and by increasing peak boost to 11.9 psi and raising the rev limit by 500 rpm, Porsche were already 30 horses stronger than the still-current 220 bhp 944 Turbo.

More power doesn't make much sense if it can't be used in a controlled fashion. It was expected Porsche would improve on the standard car's brakes, but the source of those improved parts was a surprise: the big 12-inch front rotors and ABS system from the heavyweight 928S4. It's good to have friends in high places. And those bigger brakes were only partly concealed by the flashing seven spokes of 16-inch forged aluminum rims, the kind of pattern found on the later 928 GT. The Silver Rose had the same tire sizes as the 928S4, but its rear rims were one inch wider at 9 inches.

Those big rear feet would certainly be needed once the Silver Rose's 258 lbs./ft. of torque came in at 4,000 rpm. The high-performance 2.5 Turbo did its best work at slightly higher rpm, maximum power now arrived at 6,000 rather than 5,800 rpm. Maximum torque was 15 lbs./ft. greater, but 500 rpm further up the scale. That said, the power was there and it was accessible. There had been no CR drop with the Silver Rose, and with this much boost it was only a matter of time before something big happened, and it happened sooner rather than later. Even so, this was a turbo car of smallish displacement, and in those immediate moments off the line turbo lag still reared its ugly head.

Porsche favored the single large turbo route, to give the Silver Rose enough high-speed thrust to make it special. No problem for a combatant in the Turbo Cup, since one normally has the revs up and the turbo on boost, or nearly so. At traffic lights it was a different story, but at least Porsche included a beefy gearbox so that nothing got broken while the test pilot practiced hole shots. Specifically, the M44/52 engine was attached to the 016R 5-speed. As

Porsche released a mere 1,635 250-horse 944s in 1987, the first 1,000 of which were painted in the rather unusual Silver Rose's silver with pink accent (courtesy Peter en Mijnte Remeijer).

The Silver Rose's I4 aluminum engine block. A precision casting with a durable bottom end — and it would have to be, given that the 2.5 I4 achieved its 250 horses thanks to 11.9 psi worth of forced induction (courtesy Peter M. Sullivan).

ever with any 944 Turbo, automatic wasn't available, after all it would only blunt the Silver Rose's searing performance. Zero to sixty in just 5.5 seconds and a top speed a bit over 160 mph. Porsche said 161 mph, which would allow this madcap four-cylinder to sail past speed-limited Mercedes and BMW sedans boasting eight- and twelve-cylinder counts.

Zuffenhausen were very serious about the Silver Rose's handling. The normal 944 Turbo was an extremely fine road car when it came to handling, but the Silver Rose had the changes necessary to look decent on the track. Koni adjustable shocks, stiffer and shorter springing, and veritable baseball bat-sized sway bars, 26.8 mm front compared to the normal Turbo's 22.6 mm. The rear torsion bars were bigger, and reinforcing plates about the wheel housings were there to reduce wobble in the Silver Rose's monocoque structure.

Racing craft don't have much suspension travel, and neither did the Silver Rose. In the interests of keeping control and stability, the car's suspension wasn't allowed to do much, and that meant the loss of that layer of sponge between driver and road used in four-wheeled vehicles with license plates. Was there a bump in mid-turn? The Silver Rose would be the first to let the driver know. In addition, competitors would see the car from miles away, thanks to the exterior color from which this road-race refugee took its name. Porsche made 1,635 of the 250-horsepower four-pots, but the first 1,000 were coated in an odd German racing silver — with a pink accent.

The humor continued with the interior. Why would a serious out-and-out performance car be loaded with almost every 944 option possible, and why would it have this trim color

Top: The license plate says it all. By ticking the M758 option box on the order sheet one would get the upgraded 250 hp 944 with associated suspension/braking enhancements (courtesy Peter M. Sullivan). *Bottom:* By 1989 the 220 bhp 944 Turbo had been discontinued, and the 250 horsepower 944 Turbo became the regular blown 944. This 1989 edition shows that color choices were no longer restricted to pinky silver (courtesy Peter M. Sullivan).

scheme? Only Porsche knew the answer. That strange interior involved psychedelic burgundy, and cloth-faced comfortable buckets with color stripes moving from silver to plum, and there was more: the option of a "Turbo" decal script draped over the passenger-side front fender like the long-lost 924 Carrera. Was Porsche trying to tell us something? Perhaps only that, in spite of the economic malaise, it was still around and making sports cars, great ones and remarkably good value for money.

How could such an expensive car be good value? Was this another touch of Porsche's sense of humor? The value was easy to prove. Start with an off-the-peg 1988 944 Turbo, add all the options embodied by the Silver Rose, and watch the sticker price balloon out almost $10,000. And of course the buyer would still be on only 220 horsepower, and missing some mechanical upgrades unique to the Silver Rose, and here came the value. The Silver Rose wasn't going to cost $10,000 more than a plain 944 Turbo, not even $7,500 more, Porsche were offering this super 944 for only $5,510 over and above the price of a boring 944 Turbo!

Of course, there was just one catch — the Silver Rose cost almost $50,000. One can't live in a car, cars aren't usually a sound long-term investment, but great fast fun would be had. Value issues could be pondered in serenity seated in the Silver Rose, if the driver could find a glass-smooth highway. By selecting a very sensible 3.38 final drive Porsche obviously intended the owner to enjoy the stereo on long cruises. Tall gearing, plush interior, and rock hard suspension. With less than 2,000 delivered worldwide, some folks would have considered the Silver Rose good value.

1989 — Expand & Deliver

To appeal to a larger client base, which it would have to do for survival, 1989 was the year of change at Porsche. Out with the old, in with the new. The old was the Porsche 924S, that was out. What was in were three new 944 variants. The first rung of Porsche ownership was a new base 944, packing a larger 2.7-liter engine. Still an I4 with SOHC, but, thanks to a 4 mm bore increase to 104 mm, and a 2.5 944S-like 10.9 to one CR, the M44/13 made a lucky 165 DIN bhp and 166 lbs./ft. of torque at the respective engine speeds of 5,800 and 4,200 rpm. New digital ignition permitted the 10.9 CR for all markets.

By 1989 standards the 944 2.7 was no hotrod, and there were plenty of swifter coupes that could undercut its $36,360 price. However, this was the first revised base 944 to be actually quicker than the original 1981/82 944. Porsche claimed 0–100 kph in 8.2 seconds, undercutting the original's 8.4 seconds. In spite of having more convenience features and weighing close to 3,000 lbs., the 2.7 had restored a zeal that had been missing from the base 944 since 1984. With the extra torque of a 2.7-liter I4, 944 junior was still the only member of the 944 clan to be available with automatic, and it was still the same 3 speed Audi-sourced gearbox.

Going from the bottom to the top we had the new 944 Turbo. New because it was 1988's 250-bhp Silver Rose special, now available in a normal range of color and trim options. Formerly known as the Turbo S in America, and the Turbo SE in the U.K., the Silver Rose was now simply "Turbo." The 220-bhp 944 Turbo was dead, long live the 250-bhp 944 Turbo. The Turbo was still Porsche's specialist model in the range; for mainstream business Zuffenhausen saw the 944S as the way into the 1990s. The 2.5-liter 944 was a bit on the weak side, but the idea of a powerful un-blown DOHC 16-valve engine was a good one, so Porsche went with that to create the 944S2.

Top: Goodbye 2.5 944, hello 2.7 944. This is a 1989 8-valve 944 with the newly enlarged 2.7-liter base motor (courtesy Porsche). ***Bottom:*** Despite great outright performance figures the 944 Turbo, like this 1989 example, was turbo lag prone (courtesy Jason Mills & Jad Duncan).

The 250 bhp 944 Turbo's lag was no problem on Willow Springs International Raceway. On the track one can more easily keep the revs up and the turbo on boost (courtesy Jason Mills & Jad Duncan).

The 944S2 was all new in Porsche speak, evolved beyond a point thought possible. The S2 had a 3-liter version of the Porsche balancer-shaft I4. Its DOHC 16-valve configuration was in common with the discontinued 1988 2.5-liter 944S, but its 2,990 cc displacement was achieved by sharing a 104 mm bore with the new 2.7-liter SOHC motor and by increasing the four-cylinder stroke from the original 78.9 mm to 88 mm. To achieve this the 944S2 got a new block, one influenced by Porsche's TAG Formula One episode. Lessons from the turbo 1.5-liter V6 that powered Niki Lauda and Alain Prost's McLarens to World Championship success in the 1980s taught Porsche that water-jacket area for cooling wasn't so crucial around the bores or at their base.

The fiery kitchen of Formula One led Porsche to cast a new, lighter block with siamesed bores and water jacket area for the top part of the cylinder bores. According to Porsche, water jacket area had been reduced by one third, and the new crankcase was 33 percent stiffer with a weight reduction of 15 percent. Formula One also inspired the trick of making a hole near the cylinder's base so that the air forced down by one pair of pistons went into the space of adjacent rising pistons. Channeling this air pressure was worth an extra 3 horses, enough to cancel out the drain from the four-cylinder's counter-rotating balancer shafts.

Further design details for the 3-liter were shorter, lighter pistons and a "quadrilateral" intake manifold that used different length intake tracts to generate a discernible air boost! As a result the 3-liter had a different-shaped intake manifold compared to the 2.7, Turbo, and

Top: **The most important new 944 entrant for 1989 was the torque maximized 3 liter 944S2 (courtesy Porsche).** ***Bottom:*** **With a nod to the tastes of North America, the new 1989 3 liter 944S2 was everything one could ask for in a 944. However, as in this picture, the prospect of a car like the Boxster still loomed large (courtesy Benjamin F. Smith).**

even the previous 2.5 16 Ventiler. One thing that was similar was the turn of speed of the old 944 Turbo and the new 3.0 16 Ventiler. Porsche figures said there was a noticeable gap between the 220-bhp 944 Turbo and the new 944S2, favoring the older car. However, independent tests put the zero to sixty times of the two as near as identical. The older Turbo managed a top speed higher by 10 mph. The difference was academic for most drivers, and the speed shortfall was more attributable to the S2's short 3.88 final drive than its 9 fewer horses.

If their bare statistics were similar, there was a major difference in the way the 944 Turbo of yesteryear and the new S2 delivered their punches. The 220-horse Turbo involved driving around the off-boost situation, realizing that below a certain rpm not a lot would happen, and enjoying the before and after of turbo boost living. In contrast the 944S2 had everything ready and arranged in linear fashion for any driver: no Turbo lag and a feeling akin to a very, very strong atmospheric 2.5/2.7.

If anything, the old 16 Ventiler was closer to the 944 Turbo in its high-end power delivery. The 944S2 3.0 was perfectly suited to U.S. driving conditions, better suited than either the old or new 944 Turbos. Porsche knew and intended this, which explains why from 1990 on the S2 3-liter powerplant was the only 944 motor available in North America. And if the 944S2 should go like a 944 Turbo, and take over from the Turbo, then Porsche logic dictated that it should look and handle like one as well.

In the same way the 911 Turbo had inspired the wide-body 911 Carrera, the 944S2 adopted the styling, chassis and braking of the 1985–88 944 Turbo. This involved the smoother frontal visage, 16 × 7–and 16 × 8–inch rims shod with 205/55 and 225/50 tires, and the Turbo's

Though shown here at Daytona International Speedway, the 944S2 was a natural at production car road circuit racing (courtesy Benjamin F. Smith).

By 1990 the S2 3 liter was the only 944 engine option for North America (courtesy Benjamin F. Smith).

four-piston, fixed-caliper ventilated disk brakes. When the 944S2 was launched it was fitted with the flush, 928S4-style, forged 16-inchers, but this gave way to the cast-alloy Design 90 rims that were cheaper copies of the 7-spokers found on the Silver Rose and the 1989 944 Turbo. And the S2 still sported "16 Ventiler" badging from the 1987–88 era.

It's easy to be impressed by the S2's 211 DIN bhp and 207 lbs./ft. of torque, quick enough to deal with an L98 Corvette, with the bonus of much nicer ride comfort and handling for grown-ups, plus the socially responsible addition of, dare it be said, four-cylinder economy. However, when it came to engine refinement, things were undecided. That Porsche had directed time and some of the greatest minds to create this 3-liter engine wasn't in doubt. From its "Quad" intake to its plastic oil pan, a world production-car first, this engine's middle name was efficiency — but where was the love?

The 3-liter DOHC 16V I4 wasn't rough, it was quite smooth considering it had 4 giant pistons moving about quickly. However, as with the 2.7-liter version, the Porsche I4 didn't seem to like capacity rises. It wasn't as smooth feeling as the old 2.5s, especially the 2.5 Turbos. This development wouldn't have been of such great concern, if not for the fact a 944 was no longer under $20,000. In fact, by 1990 MY a 1990 944S2 priced out at $41,900. With each cylinder weighing in at over 10 grand, Porsche was in an exclusive club: an exclusive club, but a class of its own.

Regardless of Porsche pricing or uncommonly large 4-cylinder chambers, the 944 was still the coupe to emulate. The Japanese manufacturers seemed to think so. It is curious how the 924/944 design, though evolving, faced off against the Datsun and Nissan 280Z/280ZX/300ZX,

Top: **In a world that worships ultimates, the 944 Turbo was still respected by a determined few (courtesy Jason Mills).** ***Bottom:*** **1989 would prove to be the final year for the 250 bhp 944 Turbo (M758) in America. Zuffenhausen's Corvette muncher would be missed (courtesy Jason Mills).**

By the late 1980s 944s, like this 1988 example, were commonplace on the global roadscape, but did that equate with the 4-cylinder coupe's public acceptance as "The New Porsche"? (courtesy Porsche).

including the high-tech 300ZX introduced in 1989–1990. Each time Nissan had come up with fresh styling and electronic aids, to meet a warmed-over '70s coupe originally dismissed as a rather bland Audi in Porsche clothing. However, if the 944S2's grip over the Grand Sports Firehawk endurance series was anything to go by, Porsche had the right idea.

The front-engined, four-cylinder Porsche had long been thought of as "the other kind of Porsche," and the 944S2 continued the theme. This was in the sense that the 3-liter engine in itself was not the main point. The owner probably wouldn't have the same relationship with that engine as he might with Porsche's air-cooled flat fours or sixes. The point of the 3-liter engine was simply to move the 944 about expediently, no more, no less. This it achieved superbly, in quantifiable terms, and the same might be said of all the counterbalanced I4s, turbocharged or otherwise. The 944 and its engine were conceived at a time when Porsche felt moving quickly with the best possible control was the most important thing.

944 Cabriolet—Better Late Than Never

However, all efficiency and no play makes for a very dull toy. To infuse some romance into the four-cylinder Porsche, what could have been better than a convertible? A drop-top, so that the owner could see better, and be better seen. And whether it was Monaco or Monaco

The bulky ASC top seemed out of place amidst the sleek, muscular style of a Strosek creation. (Courtesy Strosek www.strosek.de)

di Bavaria (Munich), the 944 convertible would be worth seeing because it was the work of Porsche styling boss Tony Lapine. Indeed, many had given up hope they would ever see the 944 Cabriolet at all. It appeared so far back at the 1985 Frankfurt Show — but this was 1989! In the time that a new mainstream car could have been launched, and axed, by GM, Porsche were getting matters organised, slowly.

The best things come to those who wait. The 944 Cabriolet returned to the show circuit in 1988. The 2.5-liter, 16 Ventiler engine looked possible, then the Cabrio went away again. The prototype was done by Baur, but the car was eventually converted by the American Sunroof Corporation (ASC) at its new German factory. However, all this took time, and the funny thing was that some folks had placed orders for the cabrio long ago. This was all perfectly in keeping with expensive, low-volume car production. Putting down big money and then waiting an eternity was part of the fun. It gave the prospective owner time to build a new garage and mansion to go with the new 4-wheeled acquisition.

Things had worked out for the best, because the Cabrio would now be using the near-new 3-liter engine. To cope with the torque of the 3-liter, the decapitated 944 structure would need strengthening in the right places. To that end, the Cabrio got a second floor and reinforcement about the door apertures and monocoque area near the firewall. Even though ASC chopped the windshield area by a couple of inches to create a more rakish appearance, the Cabrio had piled on 176 lbs. Such is the lot of a convertible, and the body bracing was necessary if the 944 Cabrio wasn't to be a natural at the game of Twister!

Any performance shortfall compared to the 944S2 coupe was really minor. The most

The much anticipated 1990 944 Cabrio alongside the 944 coupe. Both cars were motivated by the businesslike S2 3-liter I4 (courtesy Porsche).

glaring problem with the Cabrio, apart from its imaginary rear seats, was the lack of a fully automatic power top. Curiously, especially since experts ASC were on board, the well-heeled owner still had to use a provided pair of wrenches to free and secure the latches attaching the leading edge of the top to the windshield. Such fumbling would continue with the subsequent 968 Cabrio. Why should such labor be expended when the Cabrio's side windows automatically lowered to half mast as the top went through its arc?

What better version of the 944 to use as a swan song than the Cabrio? The version that came so late would crown the four four's achievements with exclusivity. Even though the 944's North American lineup had been pruned to just the S2, the 2.7/Turbo carried on alongside the new Cabrio in Porsche's other markets. With the winding down of 944 sales, Porsche even moved 944 production to Zuffenhausen, not requiring the volume of the Neckarsulm factory.

Top: At $48,600 the 1990 944S2 Cabrio was far removed from the cheap and cheerful 1950s 356 Speedster (courtesy Porsche). ***Bottom:*** As a 944 swan song, what could be better than the combination of the Cabrio body and Silver Rose 250 horsepower engine? (courtesy Porsche).

Top: Strosek incorporated the 968 into its portfolio, but honored the standard car's 928 style swivel-up lamps. This 968 wears the O.Z. rims created for Strosek's cars in the early 1990s (Courtesy Strosek www.strosek.de). ***Bottom:*** Strosek's 968 body add-ons were similar to those of its earlier 944. However, Strosek respected Porsche's styling transformation and left much of the car's body cladding untouched (Courtesy Strosek www.strosek.de).

So a few hundred 944S2s were built by Porsche, starting in March of 1991. However, before that Porsche created the most collectible 944 by combining the Cabriolet body with the engine from the Silver Rose.

Featuring the 944's most powerful engine, 625 944 Turbo Cabrios were built. One hundred of these cars were right-hand-drive. Slightly softer suspension settings were the only concession Porsche made to the marriage between the Cabrio's open structure and the 2.5's 250 horses; after all, the Silver Rose was a stiff coupe shell. The smoothness of the Cabrio style, the smoothness of the turbo 2.5 — the 944 had come a long way from its early days of Cookie Cutter rims and 924 dash. In 1981 it was a model that had to earn respect after a 924 start. In the 944 Turbo Cabrio it was obvious that, by 1991, the 944 family had found acceptance. It sat there smugly, confident of the 944's family achievements. The Turbo Cabrio was king of '80s coupes.

Chapter 6

968—Zuffenhausen Wasn't Built in a Day

A Victim of Success

Be careful when making wishes, they might come true, and it's possible to be a victim of one's own success. Regardless of whether the entity at hand is Porsche or the Bee Gees, the result seems the same. Familiarity breeds a tepid response. Ferry Porsche wanted an affordable, volume sports car, and the dream came true with the 924 and 944 ranges, but dreams carry a cost. Overlooking the fact that the aforementioned four-cylinder cars were mostly constructed outside Zuffenhausen, Porsche had become a mini giant among specialty car makers. With sales exceeding 50,000 cars per annum as the 1980s settled, Porsche's output dwarfed what was being crafted at Maranello or Hethel. It was a lot for a small manufacturer, and one didn't have to go very far before seeing a Porsche parked across the street. Porsche wasn't quite King Kong, but it was almost as popular as Donkey Kong.

To add insult to injury for Ferrari, Lotus, Alpine and others, Porsche was still its own boss. It didn't need to go to Fiat, GM, Renault and other large parents for money. Yes, Porsche had avoided being swallowed up by a big benefactor anxious to slap an "engineered by Porsche" badge or decal on some econobox hatch assembled by a robot, but even legends need new material from time to time. Contrary to popular opinion, Porsche didn't have a dilution issue. The presence of the 924 and 944 had not devalued the Porsche name as such. In fact, they added to the Porsche portfolio, and complemented the 911.

As further proof, around the time Porsche was notching up the big sales figures with the 944, Spanish car maker Seat were proud to state that their new Malaga/Ibiza sedan/hatchback were powered by engines designed by Porsche. Porsche were still involved with consultancy work, and companies still felt Porsche's image was golden enough to start name-dropping. No, the real problem for Porsche by the dawn of the 1990s was that the 944 had been around for an awfully long time.

The problem was made acute by the Schutz CEO years, because Porsche had become heavily dependant on the U.S. market, with over 50 percent of production going to America at certain points. Unfortunately, many of the high flyers became low flyers after the 1987 Wall Street crash; then came the recession inside and outside the U.S., plus unfavorable exchange rates that saw Porsche prices accelerate in important export markets — and the 944 was getting old! In America at least each new model year was a chance for a car maker to make stylish revisions to jazz up its range, and the 944 wasn't sitting well with this tradition. It had been much improved since 1982 model year, but looked much the same come 1991 model year.

People didn't care that this 944 Silver Rose had 250 bhp. By the early 1990s the 944 was too ubiquitous, too practical — too boring! (courtesy James E. Foley).

In addition, the 924/944 customer was a different breed than the Corvette, or even the 911, fan. The Vette and 911 patron is really never looking for anything but a Vette or 911. This sort of person isn't too bothered if things stay roughly constant for five or even more model years. The 924/944 buyer, on the other hand, likes to shop around and compare. It's a value-conscious customer profile that observes spec sheets, the latest performance figures, high-tech gadgets and, very importantly, what's new and hot on the street today. Well, the 944S2 wasn't exactly new, it embodied '80s retro, and its outright performance figures weren't exceptional considering the sizeable showroom-window sticker price. All of which left the 944S2 owner at a disadvantage when it came to key-chain bragging rights.

All of the above was unfair because, even though newer rivals offered more obvious bang for the buck, the 944 as honed by the house of Porsche was still top banana for true driver's-car credentials. It seemed to matter little to anxious U.S. Porsche dealerships, who were discounting stock heavily: how about almost 30 percent off in New York City? Hang tradition and purist sensibilities, the struggling dealers would much rather have been pushing the latest 300ZX, or the sensational new Honda NSX. The dealer chant was repeated over and over, give us something new, or at least something that looks new. Porsche were in a high-performance pickle.

Know Your Porsche DNA

Porsche did have a new model, even if it wasn't what most dealers and some enthusiasts wanted. The new car was a bridge between the past and the future, and its architect was Harm

Lagaay. Harm Lagaay was design chief at Porsche from 1989, and brought a design philosophy that would dominate Porsche thinking, and that of other manufacturers, for the ensuing years. Indeed, this credo is still well at work today in 2007, even though Lagaay left Porsche in 2004. The idea wasn't a new one, and it sounds easy, even if it's often hard to put into practice. Simply design according to the company's core characteristics. As said by Lagaay, "It's so important to have a design philosophy nowadays. Knowing the elements that characterise your range of cars, is worth gold."*

Harm Lagaay convinced management at the start of his tenure as design chief that this philosophy was important. Against a background of falling sales, and the accusations that some of its new-age models were not true to Porsche, Porsche management was ready to listen. Lagaay refuted the idea that designing according to core characteristics could be confining. The defense was that much could still be done while remaining faithful to Porsche's design DNA. Ford gave this idea a spin by incorporating an oval theme into the U.S. 1996 Taurus, feeling that the oval badge was core Ford. With the X- and S-types, Jaguar have also tried to incorporate Jaguaresque elements into its modern cars that share its Ford family platform.

When the 1968 Jaguar XJ6 first came out, an advertisement correctly stated that the car was instantly recognizable as a Jaguar, even though there wasn't a single badge on the body saying it was a Jaguar. This was the result Lagaay was alluding to. On the dark side, it can open the door to obvious retro design, and the lack of originality that entails. So it's unlikely the future will yield a completely carte blanche concept like the Porsche 924. It is also hard to identify a model as a 1970s car, or a 1990s design, when so many elements are borrowed from the past.

In view of Harm Lagaay's mission statement, it's funny to realize he had a large hand in coming up with the 924, and was also part of Team Lapine in designing the 928. Two models often considered "anti-Porsche"—911 devotees must have thought that Lagaay had finally seen the light! Fruits of such enlightenment were the 993-redrafted 911, and the Porsche Boxster. However, there was further irony in the fact that Harm Lagaay's first job as design boss was the latest iteration of the 924, the successor to the 944: Porsche 968.

Visually the 968 was a Porsche précis. The car's front section evoked the famous split-level look of sloping hood and raised fenders so familiar from the 911. The rounded nose cap was very 928-like. The once-fashionable 924/944 pop-up headlights were ditched in favor of 928-style swivel-up lamps. The rear of the car was cleaned up, with 928-type integrated tail/bumper molding with "PORSCHE" writ large between a pair of red-lensed, neutral-density rear lamps. The 968 involved a great amount of detail work, such as new curvy rear-view side mirrors. Even the previous Volkswagen/Audi door handles that graced many a 924 and 944 were deep-sixed in favor of new 968-dedicated items. They blended in with the new car's nineties organic form.

And of course it wasn't by accident that the apertures and immediate frontal section of the 968 looked very close to the 959 supercar. However, the 968's side profile, especially its side windows, were a carbon copy of 924/944 style. Step into the 968's cabin and it was obvious that the 968 was based on the 944. The new interior was practically identical to what one would find on the outgoing 944S2. The difference was that the 968 had a square, analog clock below the stereo deck on the center console. The 944's former digital dashboard clock was replaced with an outside air temperature readout. This interior carry-over was similar to the

**CAR*, April 1993, p. 42.

Regardless of critical or public perception of the new 968, shown here at turn 10 of Putnam, here was a thoroughly designed car that concentrated on the essentials of motoring (courtesy Gary Grigsby).

days of the 924-to-944 transition, where the 944 made do with the 924's dash in its formative years.

The development of the 968 was budget constrained, and alterations to its appearance were achieved by moldings and cladding upon an unaltered base structure. The goal was a fresh look, aerodynamic performance played second fiddle to the aesthetics of the make-over. The 968 had a drag coefficient of 0.34, compared with the 944S2's 0.33. It's down to personal taste whether one prefers the bold, macho, wide-fender originality of an early 944, or the rounded form of the 968. Beyond doubt is Lagaay's achievement of bringing the four-cylinder, front-engined model range into visual harmony with the Porsche look. The lesson from the stillborn 989 four-door was that regardless of engine position, number of doors, or seats, a concept can be made to embody Porsche flavor. The 968 and Cayenne are proof that Harm Lagaay was correct on that score.

So the cat was out of the bag. In Porsche's economy drive its new 968 was a major reworking of the previous 944. Rather than launch an all-new car, Porsche prepared a developed version of an existing model. They still felt the underlying 924/944 hadn't reached its development limit and went along a path of evolution. Indeed, to accompany the latest version of the front-engined four-cylinder, the "Evolution, Not Revolution" ad campaign was instituted. The revolution lay around the corner with the 986 (Boxster), which was still the stuff of rumor. Indeed, that mid-engined car wasn't yet a slam dunk concerning the financing to make it a production reality.

Total Body & Soul Make-Over

When a car maker releases a revised version of an existing model, they go to great lengths to emphasize just how "all new" their latest is. The transition from Volvo 144 to 244, Saab 99 to 900, BMW e21 to e30 3-series, involved unrelated components and body panels that couldn't be interchanged, and so it was with the new 968. Porsche described the 968 as embodying 80 percent new content compared to the 944. Component for component, there was great change between the earliest 924 and the 968 if one is looking for direct swaps, even if the two cars shared an underlying blueprint.

In truth Porsche had a headstart because it was already the class leader for driving experience, so it only had to make technical improvements where necessary. The 944's oval office interior was still easy on the eye, so retaining that was no hardship. The same applied to the 944S2's suspension. An extremely accomplished set-up carried over to the 968 with minimal alterations to springs, shock absorbers and sway bar to reflect the 968's 154 lb weight gain over the 944S2. Tires were once again 16-inch, ZR-rated 205/55 and 225/50 covers on the front and rear respectively, with Porsche initially approving the Pirelli P700-Z, Bridgestone Expedia S-01, and Yokohama A-008P, and Michelin's MXX3 also made an appearance in the 968 family. The same tire choices as for the 928 GTS, and like its big brother the 968 used

Evolve or perish! The Boxster was still a few years away, so Porsche made detail cosmetic and mechanical improvements to the outgoing 944S2 to keep their four-cylinder coupe at the top of a driver's car wish list (courtesy Porsche).

racing Turbo Cup–style rims. These alloys were standard issue for the 968, 911 and 928 in the early nineties.

Those seeking greater thrills could specify the optional 968 sport chassis pack, which stepped up the footwear to 17-inch tires, 225/45 at the front and 255/40 at the rear. The 16- and 17-inch rims shared their style, but the springs were stiffened, shocks were adjustable, and one could play around with the 968's ride height. In addition Porsche provided larger front brakes. Standard 968 stoppers were 11.7 inches front and 11.8 inches rear, vented all around; the fronts were now upgraded to an even 12 inches. For most markets, including the U.S., the 17-inch tires/rims came with the other components of the sport chassis pack as a complete set, and were limited to the 968 coupe. In the U.K. market early coupes could be fitted with the bigger tires/rims, but the remainder of the suspension stayed stock 16-inch 968. This was in deference to the market's imperfect secondary roads and preference for ride comfort.

VarioCam, 6-Speed & Tiptronic—Technical Triumphs

With the optional sport chassis pack, the cornering ability of the 968 rose above the 944S2. If a dry, amenable skidpad was available, back-to-back testing would show a 0.85–0.87g range for the old car, and as much as 0.95g for the most fortified version of the new car riding on 17-inch rims. Certainly up there with the firmest bone-rattlers in the business, which would be good enough for most, but not satisfactory for Porsche. Porsche likes to lead, so when it came to the 968's powerplant, Porsche had a couple of world firsts. On initial inspection observers might have considered such claims a hoax, because the 944S2's 3-liter, dual-cam four-pot was also carried over to the 968, but casual observers would have overlooked the existence of "VarioCam."

Still at 2,990 cc, but punching out 236 horses (SAE), rather than the 944S2's 208, so how did Porsche achieve this? Lifting the hood gave a clue, since it revealed a very different-looking Porsche 3-liter I4. Porsche eschewed the 944's under-hood 1980s wire maze in favor of a much neater "plug and play" look familiar to owners of late-model cars. There was also a much cleaner-styled intake manifold/dress cover, rounder in appearance, bearing the block script "PORSCHE," but with one key addition. In the middle and base of the canted cam cover was a plaque stating "VarioCam," Porsche's patented device and the four-cylinder family's introduction to the world of variable valve timing.

Previously Porsche had used the Mitsubishi-style counter-rotating balancer shafts to tame the 2.5–3.0-liter big four. This placater was still in place on the 968's 3.0, but now Zuffenhausen had taken a leaf out of Honda's book and produced their own version of VTEC. In the olden times, sports performance meant a big cam with greater duration to keep those intake valves open longer to admit more fuel and air, to make more power. The downside was a rough idle, torque sacrifice, and an engine that only came on cam at high revs, that is, a pokey engine. Variable valve timing meant having a camshaft for every occasion, and Porsche's incorporation of it on the 3-liter was ingeniously simple.

VarioCam altered the valve timing in certain rev ranges by playing with a chain between the intake and exhaust camshafts of the dual-cam cylinder head. A signal was sent from the 968's Bosch DME ECU to a solenoid that activated a spring-and-piston assembly. Exert pressure on the chain between the two cams from above or below, and the inlet cam altered its

Porsche's VarioCam variable valve timing system and other refinements pushed the 3-liter I4's output up from 211 bhp to 240 DIN horses (courtesy Porsche).

angle in relation to the exhaust cam. Up to 1,500 rpm, timing was advanced to cut hydrocarbons and clean up emissions. Between 1,500 and 5,500 rpm, intake-valve timing was retarded to boost torque production. From 5,500 rpm onwards, timing was advanced once again to improve top-end power delivery: a final adjustment reaching 15 degress of advancement, and worth 5 bhp out of the 3-liter's 240 DIN-rated horsepower achieved at 6,200 rpm.

Honda had VTEC, Mitsubishi had MIVEC, but Porsche's VarioCam permitted the 968 motor to record the greatest torque per liter for a normally aspirated engine, a new world record. Maximum power was now made at 6,200 rpm, rather than the 944S2's 5,800 rpm, but torque was up from 207 to 225lbs./ft. at the same 4,100 rpm. Eighty-three percent of this slab of torque lived between 2,000 rpm and 6,600 rpm. Such characteristics made the latest 3-liter the antithesis of the old turbo 2.5, which could be pretty dead in the lower ranges. At 240 DIN bhp, the 968 was 20 horses up on the original 944 Turbo, and just ten shy of the final 250 bhp version.

More conventional items to help the 968's 3-liter outdo the old S2 included a slight CR rise from 10.9 to 11 to one. The pistons themselves were lighter, as were the connecting rods. Accurate fuel delivery was achieved by altered sequential fuel injection and a hot-wire air flow meter. Breathing in was made easier thanks to new valves and an improved version of the S2's quadrilateral intake manifold that created a pulsating movement of incoming air.

Reworked exhaust and bigger catalytic converter aided exhalation, and by this time the 968 was a catalytic converter-equipped car for all world markets, unlike the 944S2.

To harness the power of the nearly new 3-liter, there were two definitely new gearboxes. The 968 had variable valve timing, and also succumbed to the latest fad of having a six-speed manual gearbox. The Getrag box had not one, but two, overdrive ratios. However, 6th gear was the same as the overdrive fifth in the 944S2's 5-speed box, with the remaining five ratios closely spaced. A carefully balanced selection for sure, with the 968 having a slightly taller final drive of 3.78 compared to the S2's 3.88 to one. Bring the 968's surfeit of torque into the picture, and Porsche's latest four-cylinder flyer achieved its terminal velocity in sixth gear. No concessions to CAFE with this car!

Unfortunately the six-speed of the 968 used the dual-mass flywheel of the sort utilized on the "964"-type 911. A more durable version of the flywheel was used on the 968 compared to the 911, but the forces of a four-cylinder compared to a six aggravate the situation, and it's something to look out for when considering a 968 with a few miles under its belt as a classic purchase. Porsche granted a small mercy, compared to the 944, by having a slot in the clutch housing that permitted easy access to the clutch plate, if one had special Porsche service tools handy.

All of which was of little concern if the new Tiptronic automatic transmission was selected. By the early 1990s this move wouldn't brand one as a heretic, and the Tiptronic part of the equation was carrying a lot of street cred — Porsche-initiated street cred that was soon taken up by Audi. It was the pragmatic choice; in the long term, automatics, if cared for, look after themselves, and stick-shift clutch replacement isn't an issue. Tiptronic, as seen on the Carrera 2 and coming to an I4 Porsche near you soon, was a neat device that allowed 968 pilots to pretend they were racing drivers.

Look down at the automatic surround, and the usual stick in a straight fore-aft plane was there. Start the 968's motor, foot on the brake pedal, lower the handbrake and pull the stick back from P to position D. Move away, and the adaptive electronic autobox tailored itself to the driving style at hand, drawing upon 5 different shift programs. There was an 8-bit chip, not unlike the MOS 6502 family found in an Atari VCS/2600, that worked with the 3-liter's DME, running software and making notes on throttle position, engine speed and the lateral acceleration pulled in a fast corner.

Drive hard, and the system worked with you by changing up at a later point in the rev range; gentle cruising saw earlier upshifts to maintain calm and frugal economy. Similar to a normal auto, but with the precision of electronic control. As a four speed box it was a big leap from the non-electronic three-speed slushbox available on the departed 944 2.7-liter. Look down again at the 968's shift surround, and notice a second, smaller fore-and-aft slot, to the right of the main gate. This was the Tiptronic trench. One side movement of the floor shifter, and sequential manual gear changes were available in that second slot. Just knock the lever forward to change up, and knock it back once to change down a ratio. The spring-loaded shifter automatically sprang back once released, and it was impossible to skip two ratios: one push, one gear.

The world of motor racing had such sequential shifts, before it moved to having paddles behind the steering wheel. As in racing, and as with a stick shift, Tiptronic allowed one gear to be held. Useful when pushing hard through a corner when unwanted throttle disturbances could upset a fine balance, and naturally there were safeguards. Forget to shift the lever forward when on the cusp of the redline, and Tiptronic's 8-bit Atari mind shifted up auto-

Top: He's at it again — Gerhard Plattner clocks up 100,000 km in 100 days using this 1992 968 (courtesy Porsche). ***Bottom:*** Harm Lagaay's distillation of quintessential Porsche styling cues made the 968 something of a visual Porsche DNA gumbo (courtesy Porsche).

matically, and kept doing so with each subsequent redline until fourth was reached. In addition, low gear could be chosen by the PC ghost, should the wannabe racer have forgotten to get out of high gear when coasting to a halt.

Note that at the heart of Tiptronic lay a conventional, torque converter-style 4-speed automatic transmission, the German ZF 4HP 18FL to be precise. In racers, and in an increasing number of late-model cars, clutchless changes come courtesy of a hydraulic clutch working on a normal manual box. By using a conventional automatic, Tiptronic permitted the driver to play the gears like a manual transmission, but be comforted by the cushioned changes of a torque-converter autobox. Another innovative automatic chapter, since Porsche's semi-automatic Sportomatic had expired in 1977. Porsche were more interested in encouraging driver involvement in automatic cars than Ferrari, Lotus or any rival.

Off with Its Head!—968 Cabrio

Staying true to form, Porsche had an open-top 968 ready for the public. The fresh-air 968 was very similar to the 944 ragtop, in that it was a conversion done by the German subsidiary of ASC (American Sunroof Corporation). ASC reinforced the 968's decapitated structure so that the windshield surround would be a sufficient support in any unfortunate rollover. The conversion work was completed with two trips to the Heilbronn works—but trips from

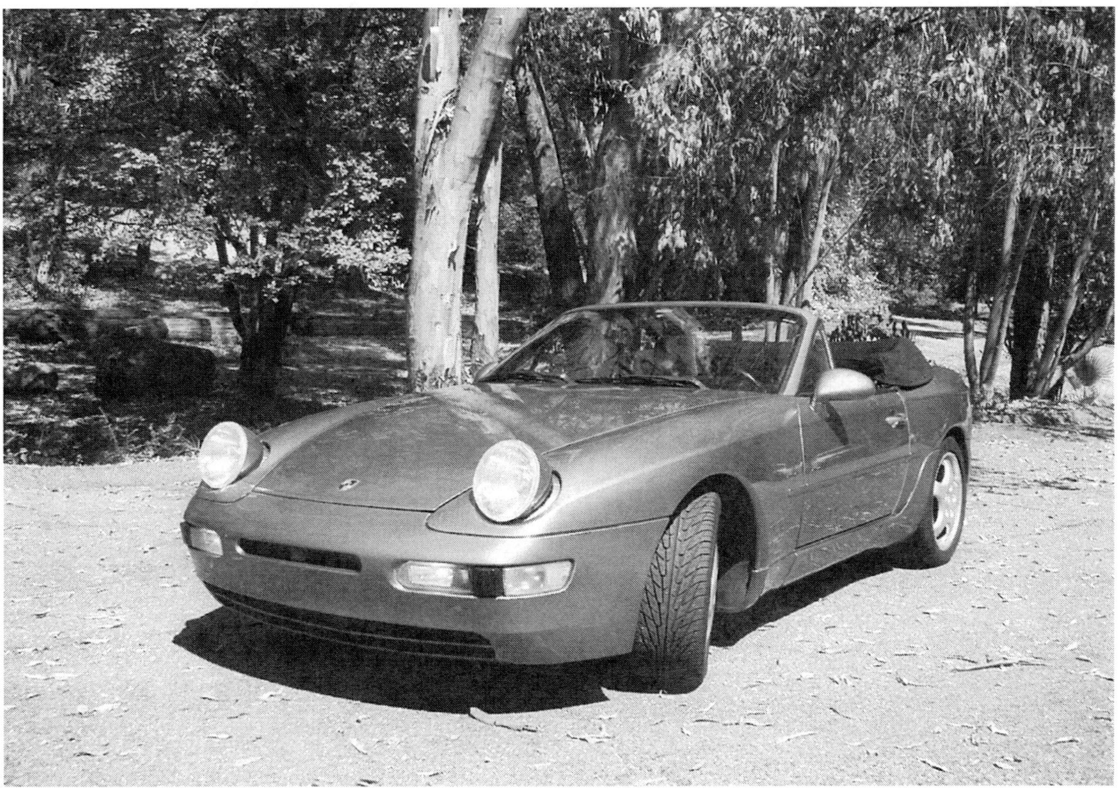

A lovely 1993 968 Cabrio. While the Corvette convertible was adept at shake, rattle and roll, Porsche and ASC ensured that the 968 Cabrio just rolled (courtesy Jeff Storey).

where? That would be Zuffenhausen, because the 968 joined the 911 and 928 in being built by Porsche themselves. Not just the 968 engine, but the entire car itself. With a curtailed production projection of seven to eight thousand cars per year, it didn't make sense to farm out production to Neckarsulm as in the 924/944 era.

Fewer four-cylinder cars from Porsche, because the family had evolved into an even more upmarket and truncated range. There were no highs and lows with the new car, just 968 coupe and convertible. No more price-leader 924S, or blown 944 Silver Rose. One 968 model, with one engine, which explained Porsche's fine-fettling to get the evolved 944S2 close to perfection. It would be the sole representative of Porsche's entry-level model. It also explained why the automatic version had been pushed to the head of the class. Previously, as in European sporty car tradition, only the base-engined 924/944s could be bought as automatics. The 944S2 and Turbos were stick-shift only. However, with only a single model version left, Porsche had little choice, and the Tiptronic would broaden the appeal of what was fast becoming a niche Porsche.

For the niche person, Porsche's 968 offered a unique driving experience by combining driver appeal with refinement: imagine a larger and more accomplished Miata. The 968 showed that Mazda and others had been imitating Porsche all along. The 968's fluid chassis invited the driver to explore its limits. This was without doubt the most neutral-handling car

Why oh why couldn't ASC have done a fully power top as per the 911? Rich folk have no time to fiddle with monkey wrenches! (courtesy Jeff Storey).

ever to wear the Porsche shield. Devoid of the 928's mass, a Weissach axle was simply unnecessary to keep the 968 on the blacktop and out of the scenery. Don't fear, but enjoy reaching the limit of adhesion where rear tires lose and regain grip under the pilot's guidance. The 968 was the ultimate drifting machine, years before the concept even took hold in the West.

Trust Porsche to realize that the enthusiast required a 6-speed—normally a fashion accessory, but so very essential in lifting the 968 above the coupe mêlée. Living up to the cliché of a gear for every situation, the torque-rich 3-liter worked with the Getrag six-speeder to maintain that ideal balance. No peaks and troughs, just a constant engine note and minimal loss of revs when going up through the gearbox. However, practice made for perfection in mastering the 6-speed's double–H shift pattern, and reverse was placed up and next to first gear. No excuses for choosing R rather than first gear, though, after all, a driver's car requires the knowledge of how to drive!

After not too many miles the 968 became an extension of the driver. So intuitive were its controls that it must rate as one of the best cars around for active safety. With this close connection to the road, it was easy to forget that the 968 still used an indirect shifter linkage, as per other transaxle Porsches. It was always good, as such devices went, but now it was even easier to palm around the close gate, and was more precise than many conventional cars with the gearbox placed directly beneath the floor shifter. As the motor was kept around the 4,000 rpm mark through challenging bends, evolution, rather than revolution, seemed perfectly acceptable. If only the same could be said for Tiptronic examples.

Negative comments concerning automatic 968s apply to most cars saddled with an auto. The Tiptronic's ECU could trip the car up by dropping two gears when the redline was much too close for the lower gear, and dropping just one would have been wiser. Humans are better at making such calls than machines. If the driver took matters into his own hands with Tiptronic mode, the situation improved—but there were too few gears. The ZF 4HP 18FL was an overdrive 4-speed auto; fourth was an indirect 0.74 to one, third was the direct one to one ratio. In contrast, the Porsche 928 had a direct one to one for its four speed auto's top gear. Therefore, the Tiptronic offered no flexibility gain over the 944's 3-speed auto. Sadly, it was no longer possible to keep engine revs constant, as with the precise 6-speed 968s.

An easy conclusion would be that the Tiptronic would be the right choice for the 968 convertible, but that would be wrong. The ragtop was very nearly as much a purist's ride as the coupe. ASC had done super work in retaining good torsional rigidity, because cowl shake was very low for a cabrio. The third-generation Camaro and C4 Corvette convertibles showed the worst things that could happen when the roof section of an automobile is disposed of. They would be better suited to that game of Twister. On the other hand, the 968 Cabrio with 6-speed was a friend even over imperfect surfaces. Porsche's decision to keep the convertible with the 16-inch rims and stock suspension was wise, the sport chassis would have upset the applecart of refinement.

One small problem, literally, with the 968 cabriolet was its extra-tiny rear seats—nicely trimmed and attractive-looking, but, as with the old S2, unusable by anyone larger than a leprechaun. And little praise once again for ASC's semi-automated hood assembly. Before one could press a button and watch the top arc overhead, those manual clamps still had to be released with those specially provided tools. Absurd! The convertible looked sharp with the top up, and because the 924/944 coupe greenhouse was gone, the 968 convertible looked even more like a fresh design. The car also appeared fine with the top down, but the top material was bulky and didn't drop down flush with the body line. It was reminiscent of the collar on an Elvis Presley jumpsuit, only less fashionable.

How fast can one travel in such Lagaay-penned style? Not 180 mph, as the 968 speedo suggested; Porsche could have left the 944S2's 160 mph instrument in place rather than pretend. In spite of the weight gain and poorer aerodynamics, the 968 was speedier than the S2: a top end of 156 mph for a 6-speed 968, compared to 149 mph for the older 5-speed car. It was also almost a second quicker to sixty, making the dash in 6.1 seconds. Tiptronic 968s were only 3 mph slower on top speed, but much tardier in acceleration, supposed to be 7.9 seconds. Fortunately, by the early nineties Porsche were back to supplying cars that could better factory figures. The 968 did manage that, but all up it was a low-14-second quarter-mile machine, and by 1991/92 people might have expected more for the price.

Sticker Shock in 968-Land

Ironically there was initial relief when the 968 arrived, because its price was lower than expected: starting from $39,850 or a $3,500 saving compared to the defunct 944S2. The

Despite performance of 156 mph and 0–60 mph in 6.1 seconds, at over $40,000 with selected options the 968 coupe's pace, if not its composure, could be matched by more plebeian transportation (courtesy Porsche).

convertible was $51,150, and Tiptronic cost $2,199 more. For the U.K. it was initially believed that the right-hand-drive 968 would enter at 40,000 pounds sterling, an incredible figure given the home-market price was the equivalent of 31,000 pounds sterling. However, the RHD 968 made its debut at 34,945 pounds sterling; better, but without the driver's-side airbag that was originally going to be standard. No such worry in the U.S., where all 968s came with dual airbags as standard equipment, but was that enough?

At first glance it didn't seem like enough; or, put another way, it seemed like too much. More expensive than the much-vaunted LT1 Vette, the twin-turbo 300ZX and, more importantly, the new Mazda RX7. Indeed, the only possible sporting rival toting a larger sticker was the exotic Honda NSX. And what is more, the Porsche was the only member of the field with a plebeian four-pot motor. A Porsche I4, but an I4 all the same. However, a Porsche I4 isn't a GM Iron Duke/2.5/Tech IV. Plus, there are convertibles, and then there are convertibles. There was the Corvette convertible with V8 at 41 grand, and the 968 convertible at 51 grand. Many thought the Porsche's price was crazy; a sensible few realized the folly of paying 41k for a 2-seater happy to shoot a driver's dental fillings from the open cabin with force commensurate with James Bond's ejector seat!

Unfortunately for Porsche, most just saw the 968's pricing as crazy. It was more economically viable to have a dental plan and buy the Vette. The buying response globally was restrained, and so too was public reaction to the 968's look. Often mistaken for its big brother the 928, the public didn't share Porsche's belief in the value of evolution. Porsche's solution was to shed unwanted baggage: a reduction of 1850 jobs, tapping into a cash stockpile, general belt-tightening economic measures to tide Zuffenhausen over hard times. Porsche applied the same lessons to the 968. Porsche's mission to clean house coincided with the exit of Chairman Arno Bohn, allegedly because of a difference of opinion concerning how the 986 project would be brought to fruition.* Bohn thought a joint deal with an auto giant was the way to go, Porsche did not. The new 986 was still some time away, and Porsche needed an answer now. The answer was Club Sport.

968 Club Sport—The Simple Porsche

The 968 was truly the bridge between Porsche past and Porsche future. First, it was the embodiment of the Zuffenhausen common look, and second, it heralded the return of the "simple" Porsche: cars not burdened by horsepower, creature comforts and a stratospheric price tag. In short, it was back to "356 skool." Back to old school, and back to Europa, because the new member of the 968 clan believing in the old minimalist ethic wasn't available in America. Burned by over-reliance on the U.S., Porsche played reverse sweep with the 968. The 1976 914 2.0 was available only in America, and the new 968 Club Sport was available only in the Rest Of The World (ROW).

U.S. 968 patrons could continue to amuse themselves with the affordable 17-inch-wheel/sport pack costing $1,352 on the coupe. For the Old World, Porsche prepared the third minimalist Club Sport, following on from the stripped 911 and 928 Club Sport. The 968 wasn't really uncompetitively priced in the ROW markets, and was actually cheaper than cars like the Renault Alpine A610 and the new Audi S2 Quattro, but the market for these luxury

**CAR*, February 1993, p. 10.

coupes, grand tourers and sports cars had softened with the recession of the early 1990s. Porsche would lead the way in bringing back value for money.

So it was that Arno Bohn's September 1992 departure was followed by the 968 Club Sport's announcement the following month. As usual with the 928CS and 911RS, the 968CS was notable more for what it didn't have than for what it did: in short, a claimed weight loss figure of 110 lbs., and a big price cut. So no more fast glass, power door mirrors, power seats, power door locks, remote hatch release, cruise control, airbags, rear hatch wiper and air conditioning. On the positive side of the ledger, the Porsche owner received a simpler and lighter wiring harness. The normal 968 vacuum-type heater controls were replaced with a more straightforward, and cheaper to fix, mechanical set-up. Open the 968CS's door and look at the big 911RS lightweight Recaro buckets, which implied the absence of the "+2" portion of the 968's 2+2.

The best part of the 968CS was in the chassis department. Here lay the optional 17-inch rims and tires available on the normal 968 coupe, but the associated sport-pack chassis was absent. This 968 hybrid rolled around on the familiar Cup rims covered by 225/45 and 255/40 tires front and rear, but the suspension was nearly stock. The small tweak Porsche's chassis gurus carried out was a 20 mm lowering of the ride height, but shocks and spring fortitude remained constant.

The lowering was simply the result of shorter front springs and an adjustment of the rear suspension's torsion bars. Since the Club Sport was lighter than an equivalent 968, the effect was that the 968CS had the feeling of a firmer ride, even though the springs and shocks possessed standard stiffness. No change either to the 968's motor and gearbox. Standard stuff here too, with the 236 SAE (240 DIN) horse, 3-liter I4 working through the 6-speed

In a car lightened by 110 lbs., the 3 liter/6 speed power team truly shone. An almost 15 percent price reduction for the 968CS really sweetened the deal (courtesy Porsche).

manual; naturally, automatic was unavailable with the Club Sport coupe. At least the price was right, almost a 15 percent price reduction.

However, the 968CS could have its price boosted by options, if not the usual options most associate with luxury sports. These were serious club-racer hardware items linked to going faster and to improved on-track visibility. For the obsessed, there was a full-scale suspension/brake package that would make you track-ready. Out went the regular Fichtel and Sachs parts, replaced with firmer, adjustable M30 Koni shocks and springs, and three-position adjustable rear sway bar. This time the CS sat up to 40 mm lower than a standard 968, and its suspension was 30 percent stiffer into the bargain. The 968's torsion-bar rear suspension was replaced with racing-style coil-overs. Bringing the whole shebang to a halt were larger, cross-drilled vented disks at all four corners, gripped by 911RS four-piston calipers.

Normally the optional 17-inch sport pack for the 968 had the bigger 12-inch (304 mm) front brakes, but the optional pack for the 968CS raised the game with 304 mm disks on all four wheels. There was a distinction between the 17-inch sport packs for the 968 and the 968CS. To help channel the 3-liter's power from the wheel that slips to the one that grips, the 968's optional Torsen limited-slip differential could be selected, but it cost almost as much as the CS's sport pack.

Then came the extrovert features, which could be deleted at no cost. Most obviously, to let others know a CS was at hand, large decal script "Club Sport" insignia adorned the lower half of the CS's body. Discreet Porsche fans just relied on the "968CS" badge below the rear hatch glass. Color choices for the CS were restricted to Maritime Blue, Speed Yellow, Indian Red, Grand Prix White and plain black, but with scope for creative color coding. The backs of the Recaros could be painted to match the exterior color, and the 17-inch Cup wheels could be color-coded too!

Make Mine Jelly-Bean Blue!!

For example, one could have a Grand Prix White 968CS with red Club Sport decals and red rims, or blue wheels, it was up to the buyer. The benefit of the 968's being built by Porsche was that special requests were not a problem. As long as it was available on the 968, the customer could have it, even air conditioning, although this meant going back to a standard and more complex wiring loom. Porsche was straddling the line between normal car maker and ultra-small-scale specialist. There was almost the exclusivity of a Morgan, without the interminable waiting list. There was the pure sports car aura of a TVR, without the suspect build quality and somewhat vulgar kit-car connotations. A galvanized body, full warranty, rock-hard residuals, and that was just the secondhand 968! After all, it was a Porsche.

For a car that was allegedly unloved, the 968 held, and holds, its value rather well. Whereas the 924/944 couldn't maintain their initially good resale value once their ubiquity became obvious, the 968 has used its limited sales to keep the dreaded depreciation demon at bay. Thank Lagaay for bestowing the Porsche link upon the 968. Its visual tie-in with his 993, 996 and Boxster has kept the 968 in the game. However, if there was one shadow cast by the 968CS, it was its unsettling of used-car values. The problem was associated with selling a new 968 at a price lower than secondhand 968s already on the scene. It didn't stop sales of used normal luxury 968s, it just added to the dealer confusion: the confusion of fudging sales figures through pre-registering new cars.

A 1995 PCA 968 racer, but this wasn't the only trackbound 968 around. After all, Porsche did have a way with turbochargers (courtesy Gary Grigsby).

The competitively priced CS also put the squeeze on any profit margin a sales outlet could make on any 968, including the CS. However, kudos to the Club Sport for saving the 968, and avoiding the fate of the slow-selling 914/6 of the early 1970s. The Club Sport allowed the 968 to recover from a glacially slow start. Not the 7,000 to 8,000 originally dreamt of, but enough of a boost to keep the car in production, and keep the wolves from Zuffenhausen's door until the 986 arrived. Removal of the 968's luxurious layer revealed the CS to be the foremost road-racer on the planet, and sparked off reciprocal paring-down and price cuts by rivals.

With the post–Savanna 3rd-generation RX7, Mazda seemed to have finally turned the tables on Porsche with an ultra-new contender. That said, even Toyo Kogyo had to bow to the commercial pressure of slow sales and follow the leader. Mazda and Renault slashed the price of their RX7 and A610 to bolster sales in export markets. The 300ZX turbo was looking like a bloated tribute to the hedonism of the eighties and was also getting ignored. Through it all the 968, the oldest competitor in the field, was teaching its high-tech rivals the secret of the sports car.

In the pre-ground effects era, the McLaren Formula One team were adept at picking up fractions and making a fast car through conventional suspension tweaking. No wholesale changes, just a matter of racecraft knowledge and setting up a car to perform. Porsche did the same with the 968: use a wealth of knowledge to make a design work. It was sobering to observe the 924/968 spec sheets and see that both cars had MacPherson struts/coil springs at the front and semi-trailing arms/torsion bar suspension at the rear. In spite of such humble apparatus, the 968CS avoided the jittery and fractious behavior of the wishboned RX7. The 968CS had the child's play, point-and-squirt handling ease of a C4 Vette with Z51 handling pack, but without the bruising ride.

Knowledge was Porsche's secret. If the bad manners of rear-engined 911s could be tamed, then the sky was the limit. Porsche brakes are seemingly limitless, too, and the 968CS's cross-drilled sports pack lived up to the legend. There are good braking systems — and then there is the racetrack. The CS's cross-drilled brakes were very track-ready to scrub off excess speed from the sub-3,000-pound coupe. Matched with the firmer Koni suspension, this was one of the few current production cars that could be driven to the track, raced, and driven home again. Other sports cars displayed decidedly nervous tendencies at the track; they were simply fast road cars.

The 968's absence of technology helped avoid the indecision. No electronic suspension forcibly holding the car parallel with the road surface come what may. No burdensome traction-control device determined to second-guess the driver. No obscene, special, artificial "nervotronic" power steering which would be magic in a K-Mart parking lot, but less useful for when the car had to be actually driven. Porsche recognized that the most sensitive stability control was the driver. Don't talk to the computer, talk to the car. The 968CS kept one really informed of all developments, with power steering that doesn't feel like power steering, and ABS brakes that intrude only when all is about to be lost, not a moment sooner.

A spine tingling road version of Porsche's racer, the fiendish 968 Turbo S. One extremely mean four-banger! (courtesy Porsche).

968 Turbo RS/S—Let's Go Racing

It seemed right for the 968 to follow the example of the successful Le Mans–entered 924/944 cars, and be backed by the factory in motorsport. Porsche turned their attention to the homeland ADAC GT Cup, and came up with a car called 968 Turbo RS, announced in February 1993. This 2,970-pound racer had a 337-bhp version of the turbo 3-liter I4, and a very similar road-going sibling known simply as 968 Turbo S. This race car with license plates was the most powerful road-legal 4-cylinder Porsche ever made, and since the 968 was the final 4-cylinder Porsche, the record remains as of 2007. Like its big brother the 968 Turbo RS, the slightly detuned 968 Turbo S was put together by hand in the Weissach racing shop.

The DIN outputs from the 3-liter, blown four-cylinder were surprising enough, 305 bhp at 5,600 rpm and 369 lbs./ft. at 3,000 rpm, but the I4's configuration was a real conundrum. Porsche retained the 3-liter capacity of the normal 968, but bypassed the DOHC 16-valve cylinder head in favor of a SOHC 8-valve head. Yes, lift the lid on the 968 Turbo S or RS, and the apex of the powerplant was a copy of the old-style 2.5-liter 944 Turbo. The official explanation from Porsche's Jurgen Pippig was that the racer's accelerated development program meant there was no time to prepare the S2/968 4-valve head for the racing rigors of forced induction.

R&D king Horst Marchart and Porsche's PR man Gerd Schmid said they just didn't need the DOHC 4-valve head, because Porsche got all the power it required from the 944 Turbo arrangement. However, the turbo set-up had a larger intercooler compared to the 944 days. The 3-liter had 7.5 to one, low–CR pistons to cope with the onslaught of maximum boost

With zero to sixty in 4.5 seconds and a terminal velocity of 174 mph, the 968 Turbo S was in the Dodge Viper class for thrust, but with better brakes and chassis (courtesy Konstantin from Germany).

With only 16 built, the 968 Turbo S is a rare example of the wildest four-cylinder technology that was current in the early 1990s. However, a 968CS yielded driver enjoyment at more realistic road velocities (courtesy Konstantin from Germany).

pressure, well up on the 944 Silver Rose era. Boost pressure on the old 250-horse 2.5-liter turbo I4 had been 11.9 psi, it was now a very serious 14.5 psi. Fearsome as the Turbo S's performance bark was, its environmental bite was subdued thanks to a catalytic converter.

Look at the Turbo S's performance figures and one is likely to agree with Porsche that 2 valves were sufficient. A genuine 0–60 mph time clocked in a scant 4.5 seconds, a top speed of 174 mph, and Porsche welcomed anyone with sufficient funds to put the car to the test. The Turbo S, like all Porsches, wasn't speed-limited to 155 mph. So what are you waiting for? Find an Autobahn and frighten a Mangusta, a Cobra, a Viper or any other wild nameplate. The driver could do it in safety, because it was a Porsche. The 968 Turbo S was an ultra-low-volume, left-hand-drive custom job, yours for $135,000 if you lived outside the U.S. The Turbo S shared its minimalist interior with the spartan 968CS, and was 110 lbs. lighter than even the Turbo RS.

As familiar as the Turbo S interior and Recaros were, its exterior showed signs of its new-found power. The front nosecone section was revised, with a deep snowplow spoiler and a larger air aperture above the front license plate. Two NACA hood ducts were present, and on the rear was a very noticeable rear wing that could adjust through 10 degrees. This was definitely downforce for go rather than show. As a chassis upgrade, the Turbo S sat 25 mm lower than the CS and had even bigger alloys. Eighteen-inch polished Cup rims had Dunlop SP Sport 8000 ZR-rated tires, 235/40 section front, 265/35 covers at the back. They sounded wide, but the blown 3-liter had the power to melt the tires in surprisingly many gears if the driver got carried away.

Top: It's Big Daddy, the 337 bhp 968 Turbo RS that Zuffenhausen hoped would set the German ADAC GT Cup alight (courtesy Porsche). ***Bottom:*** The racing interior of the 968 Turbo RS. Porsche built only three cars (courtesy Porsche).

However, the fastest 968 of all time was something of a mild disappointment on the road. Sit in the usual CS Recaro buckets, work away at the 6-speed transmission, and as one glides along the realization occurs that not much is happening. Gentle driving, even fast driving, didn't bring the pleasure level promised by the Turbo S specs. The retention of the normal driver's-side-airbag steering wheel only added to the banal experience, as did a turbo motor that didn't so much as lag, as pause. The turbo four was responsive, especially considering the low CR necessary with almost 15 pounds of boost. The car itself was extremely competent and wouldn't put a foot wrong, and therein lay the problem.

Porsche's racing department had cunningly disguised a race car as a road car, and those 911 Turbo–sourced brakes had to be stepped on very heavily to wake the Turbo S up. This was a car that had to be driven to insanely high limits before joy could be derived; below such limits the Turbo S was strangely inert. As an exercise in what could be achieved from 924 DNA, the Turbo S was a success; as a car with greater "go" than a Vauxhall Lotus Carlton its ability on real life roads was academic. It seemed little could go right with Porsche's attempt to push the 968, because the 968 Turbo RS didn't do well in the ADAC GT Cup. The victim of rule changes, like the BMW M1, it wasn't competitive and made little impact on the German series. It became clearer that Porsche's survival lay in what it could come up with for people not wearing race helmets.

With production totals of 3 and 16 for the 968 Turbo RS and Turbo S respectively, haute

The 968 Turbo RS engine. The curious thing about the turbo 3-liter in the 968 Turbo S and RS was the retention of the old blown 2.5 liter's SOHC head. The official word from Porsche was that there was no time to develop the 944S2/968's DOHC head, and that it wasn't necessary (courtesy Porsche).

couture wasn't serving Porsche anywhere near as well as the spartan CS. We will never know if the CS could have turned 968 sales around in the U.S. A low-priced 968 might have provided the excuse needed to sign up to the 968 club. As things stood, lightweight Porsches in the U.S. were limited to how many 911RS Americas could be sold. While Porsche banked on support for the 911 in the U.S., 968CS supporters in the U.K. provided the impetus for a special 968CS for that market. The 968 Sport was a CS with some of the regular 968's luxuries back in place.

Actually, even before the Sport came along, normal 968 seats were offered on the CS for those unable to contend with the Recaros, at no extra cost. As said earlier, the 968 was Zuffenhausen-built and Porsche didn't mind meeting different tastes. The U.K. 968S of January 1994 was a formal offering for those unwilling to stomach the CS's absence of sound deadening and 356-era manual window winders. Reinstated items were most obviously four regular 968 seats. Since the ordinary comfy front seats were back in place, it allowed room for the 968's rear buckets. Back to 2+2 status, and with our old friends power windows, power door locks, power rear-view mirrors, power sunroof, electric operation of the rear hatch release and alarm system.

The Sport was 44 lbs. heftier than the CS, thanks to its regained toys and soothing sound deadening. However, all was not lost, the "CS" and "S" variants could both be fitted with the optional sport pack containing Koni shocks, cross-drilled rotors and Carrera RS aluminum calipers. Even without this option the Sport was still high on the enthusiast's list thanks to the standard fitment of the CS 17-inch tire and rim pack.

Porsche announced the 968 Turbo RS in February 1993. Given how well the 924/944 had done on the track, there were great expectations for the new Turbo RS (courtesy Porsche).

CS appeal, with a thin veneer of civility, that was the Sport's charm. Like the CS, the Sport gave the buyer a more responsive car with better handling than the vin ordinaire 968, at a lower price—especially given one had to pay extra to obtain the 17-inch rims on the 968, when they already came standard on the CS and Sport. Priced midway between the CS and normal 968, the 968 Sport was a very happy medium.

The wild Club Sport decals were gone, but Porsche worked in a "Sport" script above the right rear lamp to distinguish this U.K. version. In Australia the 968CS continued as the only alternative to the regular 968, but took on a Sport-like, no-cost option: normal 968 seating for a tight four. For the Australian market air conditioning did cost extra, and that implied going to a normal 968 wiring loom. All in all, the plainer 968s helped the final vestige of the front-engined, four-cylinder family reach a sales total of 2,776. By the close of production in July 1995, four 968s were being built per day, compared to 2 for the also-sunset-bound 928.

968—Quality, Not Quantity

Fascinatingly few 968s made it into the collective garages of the globe. Consider the fact that as many as 2,099 912Es were sold in North America alone in 1976 model year. However, the 912E didn't commence at around $40,000. High price, and a public weary of the 924/944 theme, caused many to miss out on a great Porsche. After 20 years the great water-cooled, four-cylinder experiment had drawn to a close, the 968 would not be directly replaced. It

Among competitors on the track in the ADAC GT Cup. Sadly, Porsche's 968 Turbo RS didn't cover itself with glory in racing (courtesy Porsche).

didn't turn out to be the "new" Porsche after all; too many egos wouldn't let it. So Porsche looked to its past for its future and came up with the Boxster, because 924-to-968 had never been a good fit for Porsche image.

Models designed by Porsche that were not seen as Porsches represent a riddle for modern times. The criticism was harder to comprehend given the shortage of true sports cars by the early 1990s. The 968 faced up to warmed-up 2-door sport sedans, and grand tourers. They had a lot of power and features, but couldn't honestly claim to be sports cars. The 968CS exposed the distinction, proving that merely using modern technology doesn't make one a hero.

Chapter 7

928—Supersize Me!

The New 911?

Every era has its auto hero. The economy car with the best gas mileage going, the most practical and fashionable minivan, and, more recently, lavishly trimmed and upscale sport trucks & SUVs. Back in the late 1960s/early 1970s, the fast road car was king. Extravagant styling that necessitated a swoopy 2-door, death-defying suspension hardware, and as much horsepower as anyone could get their hands on were the order of the day. Go-faster stripes were advertised and magazines showed off Lamborghini Miuras, Ferrari Daytonas and V12 Jaguar XKEs. From the driver's seat of an Orbit Orange GTO in the 1971 film *Two-Lane Blacktop*, Warren Oates proudly proclaimed that it was all about performance and image.

Car fans were dreaming of the sporty car, and it was during this era that the U.S./Italian 8-cylinder De Tomaso Pantera was flying out of Lincoln-Mercury dealerships. It became the nation's best-selling luxury GT. A U.S. Ford 351 V8 and an Italian chassis—yes, they even had hybrids back then! Of course, speed takes power, and regardless of whether one was in the muscle car or exotic car camps, that implied larger and more numerous cylinders. By the 1970 model year there were 455-cubic-inch GM A bodies, and Daimler-Benz's new SOHC aluminum head 3.5 and 4.5 liter V8s in the early Seventies. Even Porsche were entering the party with capacity increases that saw the classic 911 flat six grow from 2.0 to 2.7 liters by 1973.

Reality was about to interrupt the speed dream. Escalating insurance costs and the first gas crunch of late 1973 teamed up to burst the bubble. Suddenly your personal escape pod had morphed from a 460-cubic-inch T-bird into a 1974 Cologne 2.8 V6-motivated Mustang II Mach 1. Well, at least real duals were still available! The era of the luxury compact was ushered in, suddenly going slow had never looked or felt so good. It was a time of rationalization, of discontinued lines and "efficient" designs.

Unfortunately, with the changes came blandness and loss of character, when cars from different countries started looking more and more the same. It was the time when GM's Bill Mitchell declared that Giugiaro's new VW Rabbit looked like a bullfrog that swallowed a box. *Thoroughbred & Classic Cars* magazine described the phenomenon in October 1989, "In America, as in Europe, however, the special character of all cars was progressively squeezed out in the Seventies and early Eighties...."*

The changing times caused existing sporty high performance models to fall away and saw plans for future hot cars shelved, but not at Zuffenhausen. Porsche had other ideas, their auto plan may have stalled, but it could and would be restarted. Porsche were looking for a

**Thoroughbred & Classic Cars*, Vol. 17, no. 1, October 1989 (supplement), p 12.

Top: The 1977 Porsche 928. In the 1970s Porsche was rewriting the rulebook, no longer just a small car company (courtesy Porsche). ***Bottom:*** In life there are leaders and followers and Porsche was showing the way with the avant-garde 928 (courtesy Porsche).

Porsche felt that 5 mph bumpers shouldn't ruin a car's appearance. Thanks to aluminum bars concealed by polyurethane nose and tail casings, the 1978 U.S. 928's styling didn't suffer (courtesy Brad Smith).

new car that would take them beyond their rear-engined, air-cooled past into the 1980s and beyond. As good as the 356, and subsequent 911, had proven to be both as road and race cars, they had their shortcomings. Having all the mechanical hardware in the one rear location didn't augur well for stiffer future federal crash testing, or drive-by noise pollution tests that were about to halt functional shaker scoops.

Perhaps equally important was the issue of traditional Porsche handling, dictated by pre–World War II ideals of rear-engine weight bias, a fundamentally unsound layout that promised bite-me-back oversteer. It had been tamed over time by canny Porsche engineering, and had even been deemed a bonus for the expert driver. However, such traits were tricky for the masses, and that rear bias was never handy for interior space efficiency. Something new was called for.

That something new would eventually surprise all as the 1977 Porsche 928, a project that started as early as 1971, and was delayed somewhat by the fuel crisis and the rather more pressing need to get a volume-selling replacement for the 914 family into car showrooms sooner rather than later. Pending federal regulations, and the practical limitations of rear- and mid-engined layouts, saw Porsche's Dr. Ernst Fuhrmann guide the 928 towards the power game. It was a car that conformed to the fast road car dream of 1970. As such it was expectedly a coupe, less expectedly for Porsche front-engined, and, completely unexpectedly—a V8!!

It all made good engineering and business sense. By the time the project commenced the Corvette was selling around 30,000 units per annum. North America had always been a very important market for Porsche. From the Triumph Stag V8 of the U.K. to the plastic

Top: **It was commonly thought Porsche had designed a car with a back that looked like it could be the front. In fact, the 928's rear end was influenced by the 1975 AMC Pacer! (courtesy Brad Smith).** ***Bottom:*** **Lots of original thinking went into the 928, but those swivel-up headlights looked suspiciously like the ones used on the Lamborghini Miura (courtesy Brad Smith).**

Chevy of the U.S., that was the sort of car the people wanted. So Porsche decided to say yes, and opened up an engineering avenue that was so un–Porsche like. The 911 was declared old hat, and rumored to die out by 1980. With the 928 waiting in the wings Porsche obviously felt a change was as good as a rest.

Build Me a V8

The V8 motor was an all-aluminum, single-overhead-cam unit of oversquare configuration, 95 mm bore and 78.9 mm stroke, displacing 4,474 cc and possessing a traditional 90 degree vee angle between the cylinder banks. More unusually, it was a linerless design; the steel-coated aluminum pistons ran up and down the bores thanks to the use of the Reynolds 390 high-silicon alloy. This special material originated from use on the I4 motor used in the Chevy Vega subcompact. For ease of maintenance, to eliminate valve clearance adjustments the new V8 also featured hydraulic tappets.

The Porsche V8 had a two-plane, forged steel crankshaft with 5 main bearings. It followed contemporary practice by using a one-piece ladder frame to support the lower halves of the main bearings. The camshafts were driven by a single toothed rubber cambelt. The new V8 represented generational change from the 911's flat 6. A rubber belt rather than chain drive for the cams, the adoption of hydraulic tappets, a conventional wet sump instead of a racing style dry sump. The V8's fuel measuring apparatus underlined the new performance era. In place of the 911's original 6 Solex 40PI single-throat downdraft carbs there was Bosch K-Jetronic mechanical fuel injection.

The 4.5 V8 made 240 bhp (DIN) at 5,250 rpm, and maximum torque of 267.5 lbs./ft. arrived at 3,600 rpm. Not class-leading output per liter, but a tractable and easy-going motor in tune with emissions concerns and the needs of world markets. Porsche wanted their new design to be adaptable to any future pollution control scenario. To this end the engine was set up to deliver its performance using gasoline of modest octane. It featured a wedge-shaped combustion chamber and a piston with a mostly flat top, except for little indentations for the valves, in effect creating mini-hemispheres around the valves. The goal was to reduce the squish area and promote turbulence so that the relatively high compression ratio of 8.5 to one could be used with low-lead and no-lead gas.

This was a modern engine designed from the pan up for emissions compliance. Large displacement to power a large, heavy GT coupe, and large displacement to soak up the effect of U.S. pollution controls when fitted. Results were exceptional for the time, as the 928s sold in the U.S. and Europe both had the same compression ratios and nearly identical power outputs, 240 bhp versus 219 bhp. The difference in these net power figures largely came from the fact that the former was in slightly more exaggerated DIN form, whereas the latter was an SAE figure. By comparison the Jaguar XJ-S 5.3 V12 produced 285 horses in its home market, and 244 bhp when in U.S. trim, both net figures in SAE form.

So, the 928 avoided the pitfall of "U.S. dilution" common at the time, but power in itself is meaningless unless it can be harnessed to produce total performance. In this respect the 928 remained true to Porsche practice, but with some variations from the norm. A transaxle was present and accounted for, but to avoid the 911's sudden oversteer, the 928's V8 motor lived at the front of the car. There was a solid hook-up between the front-engine and rear gearbox, mounted in front of the final drive: within a torque tube turned a slim driveshaft

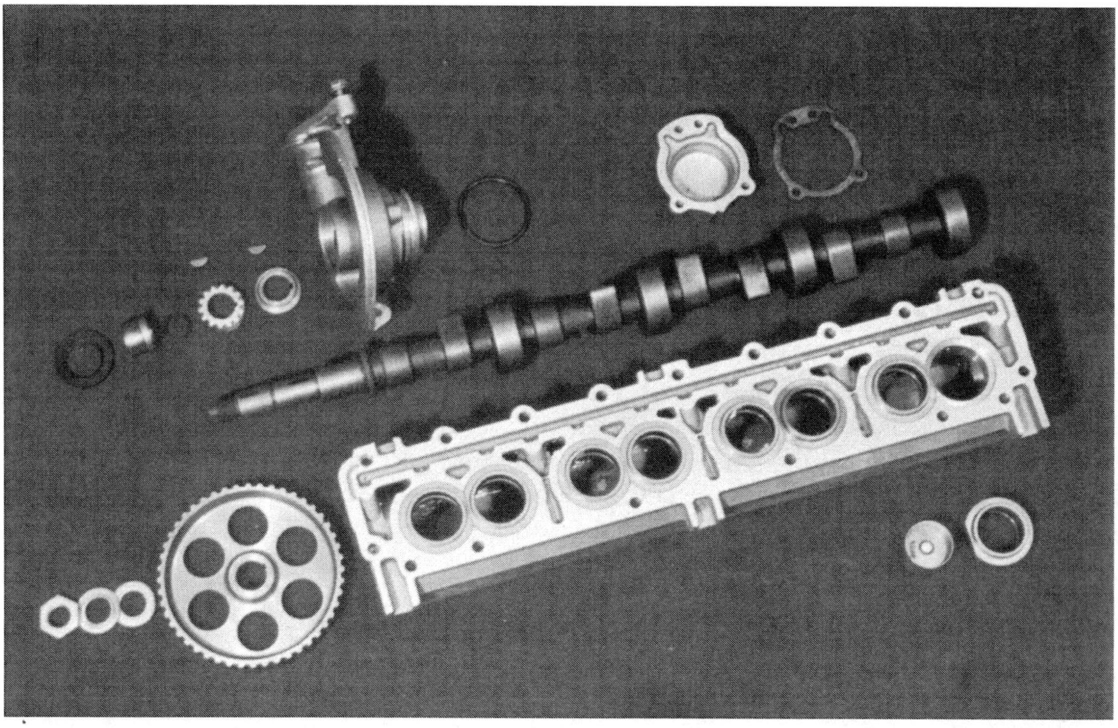

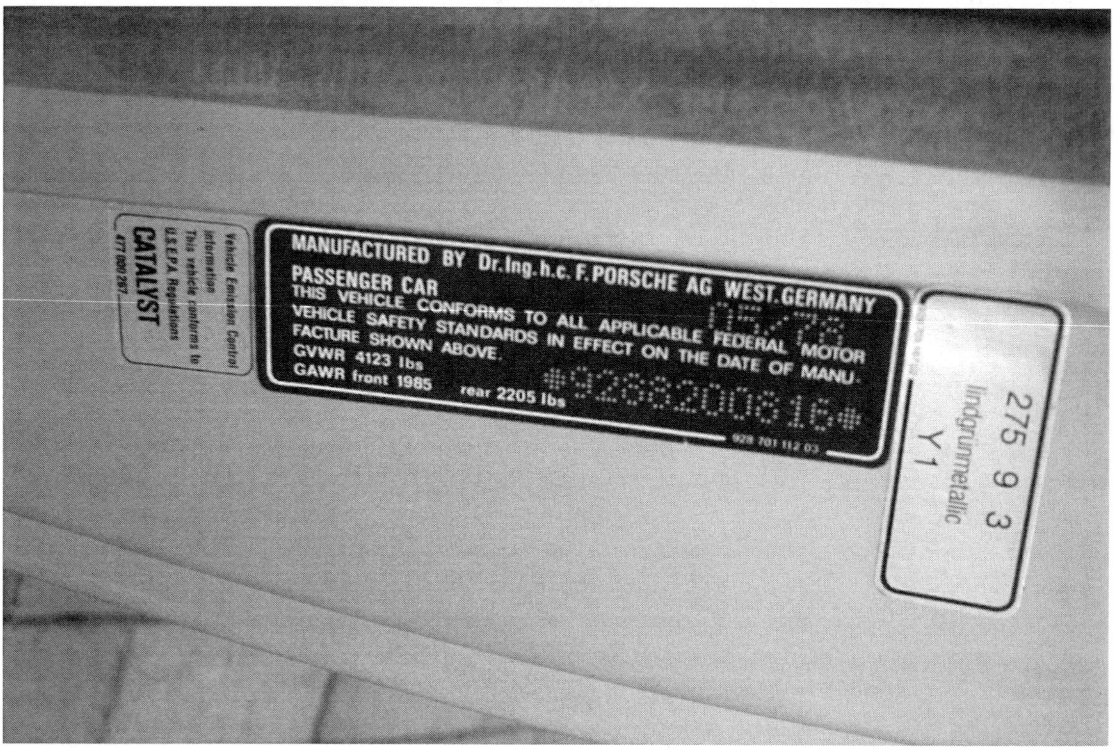

Top: The two valve per cylinder componentry used to produce the 928's SOHC arrangement. Not exactly a high performance V8 yet, it would become one in time (courtesy Porsche). ***Bottom:*** The 928 had no reason to fear the catalytic converter. In spite of power rating differences the 1978 Euro and U.S. spec 5-speeds had equal performance, thanks to Porsche's low tune 4.5 V8 (courtesy Chuck & Tina Zachman).

running in two sealed bearings. The slim driveshaft and the use of a twin-plate clutch, mounted at the motor end, helped to cut the inertia and vagueness associated with transaxle layouts. Having the transaxle ahead of the final drive was of benefit to interior seating efficiency.

The Weissach Axle

The upshot of such drivetrain furniture rearrangement was almost-even weight distribution for the 928, 50.3/49.7 percent compared to 36.2/63.8 percent for a contemporary Porsche 930. The first step towards neutral handling had been taken, the second was the use of the new magic "Weissach Axle." The Weissach axle was a patented Porsche design, and the world's first form of passive rear-wheel steering. It took its name from Porsche's engineering center. The 928's rear suspension consisted of independent lower wishbone, upper transverse link with coil springs, telescopic shocks and an anti-sway bar.

In regular independent-rear-suspension set-ups, the loaded outer rear wheel can toe out when a driver backs off in a corner, inducing oversteer. The Weissach axle introduced a toe-in change to ward off the oversteer. To achieve this, the lower rear wishbone axis was inclined to the 928's longitudinal axis, but the action of the upper transverse link was even more important. The forward end of the lower tubular radius arm was connected to the 928's body via the transverse link. When backing off in a corner, the radius arm and link were pulled back to achieve the counterbalancing toe-in. The flexibility of movement was kept in check by rubber bushes.

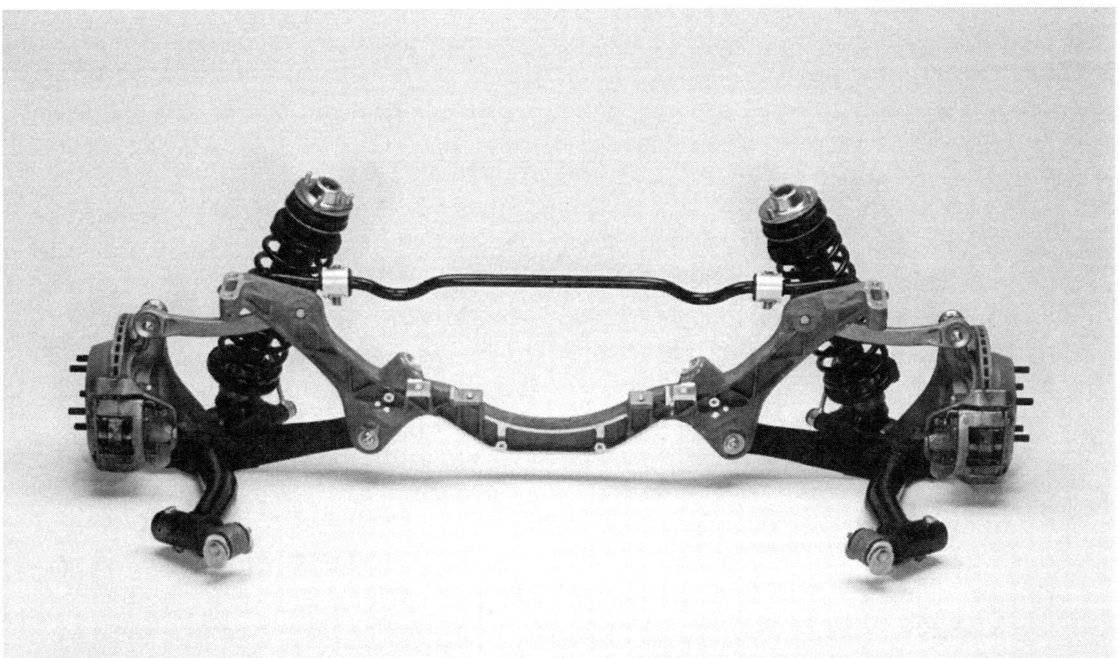

Named after Porsche's engineering HQ, the magic Weissach axle provided rear wheel steer at a time when the concept was unknown to the public. It kept the heavyweight 928 nice and neutral (courtesy Porsche).

Test-bed vehicle for the Weissach axle was an Opel Admiral fitted with rear steering. This unusual test car had two drivers, with the rear driver manipulating the rear steering in response to the front driver's backing off or lifting off the throttle. It was through this experiment that Porsche's engineers discerned the amount of passive rear steer to build into the rear suspension. The front of the 928 was more regular in design, featuring double wishbones cast in aluminum alloy, with coil springs around strut-type shocks. The front anti-sway bar worked on short pushrods. The hardware kept unsprung weight down, had anti-dive properties, and used negative scrub radius to achieve stable braking when the 928's sets of wheels lay on different-textured road surfaces.

Porsche tuned the 928's suspension to work with the high-performance, wide-section, low-profile (50 series) Pirelli P7. The first generation of ultra-low-profile tire, the 1974 P7 was a sticky customer that was part of the 928's ride comfort/handling compromise. These state-of-the-art tires were wrapped around futuristic-looking "Phone Dial" cast aluminum rims of 16 × 7 inches. Unusually for the time, the Phone Dial rims showed off a fair amount of the 928's 4-wheel ventilated brake disks. Disks were 11.1 inches front, 11.4 inches rear, and used floating calipers as part of a diagonally split system.

Functional Form

The modernity of the new Phone Dial rims continued with the 928's exterior styling. Functional, clean, with no chrome work to be seen. It was up-to-date in a different way than the newish models of the day, such as the Daimler-Benz SLC, BMW 6-series and Jaguar XJ-S. It looked like a spaceship, it looked like an alien, and with those circular bug eyes it looked like a descendant of the VW Bug Dr. Ferdinand Porsche created in the 1930s! Resembling a smoothed-out, folded-over 21st-century edition of the VW Beetle, the 928 had to be a different kind of modern because Porsche doesn't like to waste time and money reworking a car's look on a whim.

Porsche's styling boss Tony Lapine was responsible for the 928's road-missile styling, but don't jump to conclusions concerning the slippery shape. Although launched after the fuel crisis, car designers hadn't yet embraced aerodynamics to improve gas mileage, that would follow in the 1980s. So even though a 928 in German racing silver might look like it could have carved its way through the air like a bullet, its drag coefficient was a mediocre 0.42. Still, out on the 'bahn, directional and crosswind stability count for a lot, and the 928 was certainly up to speed in those areas. It changed lanes only when one wanted it to.

What you could see of the 928 was the continued use of weight-saving aluminum for the coupe's doors, hood and front fenders. The rest used galvanized steel so that Porsche could offer its long-life, 6-year anti-rust warranty. The 928's most obvious visual feature was its Miura-style, magic swivel-up front headlights, felt to be a good idea because, unlike conventional pop-up lamps, they don't tend to be forgotten about when the car is cleaned. Then there was what you couldn't see, namely the 928's invisible bumpers. They were there, aluminum bars hiding behind a polyurethane nose finished off with elastic, knock-resistant paint.

The 928 came standard with impact-resistant, insurance-friendly bumpers, so U.S. 928s looked the same as their home market counterparts. Elegant, yes, but now you couldn't get your friend to use the usual extended 5-mph bumpers of Mercedes, BMW, etc., as a platform from which to look out for small animals you might accidentally run over, should your

Top: **The 928 project predated the 924 and bestowed upon the smaller car the torque tube/transaxle layout. However, with the 928 the gearbox was in front of the final drive (courtesy Porsche).** ***Bottom:*** **It's official, the user-friendly, multipurpose 928 is a friend of the furry animal! (courtesy Porsche).**

headlights fail at night and force you to crawl home at low speed. Still, the 928's soft deformable bumper would have probably bounced any furry animals safely out of the way, with damage to neither 928 nor small creature!

The Lap of Luxury

On the inside of the 928, quality materials and functional design continued. No forests were harmed so that its interior could be wood trimmed; instead the driver was greeted with Porsche all-action, three-spoke steering wheel, and a low-mounted, energy-absorbing dash molding of fine finish. You have sat down, played with the driver's seat, using manual or optional powered adjustment, but your relationship to the controls is still less than it should be? No problem, adjust the steering column rake and watch in disbelief as the entire instrument pod moves in unison!

Porsche felt that, after 15 years of 911 life, it was time to get comfy. The auto connoisseur could now maintain unobscured sight lines with speedo, tach, voltmeter, gas, coolant temp and oil pressure. The steering column stalks and pod-mounted switches also moved with rake adjustment. With the help of spacers, even the pedals could be adjusted. In total, the 928 was a triumph for driver ergonomics, and the comfort extended to a comprehensive

No wood trim appeared on the 928's space age dash molding, and the entire instrument binnacle was height adjustable (courtesy Chuck & Tina Zachman).

heating and ventilation system. The Porsche 928 came with Behr air conditioning as standard equipment, and several moveable dash, and even door-mounted, grilles to direct airflow at will.

The door-situated vent grilles were smart for demisting fogged-up side window glass, but the whole system had the all-too-common contemporary trait of the dashboard's two center vent grilles dispensing air only when the a/c mode was switched on. The alternative was to rely on the fresh air coming from the door grilles, not sufficient by itself, or open a window. The shortcoming seemed incongruous with a future-mobile like the 928.

If that's where the driver is placed, where does one store passengers, oddments and luggage? In keeping with the 911, the 928 was a 2+2 coupe. It possessed two well-shaped and -trimmed rear buckets, even if the size back there was tight for any person of reasonable size. The 928 was a bigger kind of Porsche, but for real back-seat accommodation the Mercedes 450SLC was still a better bet.

Oddments were well catered for. Below the lockable glovebox lay a parcel shelf. If the door armrests were extended they revealed convenient map pockets. Between the rear seats was a flip-up cubby storage box. For larger items, the owner resorted to the 928's rear hatch. Normal rear cargo capacity was 6.3 cubic feet, around the size of the trunk of a contemporary Camaro. However, fold forward the rear seat backs, and capacity was boosted to a commodious 20.5 cu ft. A luggage cover prevented unwanted eyes from observing the hatch's contents through the rear glass.

A classier display than the VW Rabbit–like 924's, and the absence of Porsche's counterclockwise tach gave the 928 the sedate air of a grand tourer (courtesy Chuck & Tina Zachman).

Once the rear seats were folded down the 928 was a two-seater with 20.5 cu ft worth of load space, and a luggage cover to conceal items. Porsche also included rear sunvisors for rear seat passengers to use on sunny days (courtesy Chuck & Tina Zachman).

Thoughtful Porsche touches were here and there for driver and passenger. Front sunvisors are everywhere, but what about rear sunvisors so that back-seat passengers don't catch too much sunlight from the 928's expansive rear hatch glass? Six high-pressure water jets were provided, four for the windshield and two for the 928's headlights. Beyond that, an auxiliary supply of concentrated washer fluid was rigged up to squirt extra-stubborn windshield insect splat. Strangely enough there was no washer jet for the rear hatch glass.

As per sports car practice, the handbrake was located to the left of the driver's seat on left-hand-drive 928s. At this location were adjusters for front and rear speaker balance, and headlamp beam height adjustment, the latter useful when the car's body angle became affected by different passenger and luggage loads. On the driver's armrest existed an adjuster and toggle switch for the powered and heated rear-view mirrors.

Time to Change Gear

Was the 928 really a sports car? Its specification seemed to show Porsche was having a hard time deciding. Standard air conditioning — but also an air-conditioned glovebox? And what was this, power-assisted steering in a Porsche? All happened to be true, for the 928 was the first Porsche road car with power steering: a speed-sensitive ZF rack and pinion system so fully weighted and communicative of road feel that it didn't feel powered at all, but it was. And if one could have power steering, then why not automatic transmission? Not semi-automatic, but a fully automatic, stick-it-in-"D"-and-forget-it set up, with the cushioning comfort of a torque converter. The 928 had this available as well.

There were rumors that Porsche's 4.5 V8 was related to Daimler-Benz's 1970s SOHC 4.5 V8, in much the same way that some thought the Rolls-Royce aluminum V8 was a copy of a U.S. OHV design. Not so, Rolls-Royce and Porsche had come up with their own unique powerplants in-house. Nothing less would have been suitable for such esteemed marques. However, when it came to sourcing a slushbox, such small specialist car makers were open to outside assistance.

Rolls-Royce turned to the GM THM 400 automatic, Porsche looked to the 3-speed auto of the Mercedes 450SEL 6.9. Porsche were really after those heavy-duty gearbox internals designed to cope with the onslaught of 6.9-liter torque. In other respects the 928's 3 speed automatic was a custom job. To be precise, a special 928 housing for the MB gearbox internals, which incorporated the torque converter and fitted onto the final drive unit. That said, the same bell housing was used at the engine end as in a normal 928 5-speed manual. However, this housing now carried only the ring gear for the starter motor to engage with.

The 928's luxurious rear compartment exceeded that of any previous Porsche, but space was still tight for anyone except kids and pets (courtesy Chuck & Tina Zachman).

Porsche made their adjustments, and chose their own ratios, so that the 3 speed auto behaved in a Porsche-like manner. That meant starting off in first even on a light throttle, whereas Daimler-Benz tradition had been towards 2nd gear take-offs for seamless plutocratic progress unless the gas pedal was tromped on very hard. The two marques also diverged in the shifter department, with Porsche eschewing the Daimler-Benz trademark zig-zag gate in favor of a regular fore/aft, straight-plane, T-bar automatic handle.

Hmmm, a T-bar automatic, just the thing to keep your hands free when receiving drive-thru service at McDonalds. No one wants to handle a shift while trying to avoid being scalded by a cup of super-heated java! So far we have power steering, automatic, and — the third member of the holy trinity of snooze? That would be the 928's standard "Tempostat" cruise control, activated by the little stalk below the wash/wipe steering-column controller. But Porsche still sent gentle reminders as to what it was all about in their cyber coupe.

The 928 marked the first appearance of Phone Dial aluminum rims. It was also a first for the madcap checkered flag-style seat and door trim cloth inlays known as Pasha. Porsche further stirred the enthusiast into action with the availability of a new 5-speed manual box. It naturally had Porsche synchromesh and a direct one-to-one fifth gear. No sleepy overdrive ratios for this car, and with a flourish of nostalgic style, a racing shift. Yes, the old trick of putting first down and left below reverse, keeping 2nd through 5th in the handy H pattern where racers spend most of their day.

928 Dreaming

The psychedelic Pasha pattern seemed to be moving, you had used first's 3.60 mountain-master ratio to escape pit lane, and had skillfully managed to avoid snicking reverse on the way into 2nd. Was it Jacky Ickx, Hurley Haywood, or you commanding the 540-horse Porsche 936 to victory at Le Mans 1977? In the midst of all that padding the 928 could still awaken the racer in one. Dr. Fuhrmann's promise of bringing Porsche's road and race cars closer together was being delivered. It was genuine Porsche, according to *Road & Track*; "... how Porsche manages to make the heater smell the same as it does in its air-cooled cars is a perplexing question."*

With a base sticker price of $28,500 U.S., or 19,499 pounds sterling U.K., the new 928 was a lot of money, priced between a 911SC and 930 turbo, but it was also a lot of Porsche. Its length was 175 in., height 51.9 in., and width an AMC Pacer–like 72.3 in. As a side note, the 1975 AMC Pacer's rear styling influenced the same part of the 928! Porsche's heavyweight tipped the scales at 3,197 lbs. in European trim. The few extra pounds of the U.S. version, 3,410 lbs., made it generally on a par with the 1977 L82 350 Corvette in size, weight and raw performance figures. However, the 928 was never just a bunch of stats. Weighty compared to the lithe 911. Tough to compare with other Porsches, or indeed with cars from other manufacturers.

The 928 was well equipped, and when compared to the 911 its luxury could be described as the difference between "built in" and "added on." Hydraulic tappets and water jackets to quieten, a Bosch 4-speaker cassette-deck stereo to soothe, and numerous rubber bushings used to good effect. Front and rear subframes were utilized for refinement. The transverse link and

*R.M. Clarke, *Porsche 928 Performance Portfolio 1977-1994* (Brooklands Books, 1995) p. 20.

lower wishbones' rear pivot were attached to the rear sub-frame. So too were the gearbox and final drive, creating a rigid unit in association with the torque tube/motor, battery and exhaust-system rear section. Between the rear subframe and gearbox was another set of hydraulic shocks.

Rightly in control, isolated in your speed capsule, but all the while big brother was watching. The 928's "big brother" came in the form of a dash warning-light system far beyond mere idiot lights. As one powered along in this automotive Lockheed SR-71 Blackbird, a system error was brought to your attention by a flashing light. As test pilot your gaze fell upon the 928's instrument panel. Problems could be priority 1 (brake circuit pressure, brake fluid level, low engine oil, etc.), or priority 2 (windshield washer fluid level, coolant temp, brake pad wear, etc.). With the latter you could cancel the flashing light and deal with it at your leisure, but priority 1 stuff had to be fixed there and then. The light kept on flashing until the problem had been rectified.

928 — Car of the Year

The 928 wasn't the sort of car that left things to chance. It was that thoroughness that helped it become European Car of the Year for 1978. The COTY title normally throws up mainstream vehicles as winners. Quite often those extreme character traits, or perhaps even flaws, that endear a vehicle to the driver are the qualities that screen out an enthusiast machine

The sign of a champion — in 1978 the 928 had achieved something that even the much vaunted 911 had failed to do on debut (courtesy Chuck & Tina Zachman).

from winning the title. After all, the 911 itself had failed to win European COTY when it was a debutante.

The 928 had the practical side of things down cold. It could make as much sense as a 1-liter, 4-cylinder supermini if it had to, and it was this cover-all-bases game plan that saw a panel of automotive scribes give it two thumbs up. Perhaps it was the way the 928 flattered the driving skills of the judges? Perhaps they were grateful it didn't send them oversteering backwards into a bush like their first 911 encounter? We will never know. What we do know is that the 928 became the first sports car to win Car of the Year Europe. The car that actually predated the 924's development had earned a come-from-behind victory.

Chapter 8

V8 Evolution—Adding a Little, and a Little...

1964 911 2.0 vs. 1977 928

So there you were on a continental autoroute doing some high-speed cruising in a new 928 5-speeder. In the rear-view mirror was a fast-approaching speck that turned out to be an early Porsche 911 2.0. Time to see what the 928 could do! Speed rose up from 90 mph gradually, and to your slight surprise the 928's older brother was still holding on, as you slotted the shift lever down to the right into fifth, with six grand on the tach at nearly 120 mph. The gas pedal still had some travel left, and finally the 911 was losing grasp of your slipstream as the 928 edged over 130 mph.

Honor had been upheld for both parties, but where exactly had all those stock-market dollars got one, and what had they purchased? The build quality was everything hoped for, and the bark of the 4.5-liter V8 by Porsche always delighted on start up. That first throttle blip produced a sound akin to the finest Trans Am 6.6 motor ever hand-assembled. All in all, the buyer was happy he traded in the MB 450 SL. The three-pointed star made one seem older than really necessary, and the 928's rear seats had their uses. Plus, the 928 even ran on low-grade gas like an old late–'60s 911T, and a penny saved was a penny earned.

However, how far up the road had Porsche, and the world, come since the early 1960s? The first 911 2-liter cranked out 130 horses and galloped with flat-six zeal on up to 130 mph. Now, in the late '70s, a 240-horse soft eight glided up to 140 mph with muted roar. A victory had been earned over the pursuing 911, but the 928 was feeling the heat. The falling gas gauge needle reminded one that overall mpg was no longer in the 911's 20s, it was now in the teens.

But the 928's refinement was appreciated. The fact the pursuing 911's flat six could be heard above the 928 V8 was the source of some mirth. However, uneasiness remained: where to now for the 928? Would one have to wait for the aging Maserati Mistral's I6 motor to overheat before delivering a crushing blow on the Autobahn, and what if it was winter? As is usually the case, the past provided the solution. Porsche and power begin with "P," and they both imply speed. Speed begins with the letter "S."

Pump Up the Volume

Porsche had feverishly redeployed the 911's 1,991 cc, 130 bhp flat six. They raised the compression ratio, fitted more aggressive cams and altered the valves to improve breathing. Different carburetion for greater fuel delivery, it added up to the first hot 911, the 911S of July

PORSCHE

1966. One could do that sort of thing in the carefree sixties, but what about now? Surely the second fuel crisis of 1979 would see performance go down, not up? Such was the case for most other car makers, but Porsche wasn't like other car makers!

For Porsche, the recent doubling in world oil prices spurred them to seek greater efficiency with two new versions of the 928, introduced in the fall of 1979. The high-profile version provided what would be the 928's biggest single power jump in its entire life, the new 928S. Recognizing the need to make a good thing faster, Porsche introduced a series of upgrades to arm the 928 against fierce competition and the 1980s. For the 928S, Porsche reworked the usual 4.5-liter motor into a 300-horsepower 4.7 V8. Displacement rose from 4,474 cc to 4,664 cc, thanks to a bore-size rise from 95 to 97 mm, making the Porsche V8 even more oversquare. Compression ratio of the V8 increased from 8.5 to 10 to one, and was accompanied by hotter camshafts.

Previously max power was produced at 5,500 rpm, now the full 300 horses arrived further up at 5,900 rpm. Peak torque used to come in at 3,600 rpm, now the larger figure of 283.4 lbs./ft. was produced at 4,500 rpm. To rein in the extra punch the 928's brake disks were thicker, and the calipers were also strengthened. Visually the 928 was no longer such a clean-looking, unadorned sculpture. The 928S had a front airdam incorporating two front-brake cooling apertures. At the rear a modest polyurethane spoiler framed the base of the rear hatch glass and rear 3/4 glazing.

These aero aids lowered the 928's drag factor from 0.42 to 0.38. Slippery through the air, and with more horses under the hood, the 5-speed 928S had a claimed top speed of 156 mph, a claim which was backed up by independent testing. There was little doubt that the extra "S" had transformed the 928 into a much more focused performance machine. It had the measure of the by-now 3-liter 911 for acceleration, and top speed was knocking on the door of the 160 mph 911 Turbo. The latter 911 had been up-gunned to 3.3 liters and an even 300 horses in 1978.

Compared to the normal 928, acceleration times for 0–60 mph and 1/4 mile were down from 7 and 15.2 seconds to 6.2 and 14.2 seconds. As acceleration times fell, gas mileage rose from 14.9 to 16 mpg. These were the efficiency improvements brought by the more powerful high–CR engine. The downside was that the European spec 928S was forced to use 98 octane Superbenzin. However, for the rich individual such trifles didn't trouble the mind while the temperature of the 928's new climate control a/c, with larger center console dash vents, automatically adjusted for a long summer jaunt down to the South of France.

The other revised version of the 928 was the regular 928. It shared the 928S's CR hike up to 10 to one, and with it an improvement in peak torque to 280 lbs./ft. at the same 3,600 rpm. Power output of the 4.5-liter V8 stayed at 240 horses, coming in at 5,250 rpm. This made the 4.5 V8 an even better match for the 3 speed automatic, which received the same alterations made to handle the "S" version's extra moxie. Both 928 editions sported different rolling stock to suit their character in the expanded model range.

The 928S now wore forged 16-inch "Disc" style aluminum rims, but still with the 225/50

Opposite, top: **In the late 1970s the 928 was the cutting edge grand tourer to have while cruising Continental autoroutes at 120 mph+ (courtesy Chuck & Tina Zachman).** ***Opposite, bottom:*** **Never one to rest on its laurels, Porsche was keen to incorporate the 928 into its "S" mechanical enhancement program. In doing so some of the clean form of Tony Lapine's styling would be lost (courtesy Chuck & Tina Zachman).**

Porsche used the traditional hot rodder tricks of higher compression ratio, big cams and displacement to bring the Porsche V8 up to 4.7 liters and an even 300 ponies — in Europe (courtesy Porsche).

VR-rated Pirelli P7s that the 928 commenced life with. As the soft member of the clan, the regular 928 was now delivered with 15 × 7–inch Phone Dials, wrapped with less-extravagant VR-rated Pirelli P6s of 215/60 size, but the old P7s could still be ordered. The smaller rims and tires improved the refinement of the 928's ride comfort, without compromising the car's already sound handling. Porsche let the big brother 928S make all the noise from this point on.

And the 928 would have to make some noise, given the upgrades embraced by its Swabian and Bavarian rivals. Regardless of the second gas crunch, prestigious auto makers knew that the only way to lead is from the front. To this end Daimler-Benz was testing out its own new lightweight, all-aluminum, 5-liter 240-horse V8, replacing the trusty cast iron–block, 225

Impressive as this 1978 928 4.5 was, it would soon become the base model in a two-car range in which the 928S was the hot one (courtesy Porsche).

bhp 4.5 V8, in their 1979 450SLC. BMW had up-engined the 633CSi into the 140 mph+ 1979 635CSi. You had to keep your wits about yourself in such high-speed 2+2 seater road games. The 928S's 300 bhp 4.7 V8 wasn't a luxury, it was a necessity. After all, one's reputation is at stake!

928 Competition Package

That was great if there was market access to the European 928 range, in the U.S. it was more a case of trying to maintain position. Starting off with the same performance figures as a Euro spec 928, Porsche had taken steps to keep the 928 equally quick in the face of

Top: Ferry Porsche in 1979, with a 70th birthday present from the Porsche workforce — the new 300 bhp 928S! Porsche's answer to the upgraded BMW 635CSi and Mercedes-Benz 450SLC (courtesy Porsche). ***Bottom:*** Aerodynamically enhanced from 0.42 to 0.38 Cd, the new 928S could reach 156 mph and hit 60 mph in a bit over 6 seconds. It was a great way to kick off the 1980s (courtesy Porsche).

tightening pollution and mileage restrictions. Initially the U.S. 928 used a 2-way catalytic converter and unleaded gas. In 1980 Porsche, as with others, upgraded to a 3-way catalytic converter with Bosch Lambda Sond exhaust-mounted oxygen sensor. To facilitate the change to the three-way cat, the 928 dumped Bosch K-Jetronic, replacing it with Bosch L-Jetronic.

Bosch L-jet had an actual engine-management computer that made it easier for the Lambda sensor to send back its corrective signal, and hold the air/fuel mix at a certain level to control nitrogen oxide, carbon monoxide and unburned hydrocarbons. It made for easier engine tuning to meet stricter emissions targets without a power drop. For 1981, the odd step of introducing the infamous air pump was taken. That back pressure-inducing harbinger of doom had never been a friend of the car enthusiast, until now. Porsche engineers decided to direct the air pump's output into the cat's oxidation chamber, actually boosting the converter's efficiency.

Everything was on the up. The U.S. version couldn't match the Euro CR level of 10 to one, but in 1980 it had risen from the original 8.5 up to 9 to one. The U.S. 928 was featuring power and torque figures of 220 bhp at 5,500 rpm and 265 lbs./ft. at 4,000 rpm. Plus its 1981 EPA gas mileage rating had improved by one. The five-speed manual was still available, a feature dropped by many rivals who went to auto only. The front suspension wishbone geometry changes of 1981 European 928s also appeared on the U.S. car, as did stiffer brake calipers and the weight savings of replacing a solid 20 mm rear anti-sway bar with a tubular 22.5 mm equivalent.

The more powerful 928S was even more fuel efficient than the standard 928, a useful quality in the aftermath of the second world fuel crisis of 1979 (courtesy Porsche).

However, there was something missing: a real 928S. Yes, the best 928 sold in North America in the early '80s was equivalent to the normal 928, at least in a straight line. Porsche didn't want to sully the U.S. 928 with a phony label, but they saw no reason why the car's over-the-road reflexes couldn't be sharpened. The result was the $1,100 Competition Package, which gave one the look of a Euro 928S for relatively modest outlay. The pack included front air dam, rear spoiler, 16 × 7 forged Disc alloys with Pirelli P7 225/50 VR or Goodyear NCT 16-inch tires, firmer shock absorbers and leather-covered, 930-flavor steering wheel.

So there was now a fair distinction between the automatic U.S. 928, and a 5-speed 928 with the Competition Package. The former had been rolling around on 15-inch rims with Dunlop SP Sport 215/60 VR tires since 1979 model year. The fat-cat buyers could enjoy their softer ride comfort and play with their optional powered seats. No power seat option with the Competition Package, just single-minded sports seats with side bolsters that invited one to exploit the handling advantages of the CP. With CP you had all the right pieces to deal with a FE7 Gymkhana pack–equipped C3 Corvette out on a twisty back road.

The 928 was making its way through tough times as the company *Flaggschiff* in the U.S. The blown 930 had departed in 1979 model year, the 4-speed and turbo flat six not in keeping with CAFE or tightening pollution law. The 911SC was still running around, faster and cheaper than the 928, it has to be said. Uncertain and uneasy times at Porsche too. Dr.

All well and good for Europe with its 928S, but the relatively calm U.S. 928 4.5 also needed a power boost to stay in touch with the movers and shakers (courtesy www.928registry.org).

A 1983 automatic example of the new 234 bhp U.S. 928S, a real "S" for the U.S. at long last (courtesy Gary Quayle).

Fuhrmann had pushed the case for the front-engined cars, but as of November 1980 he had departed from the position of Porsche Chairman. The Porsche 911 was supposed to be dead by now, but it wasn't.

A Real U.S. 928S

In convoluted Porsche land there was only one way for the 928 to go, and that was up, with a real 928S for the U.S. Porsche started a good thing with the multi-market, sensible-compression, 180 and 240 horse, 3-liter flat 6 and 4.5 V8. Tightening emissions law outpaced Porsche's desire to offer the same to all. As with rivals, it started to withhold its best hardware from North America, opening the doors to the grubby gray marketers. Getting the 944 a half-decent powerplant that could cope with unleaded gas helped the 928's cause.

Lessons from the TOP (Thermodynamically Optimized Porsche) 2.5 I4 944 motor were transferred to come up with the 1983 U.S. 928S. This model had the same 4.7-liter capacity as the Euro 928S, courtesy of the 2 mm bore increase, but a compression ratio of 9.3 rather than 10 to one. Flywheel horsepower climbed from 220 to 234 bhp at 5,500 rpm, whereas torque was marginally down from 1981's 265 to 263 lbs./ft. at the same 4,000 rpm. The TOP cylinder head was trying to get good performance with unleaded gas and a relatively high compression ratio. The efficiency gain added up to even better EPA city and highway mileage figures of 16/27.

The prize for being frugal was a longer cruising range on a 22.7-gallon tankful of 91 octane unleaded. Convenient, but the real bonus was sparking some life into the 928's V8. The mellow V8 had been energized into a purposeful go-getter. And Porsche showed their

Top: Sitting in the driver's seat of the new U.S. 928S placed one in charge of the fastest production car sold in America at the time (courtesy Gary Quayle). ***Bottom:*** Improvements in the U.S. 928's power came courtesy of the 944's "TOP" combustion chamber design, giving rise to a high performance unleaded gas 4.7 liter V8 (courtesy Gary Quayle).

pride by trotting out a rather bold claim. Overcome the 928S's 43-grand sticker shock, and you would own the fastest production car for sale in the U.S. The claim was no lie, and would hold true even when the 4-valve Ferrari 308 Quattrovalvole and 1984 C4 TBI 350 Corvette were introduced.

At the time the national speed limit was still 55 mph to save lives and gas, so speed shootouts were hypothetical. However, if there was a stretch of clear, glass-smooth highway (the Vette needed it smooth), and one could max them out without fear from the cops, the new Corvette would get a little under 140 mph, the Ferrari 308 a little over, and the U.S. 928S a few mph further still over Maranello's midget. Not bad, considering the Vette and 308 only had 2 seats to haul. The moral of the story? Magnum P.I. needed a faster car!

The 928S allowed the memory of the final 930 to fade somewhat, it seemed to give the public permission to start liking the 928. In 1983 the 928 even dazzled on the silver screen, with its headlights swivelling skywards in *Scarface* with Al Pacino, and taking part in an impromptu street drag race with a Subaru Leone 12 in *Risky Business* with Tom Cruise. The 928 won the race, by the way. The 928 was finding its feet, a purpose and direction. From this point on it would be known as—Supercar! And yet the uneasiness continued.

928—A Time to Specialize

German-born, American-raised Peter Schutz took over as Porsche Chairman on January 1, 1981. He was very pleased to preside over and be pictured with the new-in-1982 911

The $43,000 U.S. 928S was still in possession of the highest top speed in America, even after the arrival of Ferrari's 308 Quattrovalvole and the 1984 TBI Corvette (courtesy Gary Quayle).

This 928S went on to finish 22nd at 1983's Le Mans 24-hour race (courtesy Porsche).

Cabrio. Perhaps nothing underlined the curious state of affairs better than the engine of the 200-mph, 959 all-wheel-drive "Gruppe B" racer unveiled at the 1983 Frankfurt motor show. It looked like a futuristic 911, was rear-engined, but its twin-turbo 2.9-liter flat six had water-cooled heads! If the 959's motor was an each-way bet regarding Porsche's future, the 928 itself seemed settled into a pattern of power.

In the beginning it was envisaged that 928 production would settle at an initial 5,000 units per year. This level was attained, but by 1981 had yet to advance from it as originally hoped. Sales never threatened to dry out completely, as was the case with some selected rivals. However, even the optimist had to admit that the big coupe concept was floundering. Jaguar XJ-S sales were at a standstill, De Tomaso Longchamp trickling, and Chrysler-powered expresses like the English Jensen Interceptor and French Monica mere faded memories.

It seemed like the Auto Vittorio 928 SK belonged to a different time. The German tuning house of Vittorio Strosek created an aerodynamically enhanced 928 with two superchargers. In the Vee of the 4.7-liter V8 lay a couple of Roots-style blowers, taking the place of the 928's stock intake manifold. The usual 928's Bosch K-Jetronic fuel injection metered gas into the blowers, which forced air and fuel into the 8 to one CR V8. Power was a shade over 450 horses, and top speed, with a taller final drive ratio, was up to 183 mph.

The 928 SK had a large rear wing, an elaborate front spoiler which involved losing the 928's normal headlights, and sill extensions. Flared wheel arches accommodated 8-inch front and 9-inch rear three-piece BBS rims for the familiar 225/50 VR Pirelli P7s. Zero to sixty-two mph was 5.2 seconds, and the only thing going faster was your money. In Germany the entire exercise, excluding supplying your 928, cost $49,500!

Strosek's early 928 design study, which incorporated two superchargers but no headlights due to the car's frontal restyling. Note that in spite of the new larger rear wing, the regular 928S-S3 rear bib spoiler was retained (courtesy Strosek www.strosek.de).

Strosek's main business has always been the look, quality body kit, and wheels that make one's Porsche stand out from other Porsches. A worthwhile quality on German streets, and there continued to be something special for the 928 while it was a current model. This extended to an eventual convertible, and even a gullwing conversion. Strosek did have a few agents outside Germany, but the gullwing conversion could be performed only at Strosek's home in Utting am Ammersee.

Strosek liked to manipulate Porsche styling, and the stock headlights were a barrier in that respect. On the early–'80s 928 SK, the loss of the regular headlights was compensated for by Strosek by including four square spotlamps, which weren't all that bright. However, by the early '90s, the use of small projector headlights had become a Strosek trademark and permitted bright light plus styling freedom on 911s and 928S4s.

The loss of the bare-bones-spec 928 in the German home market during 1982, and sole presence of the 928S from that point on, signaled the end of Porsche's dream that the 928 would expand in volume and take over from the evergreen 911. The signs of a turning tide were there on the track, and in the dirt: the disguised Jost 908 that almost won Le Mans in 1980, and the old-time 936 that actually did win the 24-hour torture test in 1981 with Jacky Ickx at the wheel for his fifth win.

Then there was the all-wheel-drive, Rothmans-sponsored 911 rally car, whizzing along desert sand in the 1984 Paris-Dakar rally. And of course the new 231-horse, 3.2-liter engine for the 1984 Carrera. That said, the 928 could improve as well, and it would have to, given the amendments to the normally aspirated and turbocharged 911. In its new role as Porsche's other flagship, the 928 would evolve as only a Porsche could.

Top: **A year later and two baby steps better, this 928S crossed the line 20th overall in 1984's Le Mans (courtesy Porsche).** ***Bottom:*** **The arrival of the revised 911, in the form of this 1984 3.2 liter Carrera, showed the shift in Porsche thinking after Dr. Fuhrmann (courtesy Benny Proot).**

It was obvious by now that the 928 was never going to be the Lexus coupe of the GT class. Its ride comfort was fine at speed, the perfect car for storming down Germany's fabled Autobahn. However, like other Porsches, the 928 suffered from tire roar, and its suspension allowed one, if not to feel irregularities, then at the very least to hear them. The smaller-tire-and-rim approach of the plain automatic 928 of 1979–82 showed the symptoms could be curtailed, but did the hard-charging enthusiast really want that? There were no two ways about it, the 928 had to go aggressive.

928S II

With the standard 928 gone, Porsche could now concentrate on the "S" variant. The 928S was tweaked for 1984, and the new version was called 928S2 in the U.K. There was even a little "2" next to 928S on the revised car's tail. The 4.7-liter V8 had its Bosch K-Jetronic replaced by Bosch LH-Jetronic. Fuel mixture and ignition timing were now both controlled by the engine-management computer. Compression ratio was increased to 10.4 to one, power rose to 310 bhp at 5,900 rpm. Torque was now 295 lbs./ft. at 4,500 rpm.

A very worthwhile improvement came with the availability of the Daimler-Benz 4-speed automatic, replacing the previous 3 speed affair. The importance of this autobox came from the fact that the fourth ratio wasn't an overdrive top. Fourth was a direct one to one gear, so there was better flexibility and performance to be gained by having an extra intermediate

In spite of the later model wheels, this is indeed a 1985 Euro spec 928S2, the new "2" being an informal title to distinguish the revised 4.7 liter cars (courtesy John Hammer).

ratio. Naturally, the 5-speed manual continued to be available with its old-world, racing-shift-pattern charm.

Porsche-claimed performance figures were normally conservative. They suggested that a manual 928S2 could reach 159 mph and do 0–60 in 6 seconds, an improvement of 3 mph and 0.2 seconds over the K-jet Euro 928S. However, for once it seemed that independent testing had trouble matching Porsche's claims. That aside, the availability of the 4-speed auto called into question the worth of the manual gearbox.

The expected efficiency losses of the torque-converter automatic accounted for a 1/2 second worsening in 0–60 here, and 3 mph deterioration in top speed there. The gain was that even the novice test pilot could achieve the 928S2's performance figures time and again, without special techniques or abuse of machinery. It also saved one the eternal embarrassment of selecting reverse in a manual 928S2, when actually requiring 2nd for a dignified traffic-light take-off. The absence of Pasha upholstery, the sensible automatic: the 928 was growing up.

Improved though the 4-speed automatic was, it was still an intermediate ratio down on the normal close-ratio 5-speed. The 928S2 now weighed in at 3,390 lbs. Combine this fact with a final-drive ratio of 2.75, and on a tight twisty road there were occasions when the gap between the 4-speed's second-gear 2.412 and third-gear 1.436 ratios left the 928S2 feeling a bit muted. Not only that, the 286 bhp BMW M635CSi had made its presence felt at the 1983 Frankfurt motor show. Comparing manual to manual, it was just as fast as the 928S2, with slightly better rear-seat accommodation and a 5-speed stick that was easier to move

Enthusiasts used the 928S2's 5-speed to reach 159 mph and do zero to sixty in 6 seconds, but many preferred to leave matters to the newly available 4-speed Daimler-Benz automatic (courtesy John Hammer).

The new S2 4.7 liter V8 featured an improved 310 horses (DIN) and a switch from Bosch K-jet to Bosch LH-jet electronic fuel injection/ignition timing (courtesy John Hammer).

through the gate. Mind you, the Mercedes camp had largely thrown in the towel; the 350/450SLC was no more by this stage, its place taken by the stately and sleepy 380/500SEC. The SL range was still around, well-built and with the latest Daimler-Benz S-class all-alloy V8s. However, it was getting so old, and never embraced manual transmissions even in its youth.

Apart from pesky opposition, and a recalcitrant 5-speed, what was holding the 928 back? The answer was anti-lock brakes. The 928 became the first Porsche road car to offer ABS as optional equipment. So the stopping was good, but were weaknesses starting to appear in the 928's armor? As we entered the mid–1980s, the 928 didn't look old, but the bar was being raised by others who could see the value in being at the cutting edge of road-car achievement.

A new 1982 Camaro Z/28 and 1984 WS6 Fiero that registered 0.82g and 0.81g respectively on the skidpad, matching the 928S's 0.81g figure. New downsized 1984 Corvette and Nissan 300ZX V6 turbo models that did 0–60 in well under 8 seconds, and not far behind the 928S on top speed. Perhaps even more worryingly, a 1985 GT 5.0 Mustang that almost matched the 928S's acceleration, 0–60 in 7.0 vs. 7.2 seconds, quarter-mile in 15.4 vs. 15.9 seconds — and all for $9,885 base sticker!

S3 5.0— Keeping the Iron Yuppie Happy

The young upstarts were certainly putting on a show. Of course the 928 had never downsized. It came into being before others had, and back then it didn't seem that large. However,

In 1984 the 928S2 became the first Porsche road car to offer antilock brakes (courtesy Porsche).

by the year of the Apple Mac, $43,000 list was enough to make even the Iron Yuppie sweat. Something had to be done. That thing was the 928S3. The third S would redress the balance of power, and prove that the Blue Oval wasn't the only one with a hot five-point-O!

It wasn't all motivated by U.S. and Japanese competition; the 928S3 5.0 was part of Porsche's plan to be a good citizen and help the environment. Since the early '70s the West German government had stated its goal of phasing out leaded gasoline. By the mid to late '80s even this country was moving to a catalyst-equipped state of affairs, so it made sense to learn how to make clean power. The 928S 4.7's 234 ponies looked a meager achievement next to the much cheaper overhead-valve Mustang 5.0's 210 horses.

The 1986 U.S. 928S3 had a 32-valve, double-overhead-cam, 5-liter version of the 928's V8. The new version's 288 bhp arrived at 5,750 rpm and maximum torque was now 302 lbs./ft. at 2,700 rpm, compared with the old U.S. 4.7's 234 bhp at 5,500 rpm and 263 lbs./ft. at

The final year for the U.S. 928S 4.7 was 1985, before a new 5.0-liter model arrived for the '86 model year (courtesy www.928registry.org).

4,000 rpm. It was all about the torque, according to Porsche's driveline guru Paul Hensler. Improving the Porsche V8's bite at low-to-medium rpm was important for one so weighty. Compression ratio had risen from the outgoing U.S. "S" motor's 9.3 to one, to an even 10 to one, a move made possible by replacing Bosch L-jet with Bosch DME or Digital Motor Electronics fuel management. The use of a hotwire mass airflow sensor and twin-pipe exhaust system implied less restriction on the intake and exhaust sides.

And here's a change you can see, a new intake manifold! The first change to the style of the V8's intake apparatus since its 1977 introduction. The new "organ pipe" design looked oddly industrial in nature. Eight pipes of unequal length between a plenum for each of the V8's banks. No two consecutively firing cylinders drew breath from the same plenum; combined with the effect of the unequal organ pipes, the air in there got really shook up! Written on the plenum chambers in bold capital script was the warning "V8 4C 32V" and "PORSCHE." Ferrari weren't the only famous quattrovalvole now, and the S3 5.0 belted out greater torque than any 308 V8 ever did.

If only the S3 5.0 sang as sweetly as the Ferrari's little 3- and 3.2-liter V8s. It didn't, the Porsche V8 was never a silent partner to start with, but with its second capacity rise it was now a throbbing, rock-and-roll motor. Like the Mustang's 5.0 it now displaced 302 cubic inches, perhaps there was something in that connection? But if the S3 5.0's burble was questionable, the engineering conversion from two- to four-valve cylinder heads was never in doubt. The accommodations made to turn the V8 from SOHC to DOHC, and to four valves per cylinder, would be seen a little later on the 944S.

Porsche's Paul Hensler and team made way for a second camshaft in the cylinder head, specifically a cam for operating the inlet valves. The V8's usual single cam, driven by the familiar rubber cambelt, now operated just the exhaust valves. Towards the inside of the Vee were the new cams for the S3 5.0's inlet valves. They were driven by a chain from the cam operating the exhaust valves next door. The single-row chain carried its own damper and tensioner. To cope with the additional indirect load, the V8 rubber cambelt was upgraded with stronger material. In spite of the cylinder head's tight confines, space was still found to provide for hydraulic lifters. So both SOHC and DOHC Porsche V8s didn't need valve-clearance adjustments.

The Stefan Bellof 928S, a company car for Porsche works drivers. The late German Stefan Bellof was a Porsche 956 racer, and World Endurance sports car champ in 1984 (courtesy Porsche).

The 928S3 5.0 was certainly faster than its predecessor. *Road & Track* found the zero to sixty sprint was now dispensed in 6.3 rather than 7 seconds, and top speed had moved up to a respectable even 150 mph. But if the firepower under the hood was helping to move the 3,500-lb. S3 5.0 onto higher velocities, its gearing made the transition to light speed rather gradual. Initially the final drive was 2.75 to one, that became a tall 2.27 for the first U.S. 928S 4.7. Now the 928S3 5.0's rear ratio was an intergalactic 2.20, a bit too CAFE friendly. Porsche might have had plans for the 928 to go to Mars!

If the 928 was on its way to the red planet, another spacecraft in German racing silver would have beaten it to the finish line. Whizzing past the 928 module was a famous Apollo mission–dated design, with turbo thrust flames issuing from its whale-tail spoiler. Unfortunately for the 928S3 5.0, the 911 Turbo had returned to the U.S. market at the same time. The older car was a scant 6 horses down on the S3 5.0's power. However, the blown 911 could blast its way to sixty in 5 seconds flat, was 1 mph speedier in terminal velocity, and at $48,000 was 2 grand cheaper than the 928S3 5.0: a reversal of fortune from 1978, when the 930 was $34,150, and the U.S. 928 was a budget-friendly sub–30K. Even so, staying true to past form, the 928 was just a tad slower in acceleration than the non-turbo 911, which was itself up to 200 horses in U.S. trim.

The S3 5.0 allowed the U.S. 928 to become more boulevard bruiser than cruiser. It could almost match the Euro 4.7-liter 928S2 for acceleration and top speed, but it was still 288 SAE versus 310 DIN horsepower. More than that, it was a question of throttle response. For all its displacement and multivalve trickery, the U.S. S3 5.0 lacked the crispness of the Euro S2 4.7-liter. It was a trait noticeable in West Germany's switch to the catalytic converter

It was left to the 1987 928S4 to bring the DOHC 4-valve 5-liter V8 to all world markets, and with it several other 928 upgrades (courtesy Porsche).

route: larger-capacity versions of existing engine designs that could run on unleaded without adjustment, with or without cat. But the VW Golf GTi 2.0 16-valve I4 was never quite as sweet, or as willing, as the final U.K. leaded 1.8-liter, 16-valve equivalents. The up-displacement "clean" motors had big torque, but strained to reach their redline; they lacked enthusiasm.

And if ever there was a time for go rather than show, it was now. In the mid–1980s the price of oil was falling appreciably. The U.S. CAFE plan to move us along the road from gas hog to good citizen had stalled somewhat. It looked like it wouldn't be necessary. Time to party, with a booming performance-car market: annual revisions that made the L98 5.7 Corvette a road rocket, Mustang 5.0 GTs fighting Camaro Z/28 TPI 5.0s, a Mercedes 560SEC, and news of an all-new Jaguar sedan on the horizon. If ever the 928 needed a shot in the arm it was now.

Europe—2 Valves Good, 4 Valves Better

Since 1980 there were moments when one looked at the 928S's four-spoke steering wheel with "928" superimposed on the hub's big "S," and pondered what it would take to put the 928 back in the lead. Trying to pass the time by playing with the auto's accordion shift gaiter was no good. It seemed like others were closing in. Porsche had the remedy with the 928S4. It was time to bounce! Zuffenhausen celebrated 10 years of 928 living with the most substantial changes seen to the V8 leviathan so far, and it wasn't just about the power.

For those drivers determined to take their cars out after dark, Strosek would keep the 928's normal headlamps in the interests of road safety, but they were working on an alternative (courtesy Strosek www.strosek.de).

Moving into the 928S4 era (note the flush rear lamps), Strosek bought out their "Ultra" body enhancement package. Shown is the "Ultra Version 1" (courtesy Strosek www.strosek.de).

The big restyle for the 928 involved new nose and tail sections. Changes at the front involved a rounder visage with integrated ducts, with one set channeling air to the new bigger front brake disks. The front vented disks were now up from 11.1 to 12 inches like the 911 Turbo, the rear rotors were increased from 11.4 to 11.8 inches. The air also went to a selective, just-in-time cooling system. Slats between grille and radiator had their angle varied in three positions by computer on the basis of thermal load. Computer inputs were coolant temperature, air-conditioning R12 refrigerant gas pressure, and slushbox oil temp on automatic 928S4s. From this info, the slats were opened/closed, and the speed of the two electric radiator fans was varied, according to how hot the 928S4 was running.

The longer the slats could stay closed, the greater the aero benefit for the 928S4. When closed, the air flowed under both the new nose and an engine-bay-capsule pan between the car's nose and front doors. New side sills directed air around the 928S4's bigger rear rims. The 928 had gone asymmetric, with the usual 928 225/50 VR rubber on 16 × 7–inch front rims, but larger 245/45 tires wrapped around 16 × 8–inch rear hoops. The rims were the recognized Disc shape of 1980's 928S, but the fatter rear rims were slightly dished. At the tail end most things were integrated.

The rear lamps were practically flush, and the U.S. license plate surround bumperette blocks looked like they had melted slightly in the sun. In place of the previous European-style, canted-to-one-side, twin side-by-side pipes there was a single oval exhaust opening well faired into the new rear molding. The rear section looked smoother, and one could more

The before and after. The 1987 928S4 brought the 928's first major restyle since 1977. The smoother new look is apparent when comparing this 1980 U.S. 928 5-speed and Euro spec 1988 928S4 automatic (courtesy Garth Matheson).

easily make out glossy reflections on the bulbous surface. It still had the anonymity-defying "PORSCHE" tag stamped on the molding. For U.K. cars the "928S" script was placed below, and under the "S" was a little "4."

Subtle was the word to describe the 928's new look. Same rims, same general organic appearance. The casual observer would need before-and-after pics to appreciate how the car had morphed — if it wasn't for that new rear wing! Porsche designers had replaced the S-to-S3's rear glass hatch bib spoiler with a large plastic wing plank! The ultimate in function being placed before form, the 928's drag coefficient had been whittled down from 0.39 to an acceptable 0.34. Quite an achievement, given no changes had been made to the 928's actual unibody steel structure established in 1977.

Audi had made much play in European advertising of the top speed and economy benefits brought by aerodynamics. Their new 1987 Audi 80 was down to a minuscule Cd of just 0.29. Ford USA had also realized the benefits of Jello-mold styling in battling CAFE for better gas mileage with the 1983 Thunderbird. Porsche meanwhile hadn't lost out image-wise from the absence of a low drag coefficient. The 928, and Porsche's other cars, had round, swoopy visual elements, so the public thought that they were already supreme wind cheaters. Even the latest and most powerful version of the 23-year-old 911, the 911 Turbo SE, had a drop-nose racing front.

Larger, flush rear lamps and a giant rear wing easily distinguished the latest 928S4 (here, the lighter colored car) to the following traffic. With an initial claimed top end of 167 mph, they would indeed be following! (courtesy Garth Matheson).

That aside, Porsche were ready to use aero's helping hand. The 928S2 and S3 5.0 had trouble matching Porsche's claimed top speed figures. They were more powerful, but wind resistance was blunting their more powerful engines. With the S4 the 928 was back on track. Porsche claimed a top speed of 167 mph for the Euro 5-speed manual. *Motor Trend* magazine maxed a 928S4 5-speed at Ohio's Transportation Research Center facility in 1987. The result was 166.94 mph, rock steady and accurate, Porsche's claim was no lie. Maximum speed running on an oval track can be a tense experience, making some terminal velocity claims academic because of the difficulty involved. However, the S4's 'bahn background implied there was nothing to fear, and no need for sunvisor warning labels about what doom might occur when exceeding 85 mph!

When it came to sprinting, the European 928S4's 2.64 final drive helped the new car from standstill to 60 mph in 5.7 seconds. The automatic version with 2.54 rear ratio took 6.3 seconds. However, the U.S. edition was still making do with the S3 5.0's taller 2.20 rear gears, in the interest of CAFE gas mileage. With a list price of $69,380 in late 1988, the $650 gas-guzzler tax on the manual-transmission 928S4 seemed rather inconsequential. It wasn't going to deter someone with the cash from trying out this 4-wheeled missile. Even with the taller 2.20 final drive, *Road & Track*'s John Lamm bettered Porsche's claim with a 0 to 60 mph time of 5.5 seconds.

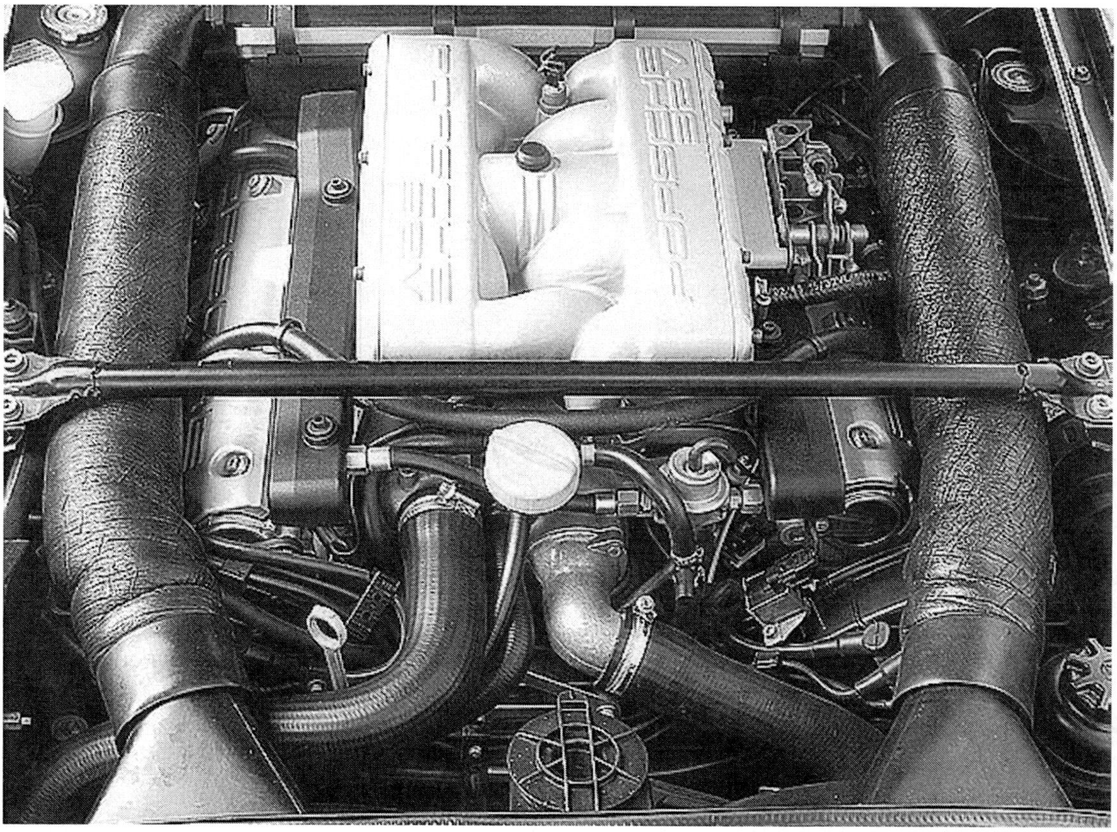

Porsche took the opportunity to alter the S3 V8's rather rudimentary looking intake manifold into the neat form seen here. However, of greater importance was the improved breathing of the 320 bhp S4 5.0 (courtesy www.928registry.org).

Behind the 928S4's performance lay a reworked version of the U.S. S3 5.0 V8 motor. The goal this time around was to make it perform. Still at the same 5-liter displacement level, but power was now 316 bhp at 6,000 rpm and torque 317 lbs./ft. at 3,000 rpm. More power and torque at slightly faster rpm, which raised a gearbox dilemma: on the one hand, the by-now heavy-duty-feeling 5-speed muscle car manual, on the other, the four-ratio slushbox. With the former, one should have invested in a body-building course beforehand. With the latter, one would lose half a second to sixty, and be neck and neck with some punk kid in his brand-new 12 grand Mustang GT 5.0. It was just as well roads have corners to separate the heroes from the pretenders! The 928S4's 3,483-lb. Euro weight spec, and those 4-speed ratios, meant it was still possible to get caught flat-footed. Regardless of the big displacement, this was one V8 that needed to be revved to give its best.

Opening the hood one was greeted by the 928's third intake manifold design. The S3 5.0's intake breathing straw resembled modern art, but looked too much like an engineering first draft. The S4 5.0 had a neater casting with just "PORSCHE 32V" cast onto the plenums. Sadly, still no Porsche crest shield as in the 1977–85 era. The new plenum chambers received air via a Y-shaped passage from the throttle body. There was also a second, shorter passage between the plenums. In the 3,500-to-5,350 rpm span, the valve (butterfly) of the shorter passage would open with certain throttle inputs to raise the resonance of the intake manifold's air. As with the S3 5.0's organ-pipe manifold, the engineers were trying to flatten the torque curve, claiming the S4 5.0 made at least 300 lbs./ft. of torque between 2,700 and 4,750 rpm.

The gains achieved were without a compression ratio rise, the S3 and S4 5.0s both having 10 to one CR. Power improvements came from deleting the engine-driven radiator fan, the new intake manifold, and the use of two knock sensors. Knock sensors were important for maintaining performance with octane-challenged gas. When used in conjunction with Bosch LH-Jetronic and DME, they allowed a precise watch over the fuel mix, and ignition control over each of the V8's cylinders. Keeping ignition timing advanced as far as it would go while avoiding detonation, it was a more sophisticated version of the earlier GM Delco Electronic Spark Control module used on the 1978 Buick Turbo Regal.

The S4 5.0 had shallower combustion chambers, bigger intake and exhaust valves, more radical valve timing, plus a narrower angle between the valves. Porsche were putting all the effort into waking up the S3 5.0, since the latest S4 5.0 wasn't just for America, it was for all markets. Europe had never seen the S3, they had still hung onto the 310-horse, phase 2, 4.7 V8 for all these years. After all, it was more powerful than the slumbering S3 5.0, in spite of the displacement shortfall.

However, with West Germany welcoming the catalytic converter, Porsche were having a third go at the world engine. This second-wave TOP motor saw Porsche policy issue the same power for cat and non-cat markets. The new S4 5.0 made 320 DIN horses, 10 more than the Euro S2 4.7, and the latest 5.0 was rated at 316 SAE bhp in the U.S. So America was getting the same 928 performance for the first time since the very early 4.5-liter 928s. In spite of the original 240 DIN-vs.-217 SAE horsepower disparity, the early Euro and U.S. 928 cars both had the same 8.5 CR and absolutely identical performance figures. With that in mind, the 928S4 was 1978 revisited. Now, if only they could have found a way to work the Porsche logo shield back onto that new intake breathing straw....

Late '80s — A Time for Excess

Sophisticated emissions controls were a means to high performance. Buyers took top-line drivability for granted, they now wanted to see the figures, and the faster the better. During those final days of their alliance with French car maker Renault, AMC were thinking of bringing in the Alpine/Renault GTA Turbo sports car from Europe. There was a white Ferrari Testarossa on *Miami Vice*. BMW had belatedly imported their Motorsport Division's M6 and M5 in 1987 and 1988 respectively. Factor in a new 1987 5.7-liter Trans Am GTA, and there was only one conclusion to reach — greed was good!

With everyone touting their ultimates, there was just one thing left for the 928S4 5.0 to do: go record breaking. A 928S4 automatic just managed to snick in on the list of cars tested by the U.K. magazine *Autocar* during 1986. At 160 mph, it was the joint fastest car they had on their books for 1986.* To get some street cred in the U.S., Al Holbert, boss of PCNA's racing side, journeyed out to the Bonneville Salt Flats. On the salt his 928S4 chalked up two FIA speed records, for both flying kilometer and flying mile, at a whisker under 172 mph.

The 928 was morphing before our eyes into an exotic supercar. It had adopted several

**Autocar, Road Test Yearbook 1986*, p. 11.

Now restored and converted into a road circuit racer, but years earlier used as a promotional exercise for the new 928S4 in America, this car set two FIA speed records on the Bonneville Salt Flats, driven by Al Holbert (courtesy Mark Kibort, www.electricsupercharger.com).

pages from the 911 Turbo's book. Asymmetric tires/rims, monster horsepower, and even a whale-tail spoiler of its very own. It was looking the part, and had a distinct acceleration and top-speed advantage over the 256-horse U.S. BMW M6. In spite of that the 928S4 5.0 was hardly thirstier than the early U.S. 928S. The 928S4 was EPA-rated at 15/23, as opposed to the M6's dire mpg tally of 10/19! As a result, the aforementioned 928S4 gas-guzzler tax of $650 paled next to the Bimmer's $2,250. It was official, the Feds condoned the purchase of a Porsche. Combined with a decent-sized 22.7-gallon tank, the civic-minded 928S4 could travel almost 350 miles on a single tank. No more gas station candy bars for you!

The 928 seemed to have "practical" and "user friendly" as DNA qualities. And however hard it tried to be its own kind of exotic car, the ghosts from the past still came back to haunt. Which was the other joint fastest car tested by *Autocar* magazine in 1986? None other than the De Tomaso Pantera GTS-5. In Europe the 928S4's release was somewhat overshadowed by the eventual availability of the 959 supercar, and the rather less esoteric 330-bhp 911 Turbo SE.

This was already a long way from the days of the association with Ford, and the Pantera was now a low-volume special. Even though its price was about equal with the 928S4, there was little chance of its toxic Ford 351 V8's meeting U.S. pollution laws these days. Even worse, it was a manual-only Pantera GTS-5 that had matched an automatic 928S4 for top-speed honors. With a U.K. starting price of 38,519 pounds sterling, the 928S4 was a relative bargain when put next to the 911 Turbo Sport Equipment which weighed in at 86,443 pounds sterling and forty pence! For over twice the outlay, one got to own the most expensive Porsche outside the 959. Performance was only marginally up with air cooling. According to Porsche figures, 0–62 mph and top speed were written down as 5.2 seconds and 171 mph, compared to the 928S4's 5.9 seconds and 167 mph.

For driver enjoyment Porsche had reworked the power seat controls for the first time in the 928's career. The old-school rectangular panel on the leading edge of the seat squab's side somewhat resembled the controller unit from the 1980 Intellivision videogame console. The new panel had the rectangular edges rounded off, and featured recessed four-way buttons. Now the panel looked like Nintendo's dog-bone controller from the NES game console. Well, at least Porsche were moving with the times.

The latest power seats had a button on the squab control panel so the user could save three different orientations for seat and rear-view mirror position. Since this memory position feature was introduced, owners have discovered that it can lead to the car's battery getting drained if the 928 at hand is allowed to sit without use.

Overall changes to the 928's interior and gadgets were restrained over the years. During 1984, the interior was graced by two power remote rear-hatch-release controls, and if the doors were unlocked the power windows could still be operated even if the key wasn't in the ignition. In the course of 1984, Porsche replaced the plain audio speaker holes at the top of the door trim panels with actual pairs of round speakers. For 1986, the Superman-style "928" superimposed on a big "S" on the steering wheel hub had given way to just a "PORSCHE" inscription on the familiar four-spoker steering wheel.

One thing that didn't change was the 928's oddly small, and expensive, power sunroof, which was standard equipment by the time the 928S4 rolled around. Power roofs cut down

Despite the license plate, one was unlikely to get jet lag when flying down the Autobahn in the luxurious 928 (courtesy J.L. Sebastian).

on interior headroom. The early 928s were often delivered without this option. One was more likely to remain cool by using the 928's air conditioning. With the 928S4 there was good reason to do so, because Porsche had built rear a/c into the big cruiser. The design staff integrated four vents into the cubbybox lid between the rear seats. Strangely enough, for a car with rear a/c, the separate temp and blower speed controls for the auxiliary a/c were placed on the front dashboard, out of reach of the rear passengers. But even with rear a/c, and those nifty rear sunvisors, the 928's rear glass hatch could double as a place to cook a turkey for Christmas in July! On the plus side, the hatch made the 928 just about the most practical supercar going, and a big improvement over the almost-zero rear visibility of mid-engined exotics.

The Devil's Advocate

However, it seemed that not everyone was pleased with the new 928S4. Although U.K.'s *Autocar* seemed to like the S4 5.0, the people at *Motor* magazine had their doubts. John Simister didn't care much for it. David Vivian, part of the team that tested the original 1980 928S which *Motor* liked, described his reservations thus: "The thrumming road roar, the harsh pattery ride, the sluggish automatic transmission, the lack of body control over crests: where had they come from? Was it the car or was it me? This was a 928, dammit, the champ. Surely these things were not of Porsche's doing?"*

The 928S4 was summed up as desirable, but flawed. The reason for its fall from grace was attributed to the advancements made by BMW, Mercedes and the tuners focusing on such brands, Alpina and AMG respectively. In an ultimate car contest, a 928, or a 911, was often going to have to face up to a tuner variant. Cars from the house of Alpina and AMG were fast, but such handbuilt specialist cars came at a price. The four-valve AMG 560E package cost 38,919.45 pounds sterling, and one still had to supply a W124 Mercedes sedan upon which to do the conversion. The starting price of a new 928S4 was 400 pounds sterling less than the AMG 560E conversion work!

The 928S4 was the cruise missile available straight off the showroom floor — any showroom floor, anywhere: the 928, and its Porsche siblings, were the only cars from that era available with exactly the same performance in the U.S. as in the rest of the world. Remember that the U.S. BMW M6 was 30 horses down from the Euro spec version at the time. With a base introductory sticker price of $58,900, the U.S. 928S4 was a genuine S4 5.0. There's little sense in paying twice the price for half the car.

Variety Is the Spice of Life — 928 Club Sport

So there was the 928, caught between super-priced cars and less exotic, but almost as speedy, machinery. And if the 928S4 couldn't be all things to all people, maybe we needed more than one 928? Porsche certainly felt that way, and extended their "less is more" Club Sport program to Porsche's largest car. The formula was simple, take a 928S4 and reconfigure it into weekend club-racer form, and voila, there you had the 1989 928 Club Sport.

First, Porsche put the 928S4 on a diet. Out went soundproofing, power door locks, power

**Motor*, Vol. 172, no. 4389, December 31, 1986, pp. 27, 30.

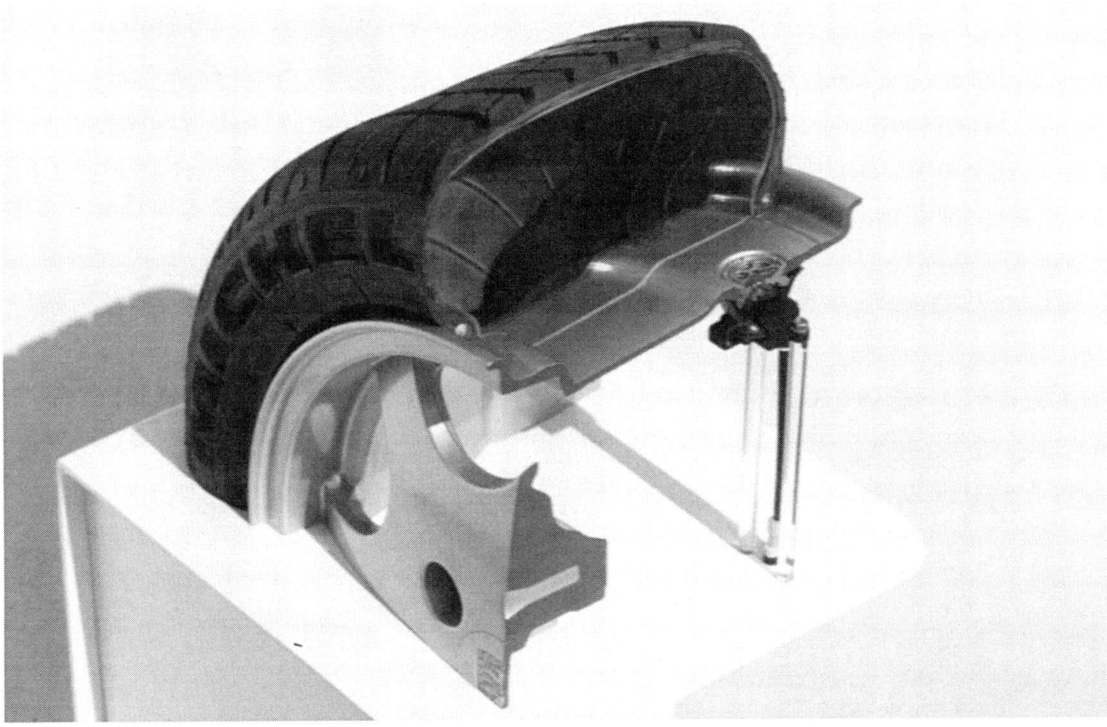

Top: For 1989 the 928S4 gained tire pressure sensors for each wheel. If pressures fell below a safe level the situation was indicated by a red dash warning light (courtesy Porsche). ***Bottom:*** Porsche thought the 928 should shake off the shackles of copious equipment and boogie! The end result was the 1989 928 Club Sport 5.0. No power or torque improvements were claimed, but the 928CS went up to 173 mph and down to 5.6 seconds for 0–62 (courtesy Porsche).

seats, rub strips, Tempostat cruise control, rear sunvisors, remote tailgate release, audio cassette box and convenience-item storage. The hatch wiper was also deep-sixed. Well, there never was a hatch washer jet, so no one was going to miss it. Even the a/c system was replaced with lighter equivalent hardware. With all these economies it became possible to use a more rudimentary and lighter wiring harness. The windshield washer assembly was jettisoned, as were some of the contents from the tool kit. Gone too was the vibration damper from the transaxle tube.

Rolling around on new 7-spoke lightweight rims, the Club Sport edition was 210 lbs. lighter than a comparable corpulent 928S4 manual, loaded up with all manner of luxury aids. For handling, the new-style rims were an inch wider at the front and rear than the normal 928S4's Disc type rims. Apart from that, the Club Sport featured shorter and 10 percent stiffer front springs. To occupy the rear arches, spacers were used to boost the rear track by one inch, and the shock absorbers were also firmer.

The S4 5.0 catalyst engine had its standard camshafts replaced with hotter items. The ECU was also rechipped to adjust fuel mixture and ignition timing, indeed the 5.0 was now redlined at 6,775 rpm rather than 6,000 rpm. The Club Sport had its own low-restriction exhaust with twin tail pipes. The 928 Club Sport was a 5-speed-manual-only model with 2.73 final drive, for sale only in Continental Europe. Its price was equal to what a U.S. owner would have paid for a 1989 928S4.

Interestingly, quoted power and torque figures for the Club Sport remained the same as the European S4 5.0's 320 bhp at 6,000 rpm and 317 lbs./ft. at 3,000 rpm. However, Porsche supplied an improved set of performance figures. Claimed 0–62 mph was down 0.3, to 5.6 seconds. Top speed was up 4 mph, to 173 mph, equal to that other front-engined monster, the old Ferrari Daytona V12. The 928 Club Sport's interior was also like a trip down memory lane. Stark, functional, devoid of trinkets the 928 had picked up during the last 10 years. It was like being back in that very first 1977 928 manual!

At least the exterior was new. Apart from the changed alloy rims, there was Porsche's use of front fender graphics in contrasting color. The bold CS script placement reminded one of the 924 Carrera, Silver Rose blown 944, and naturally the 911 Club Sport. In spite of the on-paper powerplant stagnation, the 928's unique 5.0 felt extra eager, delivering more shove beyond 4,000 rpm. The suspension was also more single-minded compared to the soft-shoe 928S4. Yes, this was indeed a true member of Porsche's sporting clan. The bond could be discerned while carving skillful cornering arcs, and making full use of the Club Sport's standard limited-slip differential.

The 928 Club Sport was Porsche's Shelby Mustang, only better. However, was Porsche willing to see its sales volume shrink, as Ford experienced, struggling to sell 3,223 1967 Shelby Mustangs, when a regular Mach 1 would suffice for most buyers? The 928 Club Sport got close to tuner specials, with such modest changes to the underlying 928S4. It was one-half second slower to sixty, but 10 mph faster on top speed than the AMG 560E. However, even in Europe tastes were swinging to powerful cars with automatic transmission. AMG's slogan at the time was "2 Pedals. No Rivals."

For the Fat Cats — Meow!

Even though the 928 iteration was the plushest member of the Club Sport family, Porsche were too small a company to risk everything on the no-compromise 928 Club Sport. Supply,

PSD (Porsche Slip Differential) was an electronic LSD present on the 1990 928S4 and GT 5.0. PSD had its technical origins with the Porsche 959 (courtesy Porsche).

and charge, what the market will bear. This seemed to apply even in the U.K. In the 1970s BMW sold a special version of their 3.0 CSL in the U.K., since they felt wealthy patrons there wouldn't wish for the back-to-basics CSL trim. So, the U.K. 3.0 CSL got bumpers, plush carpet, power windows, power steering, etc.

With this appeasement in mind, Porsche built the 928S4 SE. Special U.K.-market models seemed to go under the SE (Sports Equipment) moniker. There was the flat-nose 911 Turbo SE, and the Silver Rose 944 was denoted 944 Turbo SE in this export market, where buyers wanted both the power and the toys. So the S4 SE 5.0 was the Club Sport variant —*mit* luxury! Sadly, this undid all of Porsche's hard work to make the 928 lose weight and look great.

What the 928S4 SE did get was the Club Sport's suspension, as well as 8- and 9-inch-wide front and rear rims, plus those raucous engine mods. And just to remind wealthy Porsche patrons that they hadn't stepped into ordinary 928S4-land by mistake, observe the semi-black-leather interior with pony-car-aspirational black/red velour pinstripe seat inlays. The spirit of the checkered Pasha lived on! This was no Jag XJ-S gentleman's club. In spite of recovering much of the 928S4's excess baggage, and still no word on a spec sheet power amendment over the S4 5.0's 320 horses, the 928S4 SE felt faster and was faster in independent testing.

Motor magazine got 0–60 in 5.3 seconds with the 928S4 SE. This was equal to the fastest

During 1989 Porsche revised the 928's instrument display, converting the odometer/tripmeter to digital readouts, and introducing PIDS (Porsche Information and Diagnostic System) to inform the driver on the 928's health and serve as an electronic logbook (courtesy Chuck & Tina Zachman).

time recorded by the yet-to-arrive 5.4 liter 928 GTS, and was 0.3 seconds inside Porsche's claimed figure for the 928 Club Sport. Factor in the Club Sport's weight saving over the S4 SE 5.0, and in the right hands the 928 Club Sport could have been a 5-second-flat 0–60 car in catalysed 1989. It had reached 911 Turbo territory at last.

After some years of complacency Porsche was back to delivering on their performance claims. They were working hard for the money, and the Yuppie. Porsche had to; with the downturn in late–'80s business after the stock market crash, respect had to be earned. The days of elated money men playing with their Visicalc software, and putting a big down payment on a 928, were over. Porsche had learnt to fear the Iron Yuppie!

Scrambling to impress, Porsche worked in tire-pressure sensors for 1989. With sensors in each wheel, if pressure of any tire fell below a prescribed level, a red "BLIP" electronic game-like light on a dash diagram of the 928 showed which tire or tires were at fault. This development would have been impressive if it were not for two facts. Firstly, a tire-pressure monitoring system was available on Corvette, a.k.a. 928 nemesis, since 1987 model year. Secondly, these monitoring systems succumb to the familiar electronic gremlin and go faulty with age. The 928 is no exception, so check those pressures personally!

A more successful upgrade was to the 928's priority one/priority two driver warning

Top: The 330 bhp 1990 928 GT was a production version of the raucous 928 Club Sport, utilizing the lightweight car's revised 5.0. This 928 GT is nicknamed Zeus! (courtesy Mathew Friedman). ***Bottom:*** Now V8 coupe fans had a choice between the hard edged 928 GT 5-speed and the softly sprung auto-only 928S4 (courtesy Mathew Friedman).

In the expanded 928 range for the 1990s, the 928 GT had abandoned any grand tourer pretense to destroy the Corvette ZR-1 (courtesy Mathew Friedman).

system. This system was expanded into the new PIDS (Porsche Information and Diagnostic System). Using text and graphics, it kept tabs on 21 facets of the 928's health. Beyond that, it was also an electronic logbook that noted incidences when the user exceeded the 5.0 V8's rev limit, or drove with insufficient oil in the sump, and squealed on the owner to the service technician.

So the Porsche dealer knew if you had been good or bad. Porsche cleaned up the instrument display, getting rid of the old-school mechanical cylinder odometer and trip meter. The bottoms of the once-circular speedo and tach were cut off to make room for three LED displays at the cluster's base. The rest of the still-moveable instrument pod, dash molding, interior surround, and four-spoker tiller still said "Established 1977," and were none the worse for it ergonomically.

GT 5.0— Club Sport in Disguise

Imagine if Porsche combined the 928 Club Sport and 928S4 SE into one car? Yes, a productionized version for sale everywhere, a Rambo for the road, with the rough edges smoothed off. The result would be the 1989/90 928 GT! For the first time since 1982 the 928 was formally a 2-car range again. The 928S4 was the soft-center chocolate, continuing on with

With uprated 5 liter, PSD, rock hard suspension and 0.86g skidpad reading, the $76,500 928 GT was an ultimate car, but brutal in nature (courtesy Porsche).

automatic only. The 928 GT was the chocolate with nuts! It was also the one with the mystery: where did those ten horses come from?

The 928S4 was still on 320 horses, but the '90 MY GT's 5.0 was tweaked to a 911 Turbo–matching 330 bhp. Camshaft alteration, freer exhaust, and engine management revision conspired to produce the 10 extra ponies. The electronic redline sentry with *verboten* sign could now be found at 6,775 rpm, the same redline as the Club Sport 5.0. Maximum torque was still 317 lbs./ft., but at 4,100 rpm, rather than the S4 5.0's sedate 3,000 rpm. Once again, didn't the Club Sport show its superiority over the plebian S4 5.0 once 4 grand was dialed in on the tach?

Here was the missing power Porsche had been keeping quiet about. The 928 GT was quoting the power that the Club Sport had held all along. Porsche had also come clean on the 928's nature. By ditching the "S" tag for the top model, they had given up trying to link back to the 911 mystique. The latest and greatest 928 was now denoted by what it had always been, a Grand Tourer. The GT 5.0 took on the 2.73 final drive, suspension, and 7.5-inch front/9-inch rear rims, and incorporated a differential with a brain.

Porsche Slip Differential (PSD) constantly checked on the progress of the rear wheels, and sent the most torque to the wheel best able to grip. Sounds like a regular LSD, but this electronic driver aid had its genesis in the 959 supercar. If one consulted the dash of a new 1990 GT 5.0, or S4 5.0, during hard driving there was another indicator lamp working. This

Top: In the spirit of the lightened Club Sport models, and under the influence of the Carrera Cup racers, Strosek produced their "928 Cup" package. Present are the front projector lamps ushered in during the Ultra era (courtesy Strosek www.strosek.de). *Bottom:* As indicated by the rear body molding badge, this 928 Cup was based around Porsche's 928 GT, providing an image commensurate with the GT's rock hard driving experience (courtesy Strosek www.strosek.de).

lamp indicated that a computer had detected wheelspin, and was engaging the progressively lockable multiplate clutch in the rear differential.

The sportier suspension and trick PSD put the 928 GT into the 0.86g skidpad range, around the same as the S4 5.0 achieved on debut, but the 928's talent had always been in over-the-road handling. This task it carried out with aplomb, albeit with one qualification. The suspension's compliance was still better than anything Detroit had to offer sporty car-wise, but the GT 5.0's suspension was especially smooth Autobahn tuned. For the 'bahn, and the local racetrack, but watch out for those bumpy corners.

Take to the track, slam the shorter lever through the awkward gate to bang off fast shifts, and please make use of the revised 5.0's extended rev range. The 928 GT's full leather sport seats kept one in situ. No need for the cloth inserts of the Club Sport or S4 SE, no need either for the S4's fore-and-aft power adjustment with memory facility. The GT wasn't a car for sharing; your seat position alone was the one that counted. The memory facility only drained the battery of vital juice while you drove your Jeep Cherokee winter-beater, so good riddance to that!

Good as the GT 5.0 was, the 928 Club Sport still stands out as the best of the fourth series 5-liter clan. Its no frills interior, those exciting body graphics, and those gas-mileage-improving weight savings. The EPA would have liked the 928 Club Sport. Plus, it still came with a/c, and that taller shift lever was easier to grab when one needed to manhandle a stubborn gearchange. Yes, North American buyers may well have taken to the Club Sport's scant gadget portfolio, if enticed with, say, a 20 percent discount off the GT 5.0's list price? After all, they still had the soft-center S4 5.0 as a fallback position.

The high times of the '80s were about to give way to the recession of 1990. How much demand still existed for high priced supercars like the 928 GT? (courtesy Chuck Zachman).

Revenge of the 928

And what was the 928 GT's price? Try $76,500, which included transportation charge and a $1,300 gas-guzzler tax. CAFE didn't like the GT 5.0's camshaft duration; its EPA numbers had plummeted from a civic-minded 15/23 to a voracious 13/19. It was the price of dumping the U.S. S4's slumbering 2.20 final drive, but you weren't really worried about that. And that punk kid in the Mustang 5.0? He was still neck-and-neck with the 1983–85 U.S. 928S. No, your concerns lay elsewhere.

Elsewhere included the first all-new Daimler-Benz Sports Leicht since 1971, with ADS adaptive damping system and 326-horse, 5-liter V8. Also BMW's technological V12 wonder called 850i. Then there were the new 3.6-liter 911 Carrera 2 and 4. The marginally quicker all-wheel-drive Carrera 4 was even cheaper than the 928 GT. Of greater concern image-wise was the 380 bhp 1989 Corvette ZR-1. The bow-tie bruiser probably convinced Porsche that it was most timely to put the GT 5.0 into circulation. *Autocar & Motor* magazine said the 928 GT sacrificed refinement for excitement. Was the GT 5.0 exciting enough?

In U.S. testing, the King of The Hill Vette had the acceleration edge on the 928 GT. However, in the U.K. both manual transmission cars managed exactly 5.6 seconds for 0–60 honors under *Autocar & Motor*'s eye. The Vette tested in April and the 928 GT in August of the same year. Chevrolet claimed an extra 50 horses and a 180 mph terminal velocity. In truth there was more chance of the 928 GT's reaching its lower claimed top speed of 169 mph,

The truth was that the 13-year-old 928 was a car from the '70s, for the '90s. Obsolescence has no place in Porsche's lexicon. The 928 GT did exist earlier as a late model year 1989 entrant (as with this car), using the S4's 5.0, with over 50 cars reaching U.S. shores (courtesy Porsche).

When the 928 might have appeared to have run its course, Porsche had other plans, introducing the 928 GTS as an early 1993 model year vehicle (courtesy Joanne & Garth Hadley).

which it did reach on occasion. In a contest of speed and acceleration, it was basically a wash between the two V8 adversaries.*

Naturally, the Vette could show its sticky prowess on the skidpad, but also its trademark structural creaks and groans. And even though the C4 Corvette was designed a generation on from the 928, the plastic coupe was still looking rather 1980s cyber-like in spite of a recent styling round-off. The 928 was much harder to date. In the U.K. the Vette was around 35,000 and the Porsche 55,000 pounds sterling. That implied the ZR-1 was a car for the moment, until the next big thing came along. One would hold onto a 928 for a tad longer. The trade-off was there, so buyer beware.

As ever, the Mercedes SL was a different sort of cruiser than the 928. In initial 500 SL form it could manage 0–60 in 6.5 seconds, which would have been impressive—if it was still 1985! In addition it had a top speed of 155 mph. This was no accident, as the German manufacturers had largely agreed this was a sensible level to place a speed limiter. Porsche automobiles were the exception to the rule in Germany, in not being electronically governed for top speed.

*_Autocar & Motor_, Vol. 183, no. 8, February 21, 1990, pp. 78, 82.

A 1993 928 GTS 5-speed in action (courtesy Joanne & Garth Hadley).

The BMW 850i also had the artificial 155 mph ceiling imposed. However, with a mere 300 horses and a 4,000 lb.–plus curb weight to haul, it was doubtful if its cutting-edge aerodynamics could have allowed it to slip much beyond 160 mph. It was 1½ seconds slower to sixty than the 928 GT; in a contest of acceleration and outright speed it was beaten by the Porsche. Oddly enough, with an 8.8 to one CR, 5-liter V12 for all markets, the initial 850i was not unlike the very first 1977 928. It had roughly the same acceleration figures as the early 4.5-liter 928 as well.

As things would have it, the 928 GT was feeling the most heat from ye olde English Jaguar XJ-S. Since 1989 the property of Ford USA, Jaguar could afford to spend a little, and in recent times the XJ-S had become the 6-liter XJR-S. Even the good ol' GM THM 400 3-speed auto couldn't hold back the 318- and 333-bhp editions of the V12 coupe from Browns Lane. With a price saving of almost 16,000 pounds sterling the Jaguar was looking like exceptionally good value. However, and you knew this was coming, capable though it was the Jag wasn't the committed racetrack slot racer that the 928 GT was. It was really a coin toss: the refinement of the Coventry coupe, or the racer ways of the Stuttgart stormer, it was your money.

Avoid using personal funds to finance the commodious Daimler-Benz 560SEC. Like the BMW 850i it was a great car taken in isolation, but the shine started to wear off with value comparisons. It seemed like an expensive way to get the only full 4-seater in the premium coupe class. The opposition was always on the march, but the 928's greatest enemy was itself.

With its new 5,397 cc V8 possessing 369 lbs./ft. of torque, the 928 GTS had enough pulling power to ... climb a mountain? (courtesy Porsche).

Compared to the outgoing GT, the 928 GTS had flared rear arches, red plastic reflector between the rear lamps and a body-color rear spoiler (courtesy Chuck Zachman and Stan Meyer).

Originally at 3,197 lbs. and 240 bhp, now at 3,449 lbs. and 330 bhp, it was getting a bit too much for the Weissach rear suspension to cope with. With the mass and horsepower on hand it was certainly going to oversteer, but at least the passive rear steer increased the window of warning for correction.

The 928 GT wasn't as on-the-rails neutral as the early 928s. It also wasn't as easy for road placement as the junior 944 family, but the 928's basic layout meant it would always be easier to drive than a 911. However, like its rear-engined forbear, the 928 GT liked to follow road irregularities. Originally on 7-inch-wide rims with 225-section tires all round, the GT 5.0 had 7.5-inch front and 9-inch rear hoops with 245-section rubber at the rear. They conferred greater grip, and a propensity for the 928 GT to follow road paint markings and camber changes as blindly as any pre–1969 short-wheelbase 911.

Just because the U.S. 928 GT had dual front airbags didn't mean one was in a hurry to use them. The driver's sawing action at the wheel to maintain a given line was off-putting to passengers, as was the current ride comfort. The 928 had gradually departed from Pirelli P7s, through Goodyear NCTs, to Bridgestone RE71s or Dunlop D40s by the GT 5.0's time. Combined with the firm suspension ride, comfort wasn't quite Corvette-like, but it was getting there.

We were also getting to the point when one 928 would be enough. Porsche's volume 944 model was ageing and on the decline. Its Porsche presence in the U.S. was being pruned, with

Among German automakers Porsche doesn't speed limit its machines, so there was nothing stopping one from running a 3,590 pound 928 GTS up to 170 mph (courtesy Richard Andrade).

uncertainty arising over its replacement. The 911 was starting on an exciting new path, and that left Porsche with too many 928 flavors on the Zuffenhausen line. An auto S4 5.0 here, a manual GT 5.0 there, it was high time to take stock and consolidate. It looked like the future had arrived for the 928: it would be evolve or perish!

The 928's Last Stand—GTS 5.4

It was all a matter of following the script—tail script, that is. Key changes in the big 2-door could be discerned by observing the plastic tail section. First with a "PORSCHE" stamping to let people know it was indeed a Porsche, followed up by adding "928S." Then a "2" suffix after the "S," with Porsche getting creative by placing the "4" below and to the right of the "S," and the "T" below and to the right of the "G" on the S4 5.0 and GT editions respectively. After 15 years Porsche figured that the world knew the 928 was a Porsche, so the tail of the latest 928 iteration simply said "928 GTS" in 1990s-style Porsche script.

Porsche concentrated most of the styling alterations on the tail of the new 928, because that's what most drivers would see when they were left in the dust! There were flared rear wheel arches and a red plastic reflector lens linking up the rear lamps. Above the reflector, a body-colored rear aero wing, not looking quite so tea-tray, S4/GT–like now that it was color-coded. And below the rear wing, just plain 928 GTS.

The teardrop rear-view mirrors were a stylistic improvement over the GT's table tennis paddles, but most eyes first went to the GTS's new footwear. Many had forgotten that the 1970s 928 was riding on 16-inch rims, while others were floundering with Michelin's metric TRX system. So, for the GTS, Porsche gave the 928 17-inch "Turbo Cup" rims, 7.5 inches wide at the front, 9 inches wide at the rear, with 225/45 and 255/40 covers front and back

The red reflector lens between the rear lamps marks this Strosek car as a 928 GTS. Adding the Ultra Wing modification to the GTS' base price made for one very expensive and exclusive 928! (courtesy Strosek www.strosek.de).

respectively. Tire manufacturer choices extended to Bridgestone Expedia S-01, Yokohama A-008P, Michelin MXX3 and Pirelli's P700-Z.

Porsche described the suspension as basically GT level, with refinements: slight meddling with spring rates, shock absorber valving and ride height. For the truly committed, there were special firmer shocks as optional equipment. Open the door, hop over the rocker panel still adorned with the same "928" insignia as on the very first 928, place yourself in that full leather sport seat and activate the 5.4-liter V8. One is in charge of a 5,397 cc, 350-horse (in DIN net terms) version of the 928 V8. The capacity rise came courtesy of a 7 mm stroker package involving a crankshaft running in 8, rather than the previous 4, counterweights. Compression ratio of the new 5.4 was back up to 10.4 to one, returning to the level of the old toxic Euro S2 4.7 engine.

Lighter, and now forged, connecting rods and pistons featured alongside plastic-coated intake manifold passages, along with different cams. The goal was more even power delivery from the V8. The end result, in the most flattering DIN net terminology, was 350 bhp at 5,700 rpm and 369 lbs./ft. at 4,250 rpm. The fatter torque curve really closed up the

Opposite, top: **According to Porsche's R&D man Horst Marchart the new 928 GTS had 350 horses saying giddyup, but 1332 ponies shouting whoa, thanks to the GTS' 12.7 inch front disks and 4-piston Brembo calipers (courtesy Roger Tyson).** ***Opposite, bottom:*** **The 928 GTS rear compartment. Tight as ever back there, but the lockable cubby was useful for stashing spare krugerrands, and rear A/C kept one cool while counting the loot! (courtesy Roger Tyson).**

928 GTS
TEXAS
T82-SHR

GTS

More powerful and more frugal with U.S. EPA figures of 15 city / 19 highway, but was the purchaser of a $90,000 automobile worried about gas mileage? (courtesy Gene Bammes).

performance divide between the manual and automatic versions. Manufacturer-quoted top speed for both models was 170 mph, the manual slated as being able to go from zero to sixty-two mph in 5.7 seconds, the auto only 0.2 slower. With the extra torque, the auto 928 no longer got caught off guard on the twisties.

With this kind of pulling power on tap, the 5 ratios of new-generation slushboxes, like the Daimler-Benz D+4, were superfluous. However, Porsche still worked some improvements for both 928 gearboxes. Still with the old T-bar handle and accordion shift gaiter, the 4-speed auto was adjusted to suit the 5.4's improved torque. However, the manual gearbox had an external oil pump and oil cooler mounted at the front. Porsche had done their homework to make the 5-speed easier to use compared to the S4/GT era. The changes were effective, the 5-speed stick was passable now, as long as it wasn't hurried through the shift gate.

Porsche brakes have always been legendary, and the GTS was improved over the GT to

Opposite, top: **Since the first 928S Porsche had put one question before the public: Which was Zuffenhausen's flagship, the 911 Turbo or the 928? The 928 GTS made the question even harder to answer (courtesy Roger Tyson).** ***Opposite, bottom:*** **A U.K. advertisement for the 928 GTS was titled, "It sorts the chairmen from the managing directors." If that was the case, this must be the seat of power (courtesy Gary Quayle).**

keep the extra artillery in check, with larger front disk brake rotors of 12.7 inches and Brembo 4-piston calipers. New Porsche R&D boss Horst Marchart stated that the GTS's braking capacity was 1332 bhp, permitting the heavyweight to halt from 125 mph in a mere 5.3 seconds.

Introduced to the U.S. in spring as an early 1993 model year car, the 3,590-pound 928 GTS had a base sticker price of $89,092, and slightly better EPA gas mileage numbers of 15 city and 19 highway in spite of the larger V8. The "S" in GTS might have stood for smooth, since in many respects the 928 GTS felt like a GT 5.0 with the rough edges rounded off. The ride comfort that was formerly bordering on Corvette crude was now much more palatable. The 5-speed manual was actually a viable option again for the first time since the original 928S. Less impressive was the enlarged 5.4 motor.

Long-stroke engines normally don't like to rev, which is why racing engines traditionally have large bores and short strokes. The GTS 5.4 was still oversquare at 100 × 85.9 mm, and it would zip to the redline, but in a roguish manner. It had lost charm compared to the 4.5/4.7/5.0 family. Dare it be said, the 235-horse 5.0 Ford's SVT put together for the contemporary 1993 Ford Mustang Cobra was a sweeter deal. *Car & Driver* found it to be just 0.3 slower to sixty.

Punk boy was looking rather smug about the greater smoothness of his 302. He had just won the lottery and was there on open-track day with his brand-spanking-new SVT Cobra. He was also virtually neck-and-neck with you down the first straight, then something happened—the first chicane! Hard to believe that the 928 actually predated the 1979 Foxstang, but it did. And whereas the Cobra's structure was rattling away next to the latest GM F-body, your 928 GTS was sitting serene, because, in the words of *Thoroughbred & Classic Cars* magazine in June 1977, "... one might reasonably call the 928 a car for the nineties!"

It was the 1990s, and Chevrolet's LT1 Camaro matched the 5.3-second 0–60 time of the 928 GTS, when both cars were tested in 1993. However, the LT1 Corvette never quite matched the 928's acceleration time. No matter, there were bigger fish to fry, and not the slumbering BMW 850i, nor the Lexus SC400. No, you were after the Godfather: the Testarossa, no less! Ferrari's redhead was supposed to be good for 180 mph plus, but *Autocar & Motor* found the 512 TR to be only 7 mph faster than the 928 GTS on the Millbrook speed bowl, 175 vs. 168 mph. And the GTS 5.4 had a clear advantage over the 512 TR when it came to in-gear acceleration.

Almost as fast as a Monteverdi HAI, but less scary to drive. To make a case for the 928 GTS automatic, one needed only to drive the latest 1995 993 911s. The Tiptronic S with automatic may have been the easiest 911 to drive ever, and according to the figures only a little bit slower than the 928 GTS in acceleration and top speed. Unfortunately, something was missing, namely the GTS 5.4's torque. The 911 Tiptronic and GTS 5.4 both had four forward ratios, but the 911's 3.6 liters couldn't hope to bridge the chasm between ratios like the GTS V8 could. Then try the 6-speed Carrera 4: no performance deficiency there, but the 928 GTS could go a bit faster as an automatic. And who really liked those old-school 911 ergonomics?

Opposite, top: **The 1993 Porsche 928 GTS and contemporary Camaro LT1 both had 0–60 times of 5.3 seconds. Rapid advances in mainstream cars implies toil and trouble for specialists like Porsche to ensure their cars offer that little bit extra (courtesy Gene Bammes).** ***Opposite, bottom:*** **The 928 GTS received additional soundproofing over the GT to compensate for the more raucous 5.4 V8 motor (courtesy Chuck & Tina Zachman).**

PORSCHE

The 928 GTS was the first 928 to use 17 inch wheels. Tire recommendations for the Turbo Cup rims were Bridgestone Expedia S-01, Yokohama A-008P, Michelin MXX3 and Pirelli P700-Z (courtesy Gary Grigsby).

Two 911s in one, and half the price of a Testarossa, the 928 GTS wasn't bad value as supercars went. Then again, the 928 had always been reasonably good value new, and even better value secondhand. Without the magnet-like attraction that characterizes the 911, the 928 has always been a fast depreciator. Pre-owned, it represents a lot of exotic car for the money. However, as is par for the course with exotics, it is complex. Relatively cheap to buy perhaps, but expensive to run certainly. Drive it as it is meant to be driven, and wear-and-tear consumables like disks, pads and exhaust can add up to a pretty penny indeed. The 928 was always well equipped with gadgets, and these are not always foolproof. Plus, no 928 can ever make do with low-speed-rated tires. Even the earliest models wore 150 mph VR-rated covers.

Pitfalls to 928 motoring maybe, but if one can afford the price of admission, and the various sundries to keep the 928 in fine fettle, chances are the ride would be enjoyed. And even the critics were acknowledging that there was method in Porsche's madness with the GTS 5.4 V8. Certainly *CAR* magazine thought so, naming the 928 GTS a near icon: "The GTS was designed to go obscenely fast and thrill you through to your bone marrow, and it was

Opposite, top: **Whether the stereo was playing Bee Gees in the '70s or Nirvana in the '90s, the 15-year-old interior design coped easily with fickle fashion (courtesy Chuck & Tina Zachman).** ***Opposite, bottom:*** **In a country known for its speedy projectiles, the 928 GTS was the fastest non-turbo production car made to that point in Germany's history (courtesy Gary Grigsby).**

Top: **The Turbo Cup wheel, Porsche's default design for the 968/911/928 ranges by the early 1990s. For the 928 GTS the 17 inchers were 7.5 inches wide at the front and 9 inches wide at the rear (courtesy Chuck & Tina Zachman).** ***Bottom:*** **After the rough riding GT, Porsche had retuned the 928's suspension along more considerate lines, making the latest 928 GTS a comfy ground coverer. With Michelin MXX3s road roar was at an all time low (courtesy www.928registry.org).**

The 928 GTS represented the end of an era in that it was not equipped with traction control, ESC etc. Such features were unnecessary with a world class chassis (courtesy Jeffrey L. Frye).

wonderfully single-minded in its approach to that task. It remains one of the mysteries of the modern world that the 928 GTS has never gained the recognition it deserves."*

The U.K. advertisement for the GTS was confrontingly titled "It sorts the chairmen from the managing directors," and it was billed as the swiftest non-turbo production car ever made in Germany. Even the 928's critics would have to acknowledge the 928 GTS's high-performance proficiency. However, was this character true to original Porsche ideals of light, simple, sporty simplicity? The essence that sired the rudimentary, but beloved, 1955 356 Speedster? Yes, the 928 was far removed from such ideals, and the critics were aware of this too. L.J.K. Setright felt and said as much when praising the BMW 850i in 1992, "I quite like it anyway, nicely civilised car that it is in a market where the Porsche 928 has gone overboard in pursuit of raucous super-sports performance...."†

So the next time you go looking for a slightly ancient 911, just consider what the same outlay could achieve in 928-land. A much younger car, with loads of electronic toys to play with, and the automatic would come in handy for excursions into town. Your ego might suffer from not being able to pretend you're Steve McQueen checking out the Le Mans circuit, but your clutch leg would thank you for it!

How long would Porsche keep making the 928 GTS? The official line from Zuffenhausen was that the 928 would continue for as long as there was demand for it, but business for the 928 hadn't been kind. In spite of the introduction of the GT 5.0, three-quarters of Porsche sales in the U.S. were for the venerable 911 by the close of 1991. Improved though it was, the

**CAR, Performance Car (supplement)*, August 1998, p. 44.
†*BMW Australia Magazine,* 1/1992, p. 25.

Years of polishing the diamond had seen the 928's Cd drop from 0.42 to the 928 GTS' 0.35. In spite of its modern styling the 928 was never at the cutting edge of low drag coefficients (courtesy Jeffrey L. Frye).

GTS 5.4 seemed unable to rectify the situation. Indeed, high-end luxury didn't seem to be particularly in vogue by the early 1990s. The recession at the start of the decade was taking its toll on the extravagant. The pudgy new W140 MB S-class was denoted the wrong car for the wrong time, dubbed the Chancellor Helmut Kohl of sedandom. BMW also went large with its 6-series replacement, but by 1993 sales were so slow that the idea of a replacement was off the table as far as management was concerned.

The 928 had also taken the path of pricing itself into oblivion. As sales declined, it went more elaborate, more expensive, and sales were further eroded. In late 1989 the 928 GT was 55,441 pounds sterling in the U.K. market, by early 1995 the GTS 5.4 had climbed to 72,950 pounds sterling. At some point in its life Porsche had to make a 928 for ordinary non-turbo 911 money, and this never really happened, the stripped-down 928 for the home market being the closest to the target.

928—The Future Has Arrived

Was the Porsche 928 one of those cars that failed by trying to appeal to the U.S. market? Probably not, since the 928 was its own kind of car at heart. Early on there were noises made concerning the Corvette overtones, but these accusations were short-lived. The 928 quickly established itself as a very able car, certainly on the wish list of automotive connoisseurs around the globe for many years. Just about everyone was interested in seeing what the

Top: **Don't fear the stick shift; Porsche had reworked the 5-speed manual so that it was an easy and smooth device on the 928 GTS (courtesy Chuck & Tina Zachman).** ***Bottom:*** **Despite a length measurement of 178.1 inches, old fashioned rear wheel drive ensured that the 928 GTS possessed a reasonable turning circle of just 38.4 ft. (courtesy Chuck Zachman).**

Top: **Despite constant improvement, after 19 years and increasingly stratospheric price tags 928 GTS production reached just two cars per day. The 928 was at an end (courtesy Chuck & Tina Zachman).** ***Bottom:*** **As a no-compromise futuremobile the 928's appeal is enduring (courtesy Porsche).**

latest 928 version could do, so closely was it associated with raising the bar for high-performance cars. It can safely be said that if one walked into any Porsche showroom in 1982/83 there were two models to gravitate towards. The first would be the 911 Cabrio — and the 928S was easily the second, hardly a step in interest behind.

The 928 was the business. Some cars just give off that confident aura, and it maintained that public interest right to the end of its life, even though sales dwindled to 2 cars being built per day. Certainly it never suffered the ignominy of the BMW 8 series, which made so little impact that people were unaware that it was still being produced by the late nineties. The only regret was that Porsche didn't increase the V8's bore and stroke from 100 x 85.9 to the 3-liter 944S2/968's 104 × 88 mm. A 6-liter 928 with VarioCam would have been quite a machine, but motor refinement might have proved a headache.

Enthusiasts knew when the 928 arrived, and they knew when it departed. Perhaps we have Dr. Fuhrmann to thank for this. He was no marketing marvel, no demographics diva, he was an engineer, and cars have to be designed before they can be advertised. Little wonder that the competency of the 928 is so valued, long after a production run where it wasn't fully appreciated.

Porsche practice is the antithesis of mainstream car-maker business. The company lets a design have its chance, in this case 19 years. The 928 joins other timeless designs like the Citroen DS, NSU Ro80, and of course the original 911. Porsche also doesn't like to throw stuff away. For 1995, the 911 actually adopted the principles of the 928's Weissach axle.* If you can't beat them, join them. Good ideas have long lives, and so do Porsche 928s. Embodying Porsche's bank-vault-build quality, very early 928s are still hovering around like low-flying spaceships. This fact should come as little surprise. After all, Porsche did intend the 928 for the 21st century!

**EuroSport Car,* Vol. 2, no. 1, January 1995, p. 51.

Appendix: Quartet of Quality

1975 Porsche 924

The model that put the sourdough on the table at Zuffenhausen, as it hooked many first-time Porsche owners. A modified Audi power team took Porsche's efficient 0.36 Cd, front-engine, transaxle 2-liter coupe to a genuine 125 mph.

Body: Unibody construction
Engine: 121 cu. in. / 1,984 cc I4, cast-iron block, aluminum head with SOHC, 2 valves per cylinder, Bosch K-Jetronic mechanical fuel injection, 9.3:1 CR, 125 bhp (DIN) @ 5,800 rpm / 121.5 lbs./ft. @ 3,500 rpm.
Gearbox: Audi 4-speed (cone-type synchromesh) / 3.44 rear gears
Chassis: Front: Independent, MacPherson struts, coil springs, tube shocks.
Rear: Independent, semi-trailing arms, torsion bars, tube shocks.
Brakes: Disk (10.1 in. solid) / Drum (9.1 in.)
Steering: Rack & pinion, no power assistance.
Wheels / Tires: 14 × 5.5 in. (pressed steel rims) / 165-section HR-rated radials
Dimensions: 166 in. L / 66.3 in. W / 50 in. H
Weight: 2,380 lbs.
0–62 mph: 10.5 seconds*
Top speed: 125 mph*

1988 Porsche 944 Silver Rose

The opposite of a Club Sport, the Silver Rose was a more powerful 944 Turbo painted in dusky silver pink, with psychedelic interior and every option squeezed aboard. The other side of the Walter Mitty 924!

Body: Unibody construction with reinforcing rocker panel plates between wheel housings.
Engine: Porsche 151 cu. in. / 2,479 cc I4, all-alloy SOHC, 2 valves per cylinder, Bosch Digital Motor Electronics (DME), 8.0:1 CR, KKK turbo / 11.9 psi max. boost pressure, 250 bhp (DIN) @ 6,000 rpm / 258 lbs./ft. @ 4,000 rpm.
Gearbox: Audi 5-speed overdrive / 3.38 rear gears
Chassis: Front: Independent, MacPherson struts, coil springs, tube shocks, anti-sway bar.
Rear: Independent, semi-trailing arms, torsion bars, tube shocks, anti-sway bar.
Brakes: Disk (12.0 in. vented) / Disk (11.8 in. vented)
Steering: Rack & pinion, with power assistance.

Wheels / Tires: Flush 7-spoke forged alloy rims, 16 × 7 front & 16 × 9 rear, 225/50 VR front & 245/45 VR rear.
Dimensions: 166.5 in. L / 68.3 in. W / 50.2 in. H
Weight: 2,998 lbs.
0–62 mph: 5.7 seconds*
Top speed: 161 mph*

1993 Porsche 968 Club Sport

The famous stripped-down 968 that revived sales and interest in the bug-eyed, 3-liter I4 range. The whole is indeed greater than the sum of the parts. Those parts were assembled by Porsche, as with all 968s, so quality was assured.

Body: Unibody construction with polyurethane/body cladding.
Engine: Porsche 183 cu. in. / 2,990 cc I4, all-alloy DOHC, 4 valves per cylinder, Bosch Digital Motor Electronics (DME), 11.0:1 CR, Porsche patented "VarioCam" variable valve timing, 240 bhp (DIN) @ 6,200 rpm / 225 lbs./ft. @ 4,100 rpm.
Gearbox: 6-speed (Getrag) close ratio / 3.78 rear gears
Chassis: Front: Independent, MacPherson struts, coil springs, tube shocks, anti-sway bar.
Rear: Independent, semi-trailing arms, torsion bars, tube shocks, anti-sway bar.
Brakes: Disk (11.7 in. vented) / Disk (11.8 in. vented)
Steering: Rack & pinion, with power assistance.
Wheels / Tires: Cast alloy rims, 17 × 7.5 front & 17 × 9 rear, 225/45 ZR front & 255/40 ZR rear.
Dimensions: 170.1 in. L / 68.3 in. W / 50.1 in. H
Weight: 2,904 lbs.
0–62 mph: 6.5 seconds*
Top speed: 156 mph*

1989 Porsche 928 Club Sport 5.0

The equivalent of turning a Rolls Royce Corniche into a go-kart. Porsche pared down the weight of the 928 to the tune of 210 lbs. A glimpse of what the 928 might have been like had it replaced the 911 directly. The 928 enjoying the simple life!

Body: Unibody construction with aluminum hood, doors, front fenders and polyurethane moldings.
Engine: Porsche 302 cu. in. / 4,957 cc V8, all-alloy DOHC, 4 valves per cylinder, Bosch LH-Jetronic, 10.0:1 CR, two-stage intake manifold, 320 bhp (DIN) @ 6,000 rpm / 318 lbs./ft. @ 3,000 rpm.
Gearbox: Porsche 5-speed close ratio / 2.73 rear gears
Chassis: Front: Independent, upper A arms, lower trailing arms, coil springs, tube shocks, anti-sway bar.
Rear: Independent, upper transverse links, lower trailing arms, coil springs, tube shocks, anti-sway bar, Porsche patented "Weissach Axle" rear-wheel steering.
Brakes: Disk (12.0 in. vented) / Disk (11.8 in. vented)
Steering: Rack & pinion, with power assistance.
Wheels / Tires: Flush 7-spoke forged alloy rims, 16 × 8 front & 16 × 9 rear, 225/50 ZR front & 245/45 ZR rear.
Dimensions: 178.1 in. L / 72.3 in. W / 50.5 in. H
Weight: 3,263 lbs.
0–62 mph: 5.6 seconds*
Top speed: 173 mph*

**Porsche factory performance figures*

BIBLIOGRAPHY

Autocar. Road Test Yearbook 1986.

Autocar & Motor. Vol. 183, no. 8, February 21, 1990.

Bernstein, Edward M. "The Making and Remaking of the Bretton Woods Institutions." In *The Bretton Woods-GATT System Retrospect and Prospect after Fifty Years.* Ed. Orin Kirshner. M.E. Sharpe, 1996.

BMW Australia Magazine. 1/1992.

CAR. February 1993.

CAR. April 1993.

CAR. Performance Car (supplement), August 1998.

Clarke, R.M. *Porsche 928 Performance Portfolio 1977–1994.* Brooklands Books, 1995.

Consumer Reports. Vol. 35, no. 7, July 1970.

Consumer Reports. Vol. 35, no. 9, September 1970.

Consumer Reports. Vol. 40, no. 7, July 1975.

EuroSport Car. Vol. 2, no. 1, January 1995.

Motor. Vol. 166, no. 4253, May 16, 1984.

Motor. Vol. 172, no. 4389, December 31, 1986.

Motoring Which? January 1974.

National Geographic. Vol. 152, no. 2, August 1977.

Popular Science. Vol. 227, no. 2, August 1985.

Thoroughbred & Classic Cars. Vol. 16, no. 12, September 1989.

Thoroughbred & Classic Cars. Vol. 17, no. 1, October 1989.

Vernon, Raymond. "The U.S. Government at Bretton Woods and After." In *The Bretton Woods-GATT System, Retrospect and Prospect after Fifty Years.* Ed. Orin Kirshner. M.E. Sharpe, 1996.

Index